UTAH & ALL THAT JAZZ

CALVIN GRONDAHL

Signature Books
Salt Lake City
1989

Printed in the United States of America

95 94 93 92 91 90 89 6 5 4 3 2 1

Cover design: Randall Smith

Library of Congress Cataloging-in-Publication Data

Grondahl, Calvin.
Utah and all that jazz.

1. Utah—Social life and customs—Caricatures and cartoons. 2. American wit and humor, Pictorial.
I. Title.
F827.G76 1989 979.2 89-70028
ISBN 0-941214-86-9

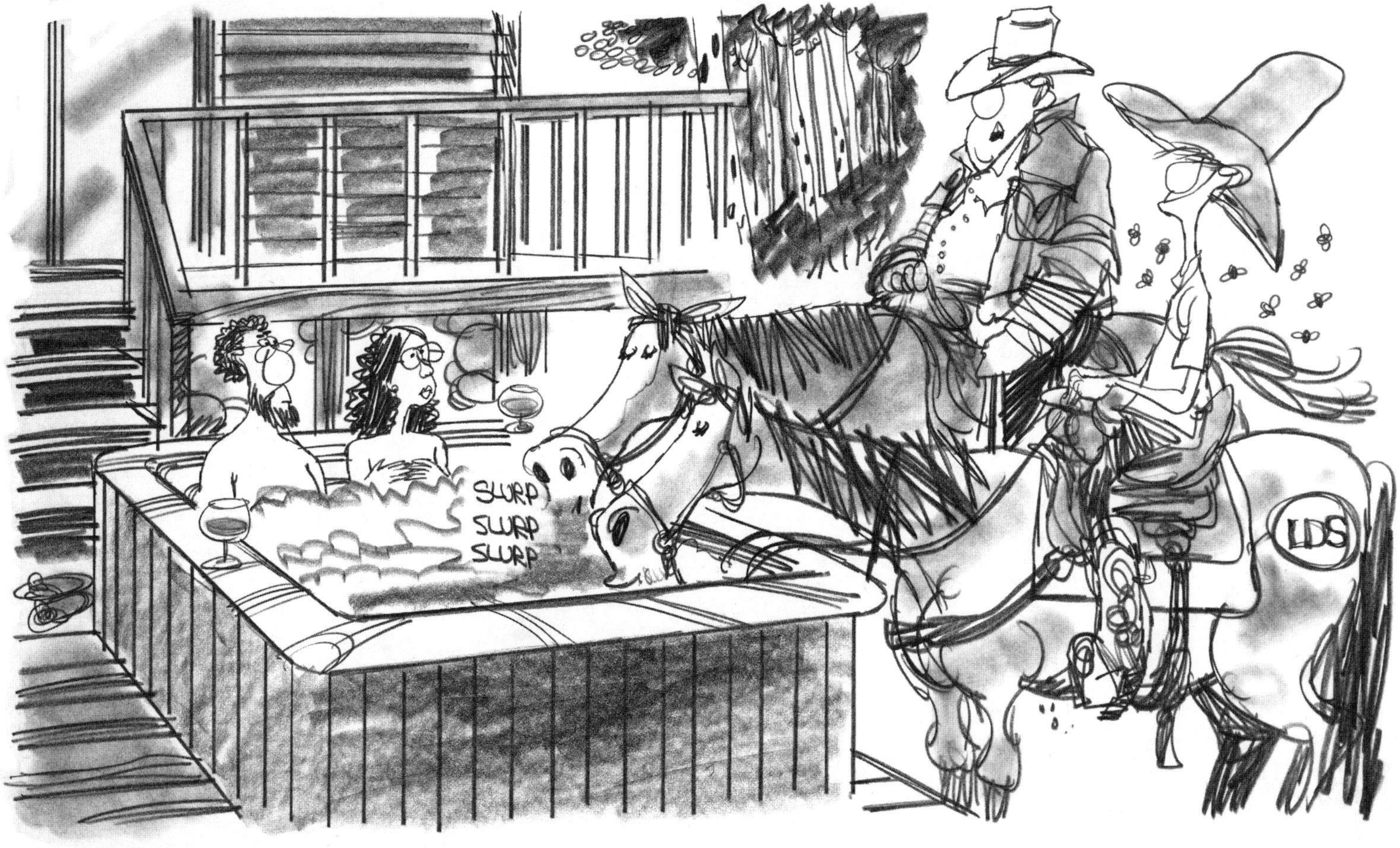
SLURP
SLURP
SLURP
LDS

"Welcome to Utah."

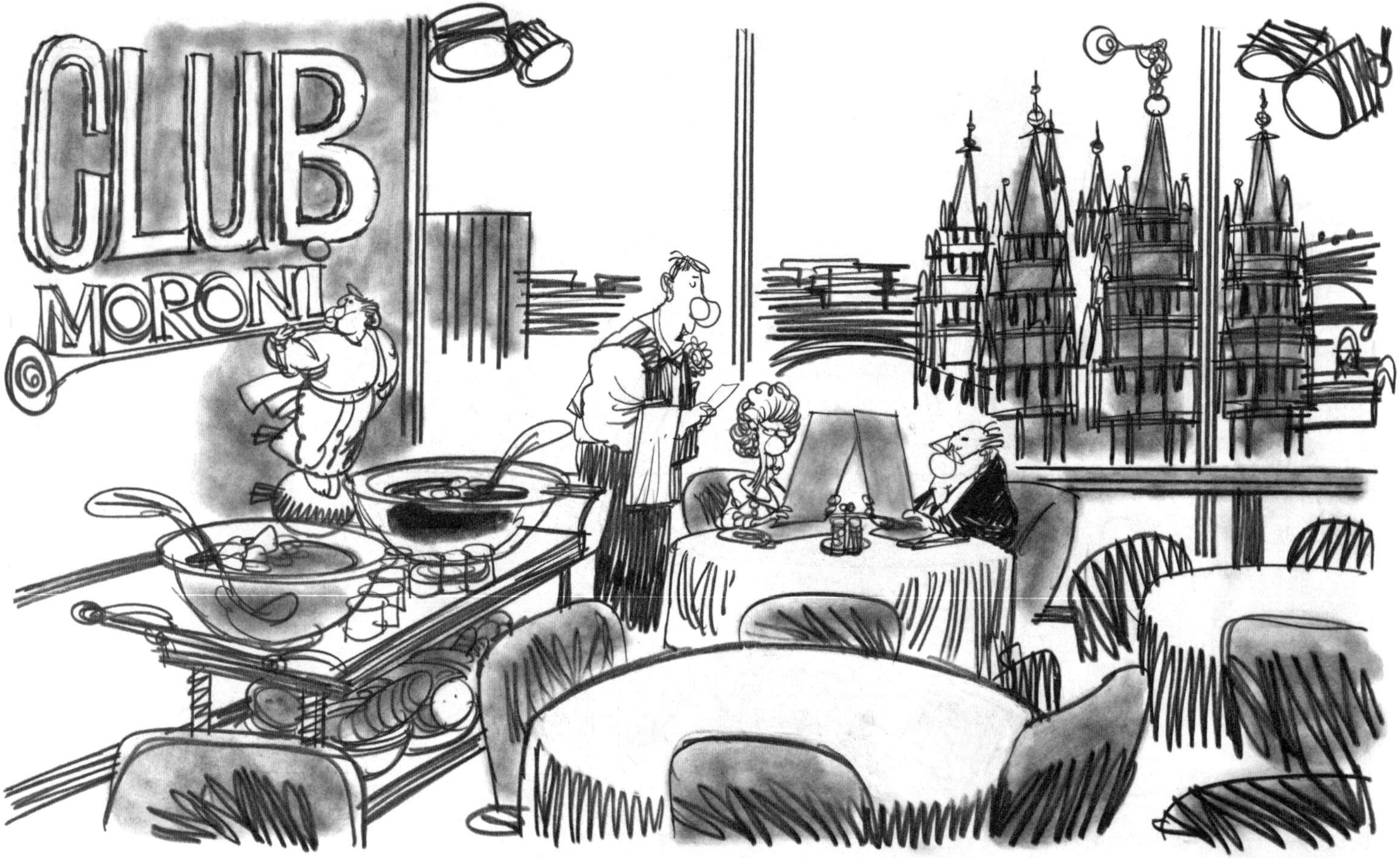
CLUB
MORONI

"My name is Levi and I'll be your waiter.
May I recommend the green punch with the fish."

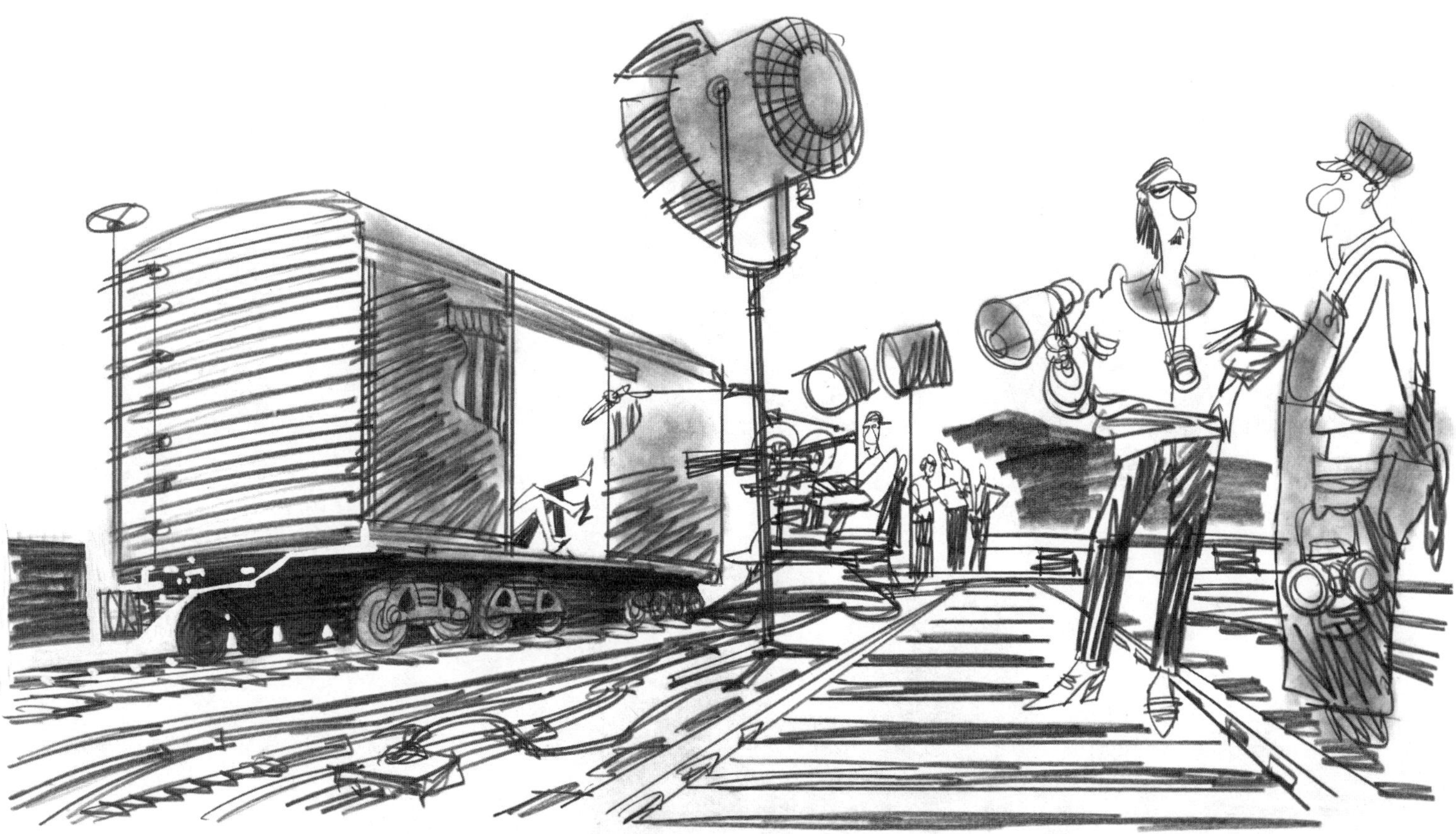

"I'm making another film here in Ogden . . .
'A Boxcar Named Desire.' "

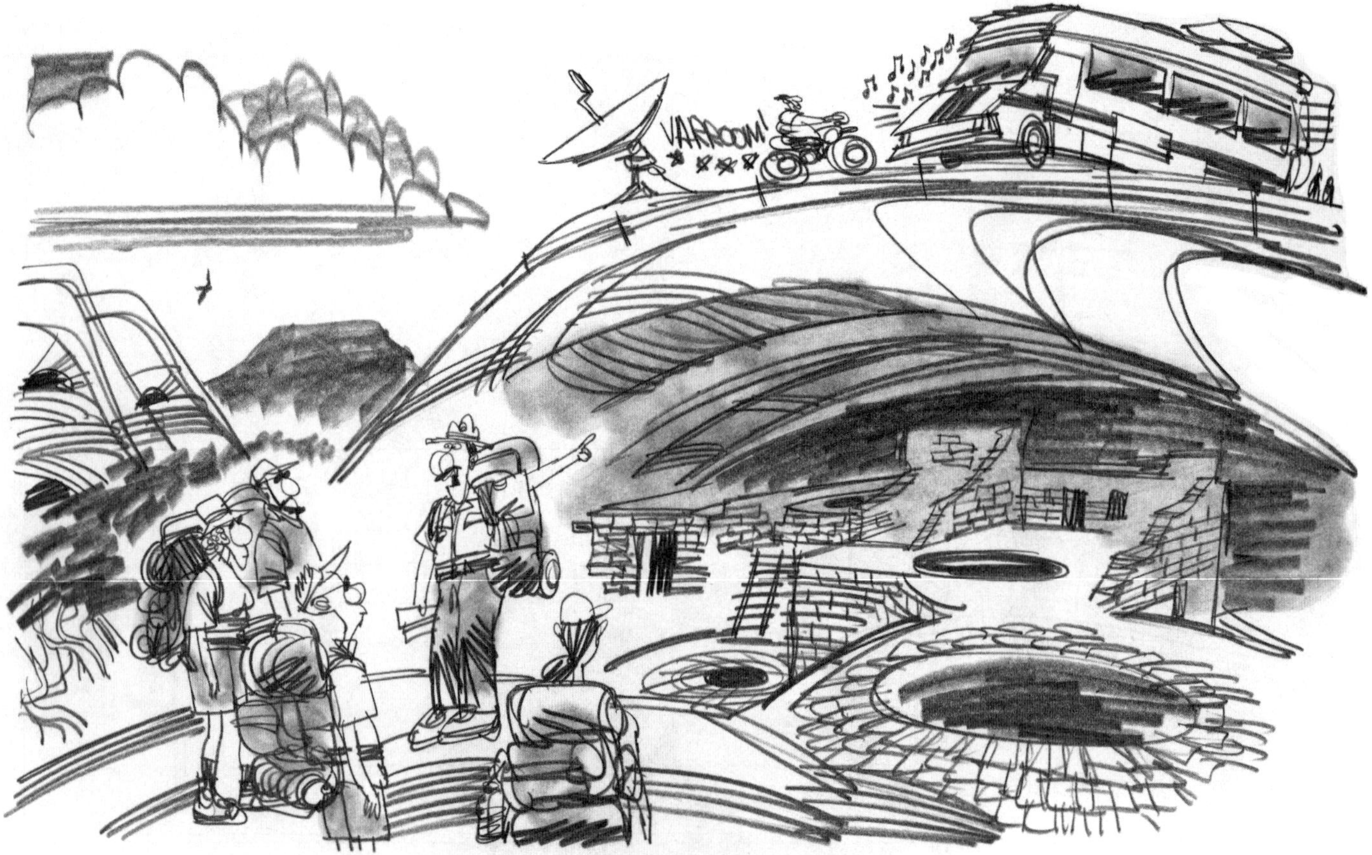
VARROOM!

"And in the layer above the Anasazi we find
the shopping mall culture."

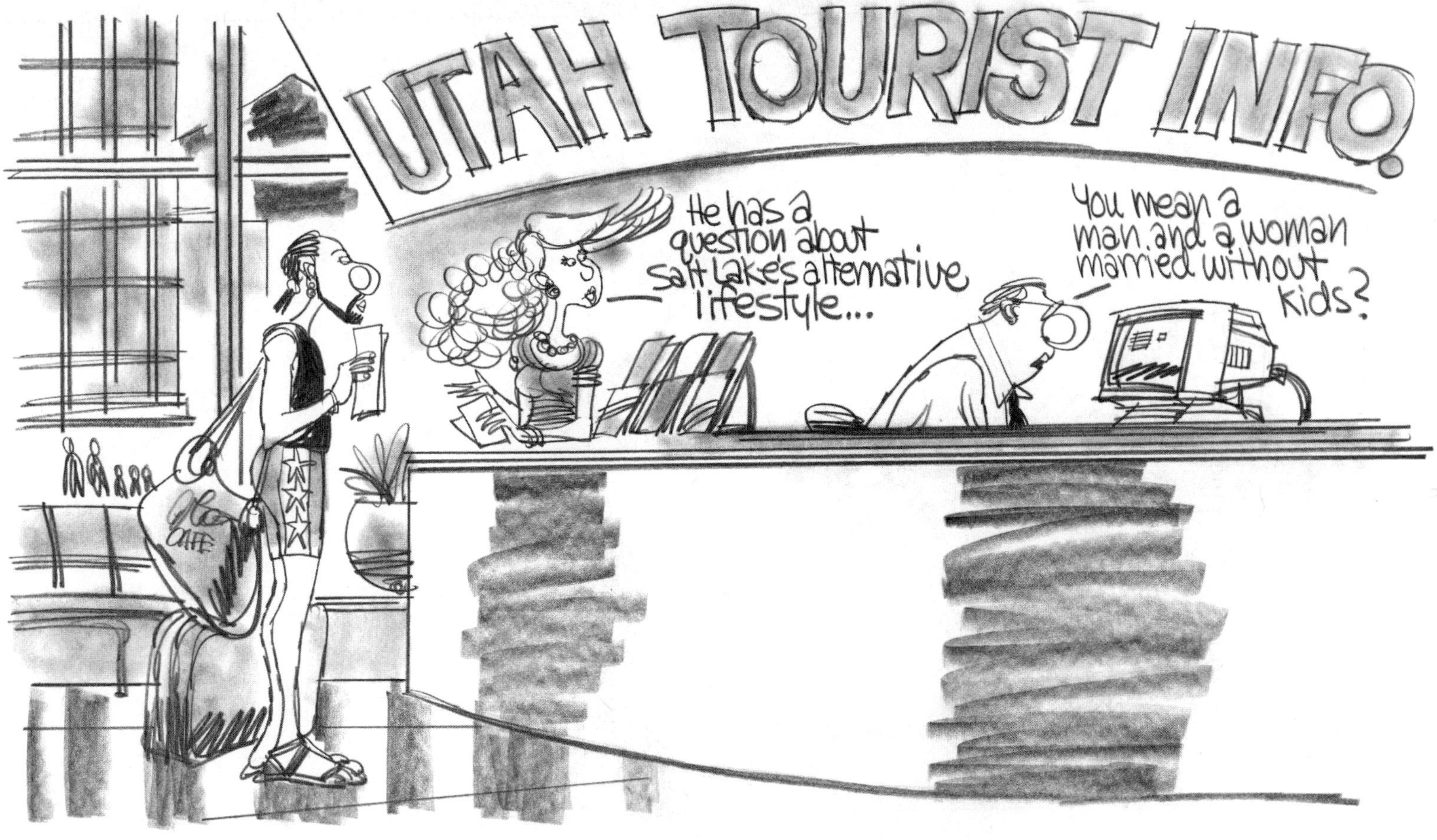
UTAH TOURIST INFO.
He has a question about Salt Lake's alternative lifestyle...
You mean a man and a woman married without kids?
CAFE

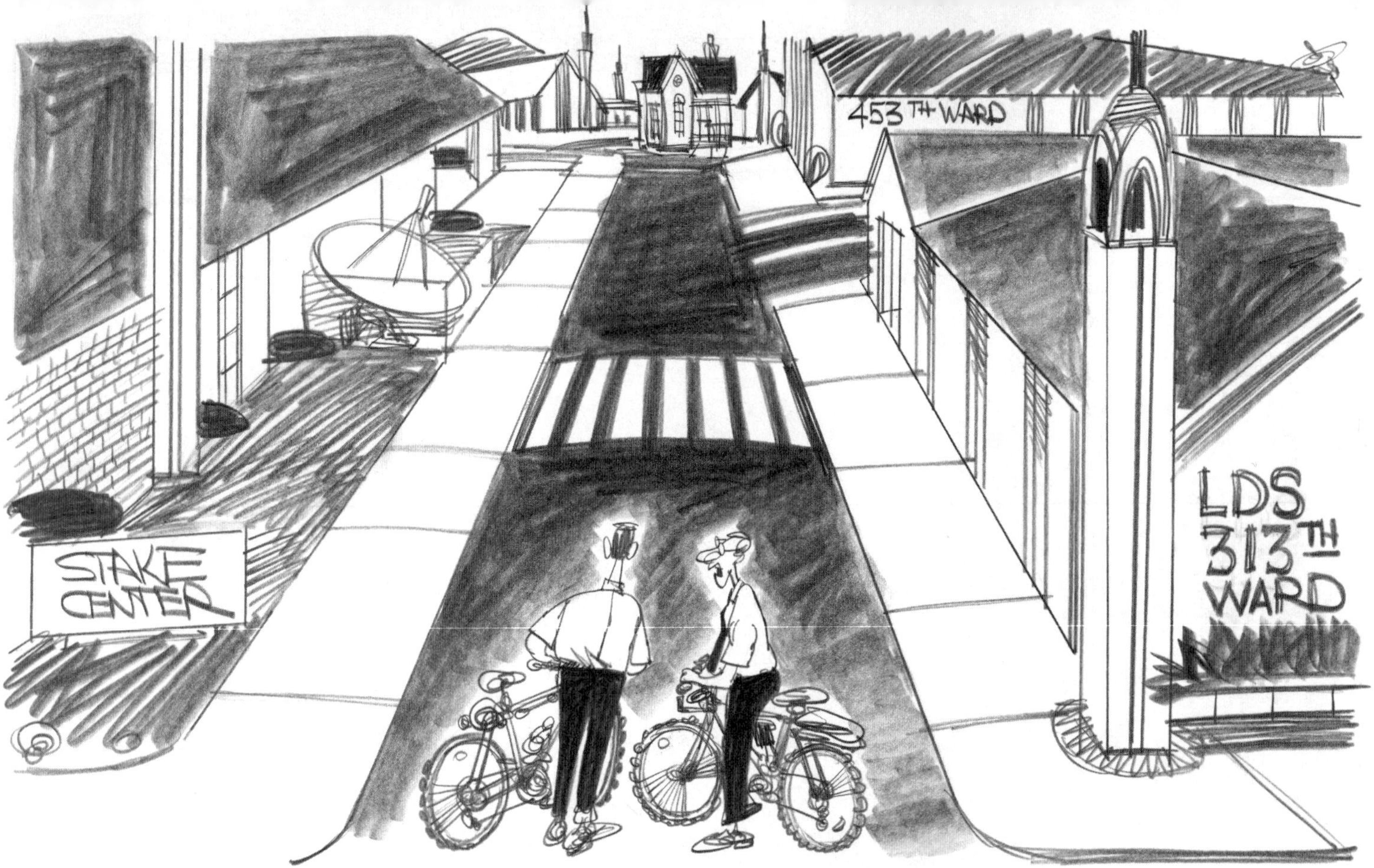
453 TH WARD
STAKE CENTER
LDS 313 TH WARD

"Elder, that's a non-member's house. Let's go ask them to surrender because they're now completely surrounded."

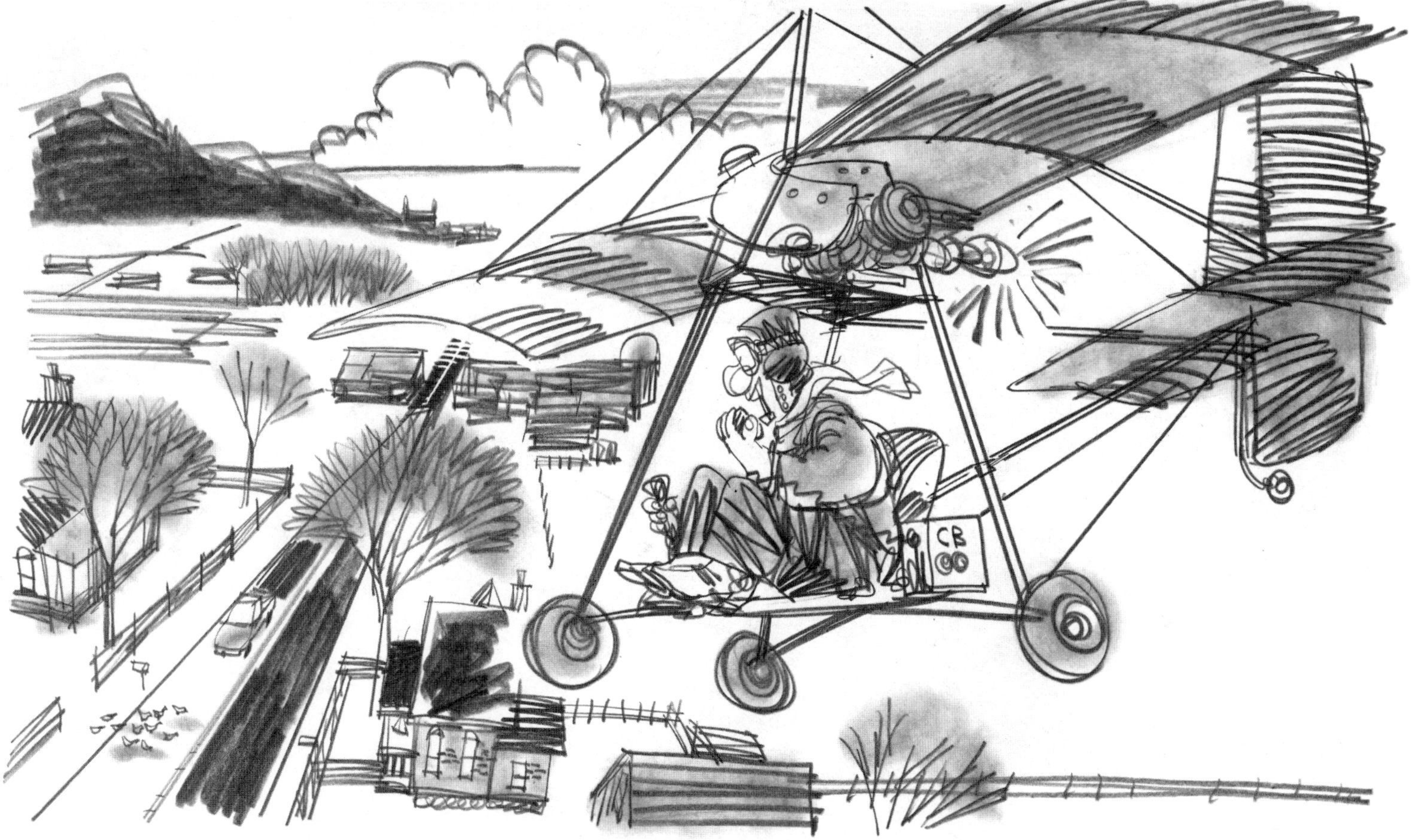
CB

"Molly Pratt's ducks are on the road again, so avoid that traffic tie up . . . This is Manti Skywatch."

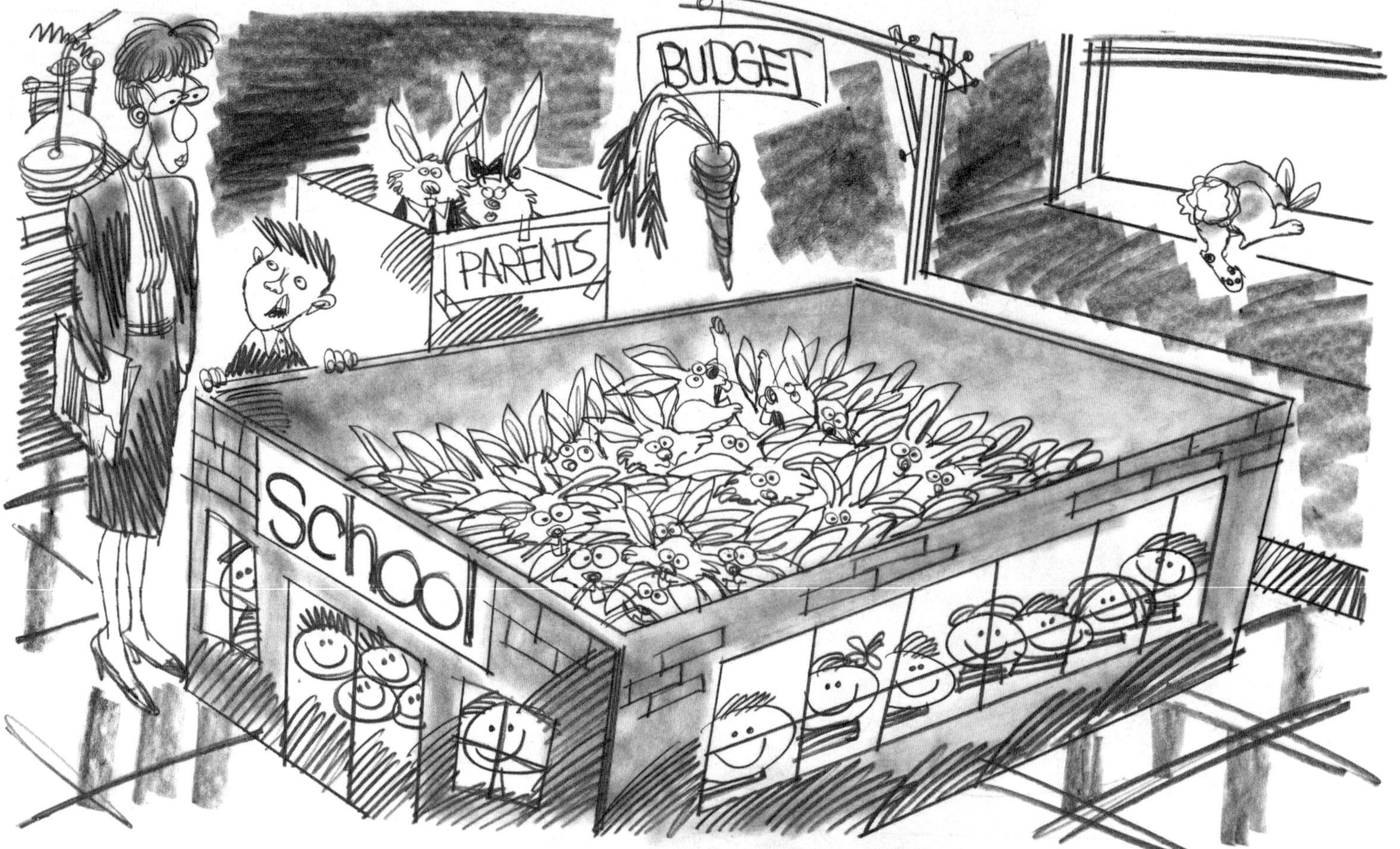
BUDGET
PARENTS
School

"For my science project I have constructed a model of the Utah education system starting with just two rabbits."

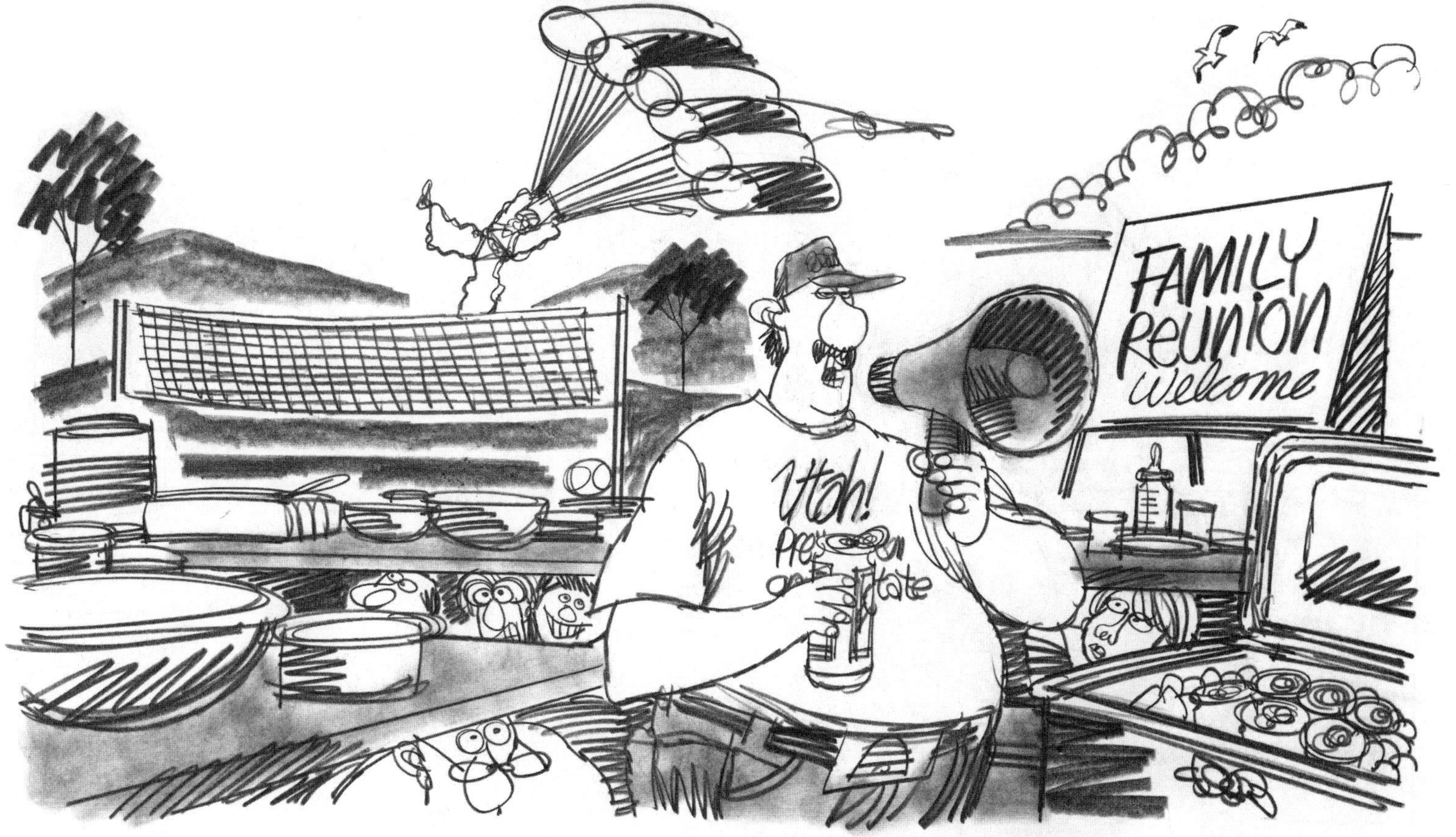
FAMILY
Reunion
Welcome
Utah!

"For your own safety, please remain under the picnic tables until Grandma has landed. Thank you."

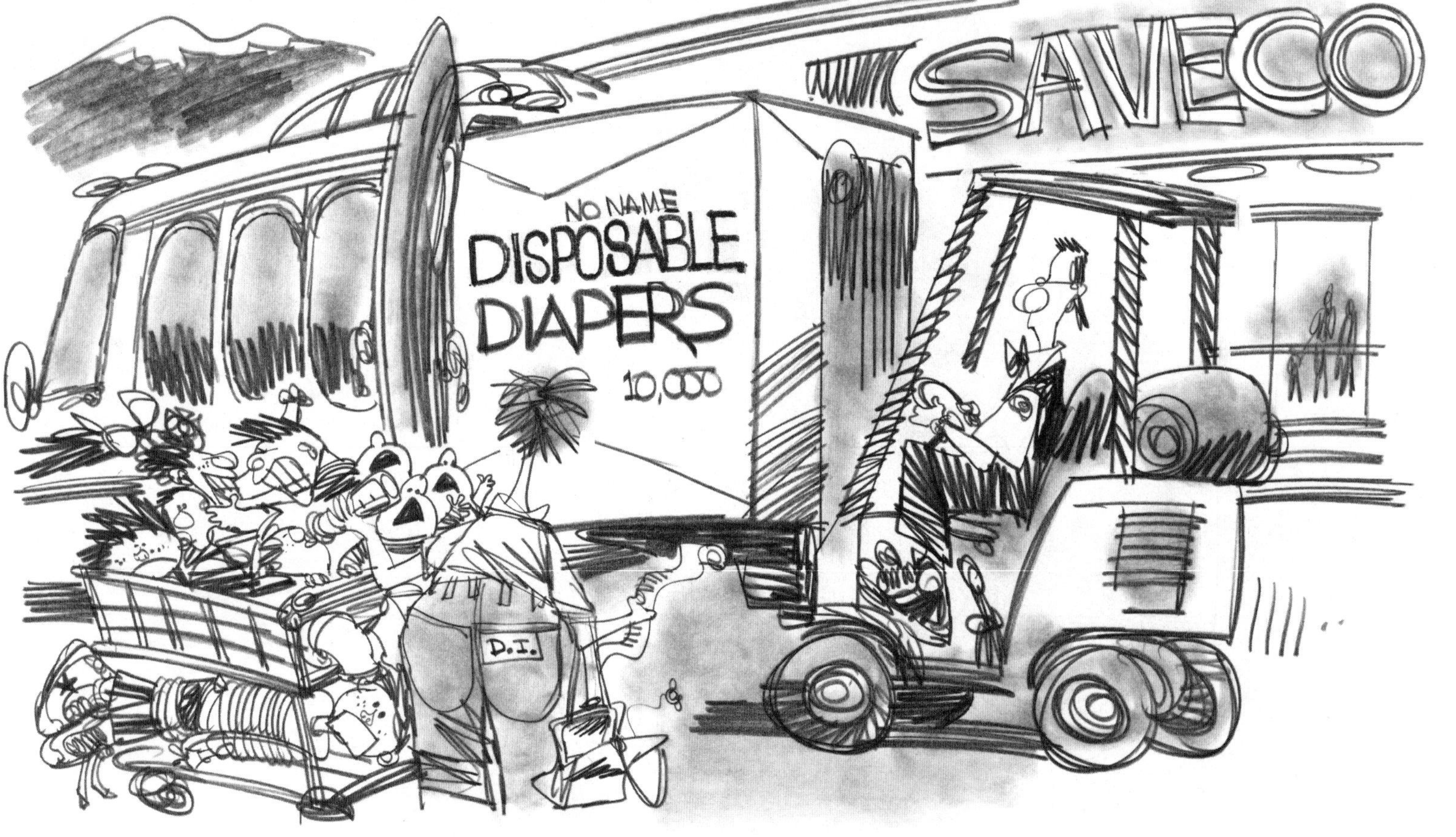
SAVECO
NO NAME
DISPOSABLE
DIAPERS
10,000
D.I.

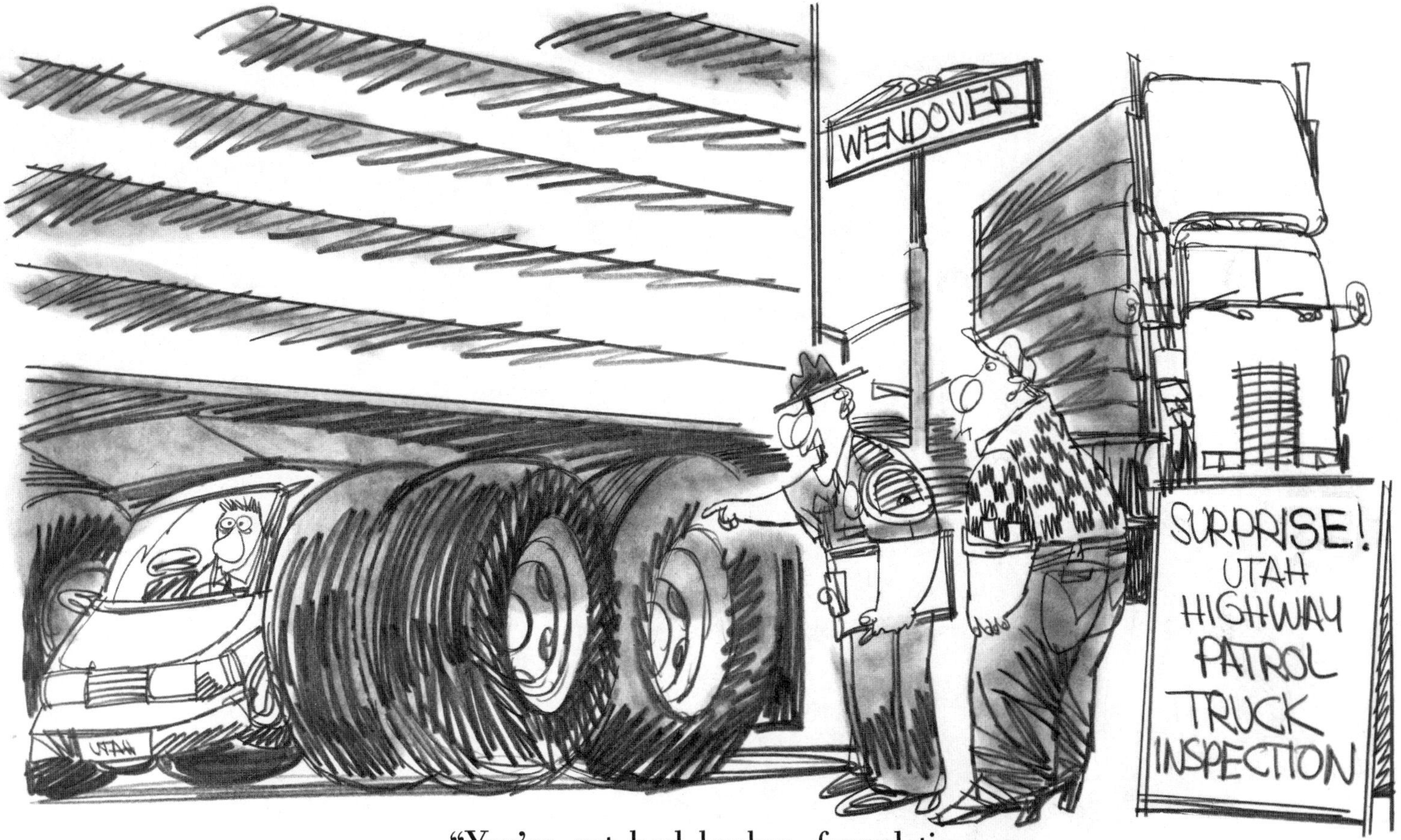
WENDOVER
UTAH
SURPRISE!
UTAH
HIGHWAY
PATROL
TRUCK
INSPECTION

"You've got bad brakes, frayed tires, and a small commuter in your rear axle."

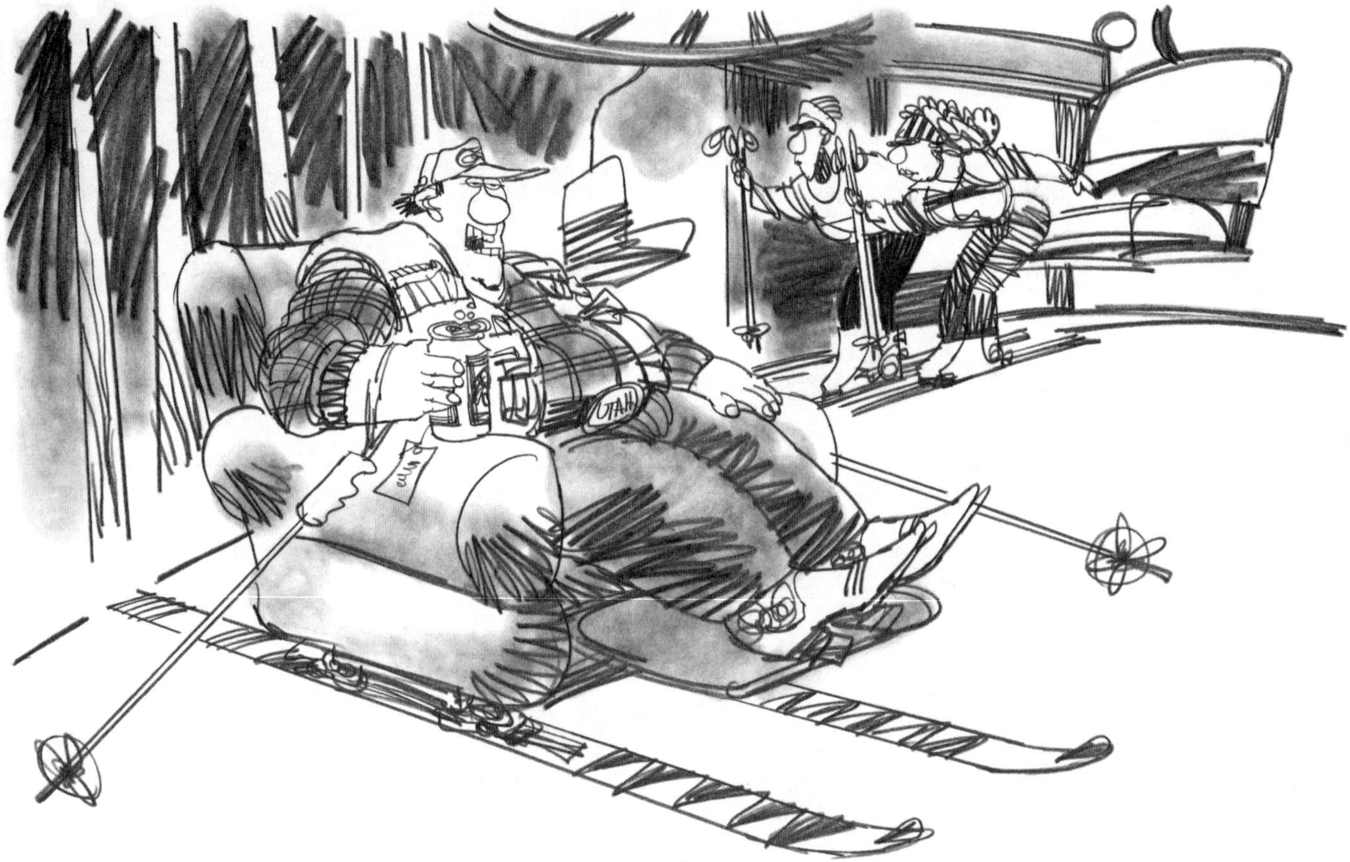
UTAH

"I said they'd never get me up here on skis . . .
Yet here I am."

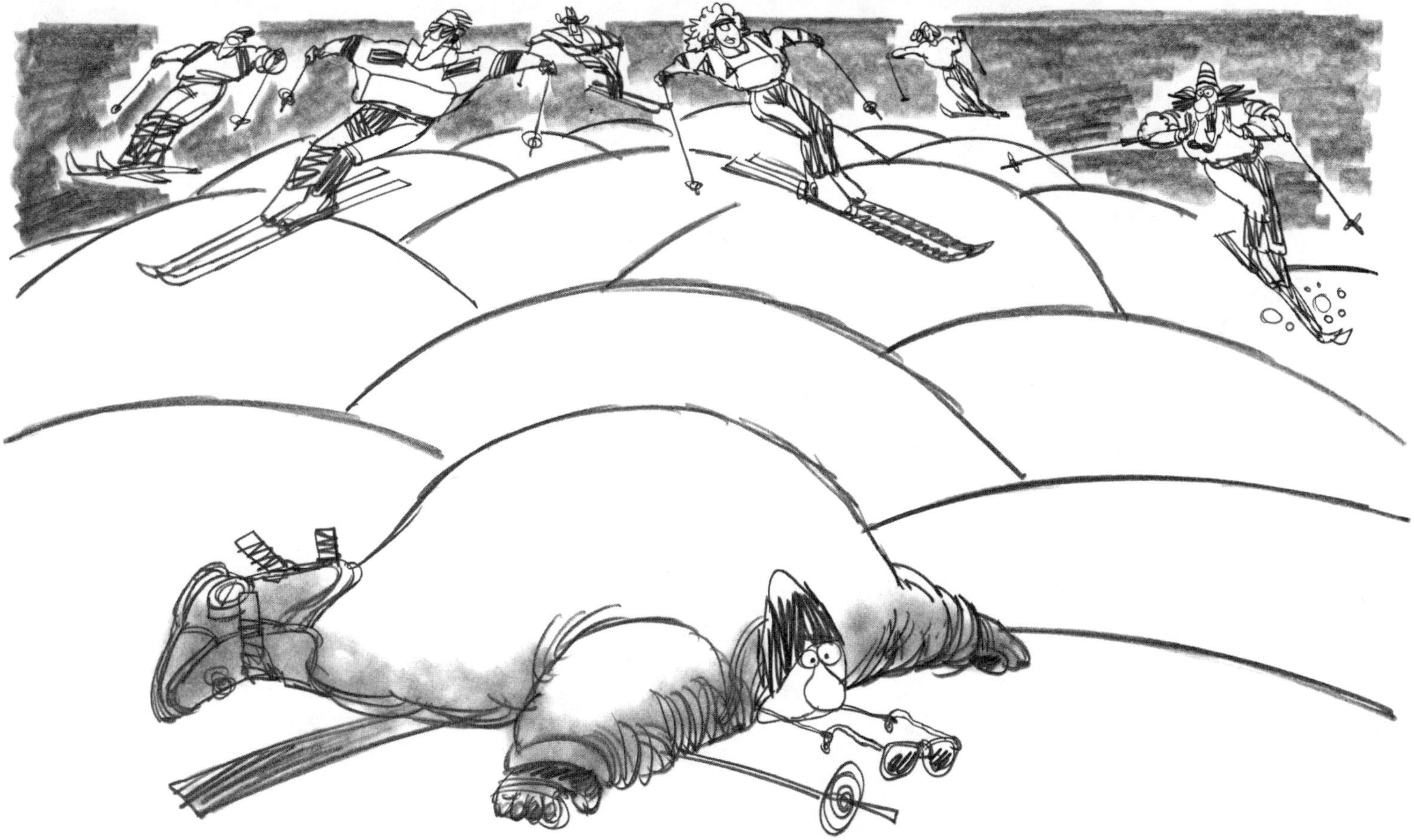

"Harry, get up! You look just like a mogul!"

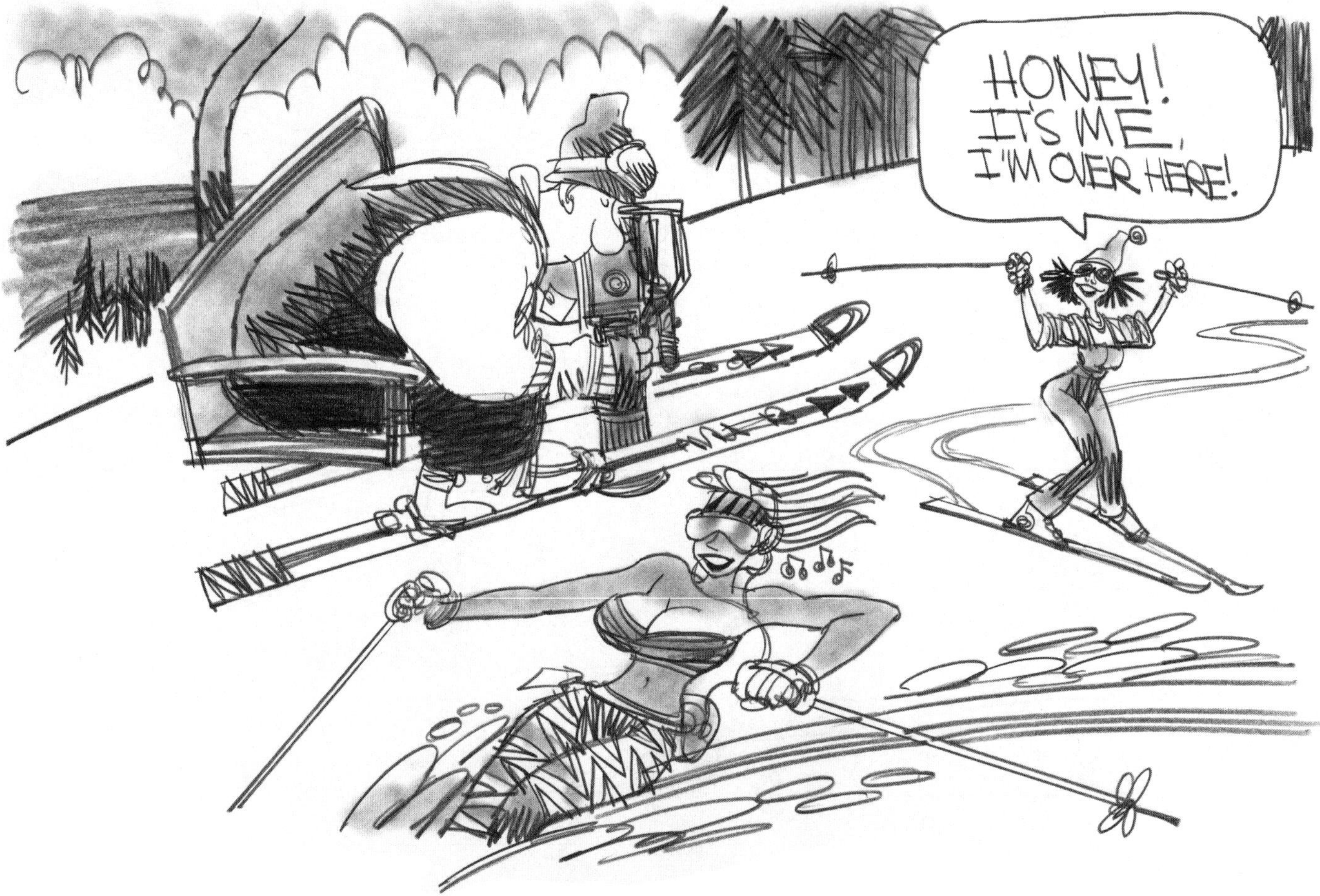
HONEY! IT'S ME, I'M OVER HERE!

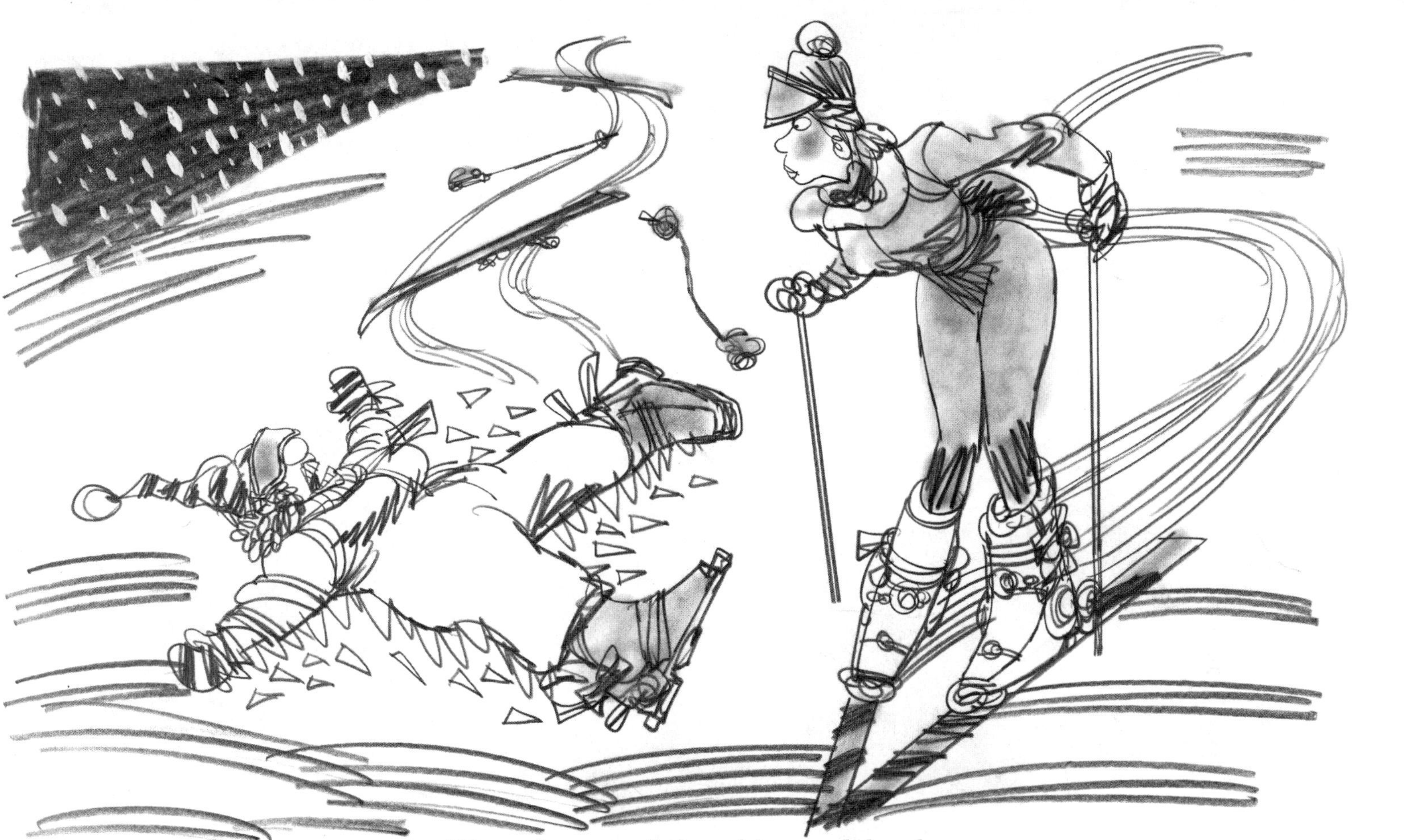

“Go ask one of the ski patrol hunks
to drag me to the nearest hot tub.”

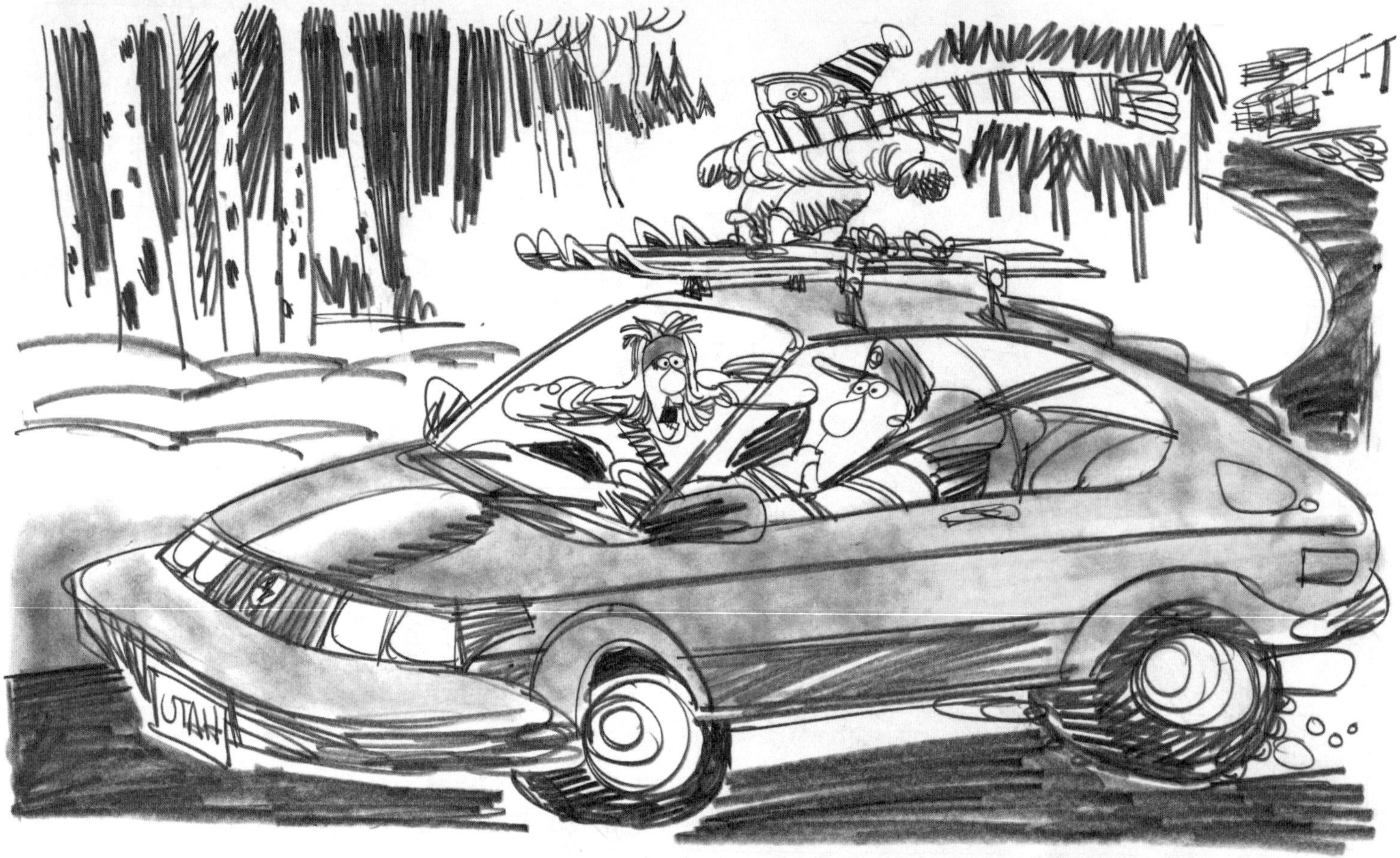
UTAH

"Stop the car!
We forgot to take little Walter out of his skis!"

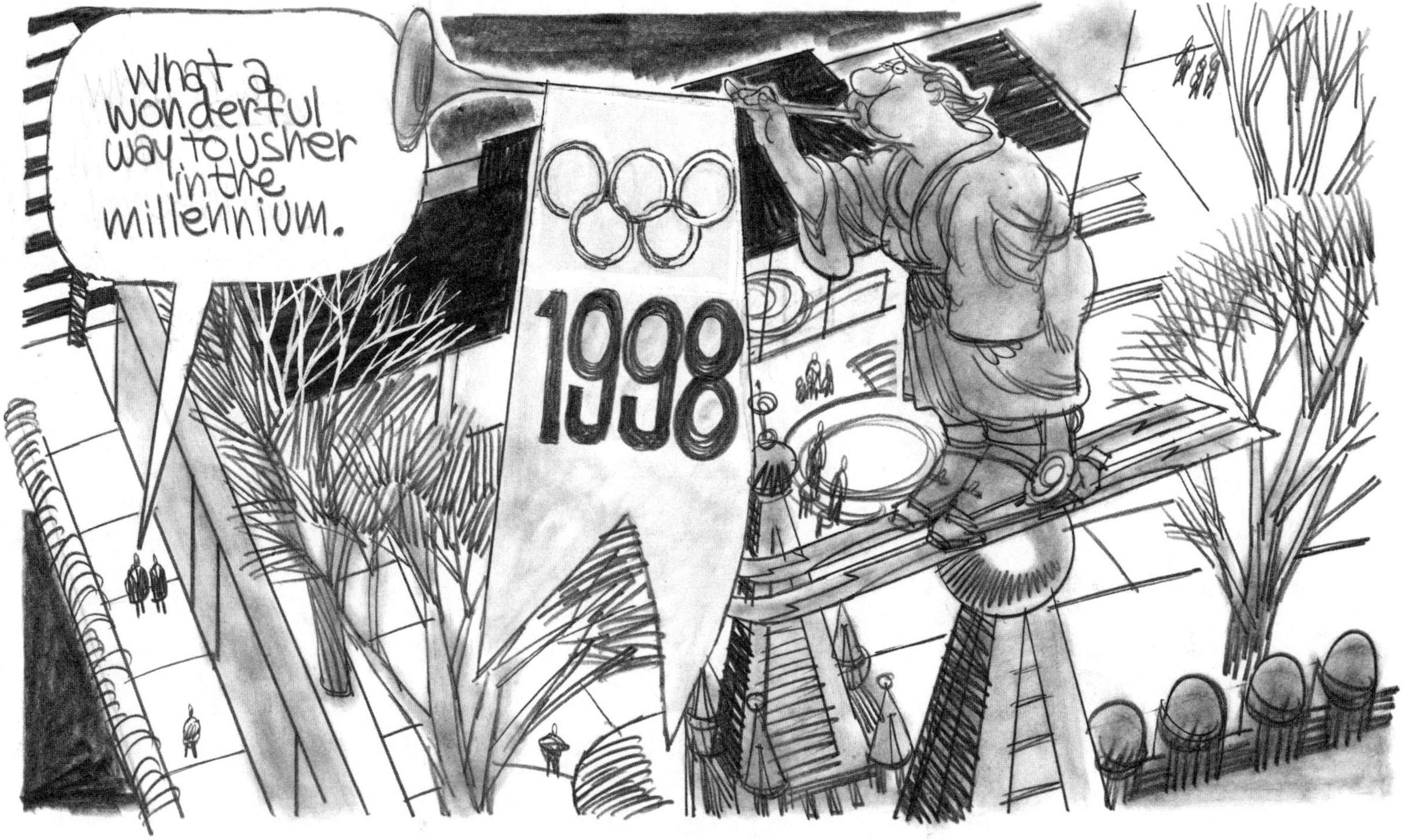
What a wonderful way to usher in the millennium.
1998

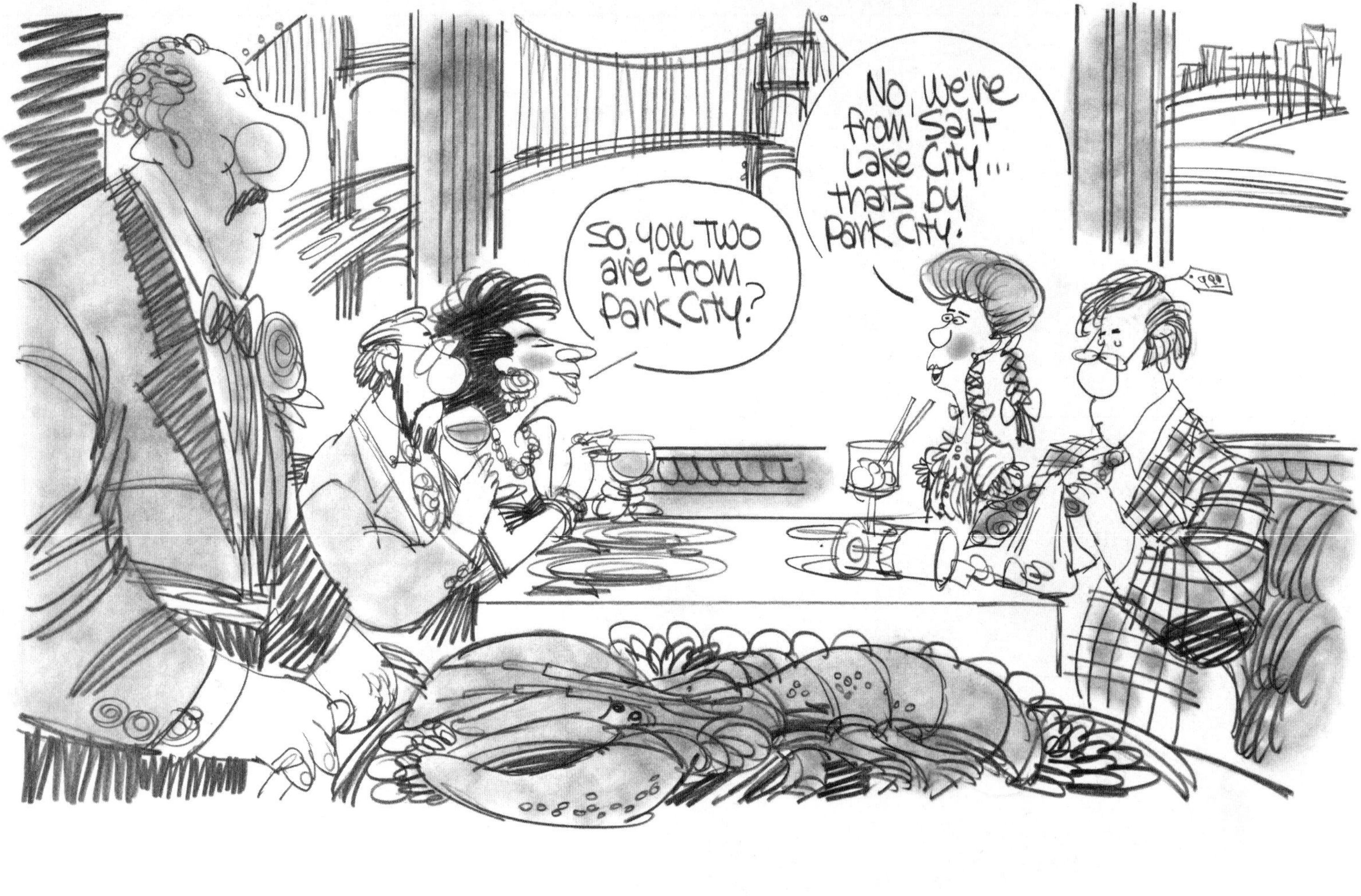
So, you TWO are from Park City?
No, we're from Salt Lake City... thats by Park City!

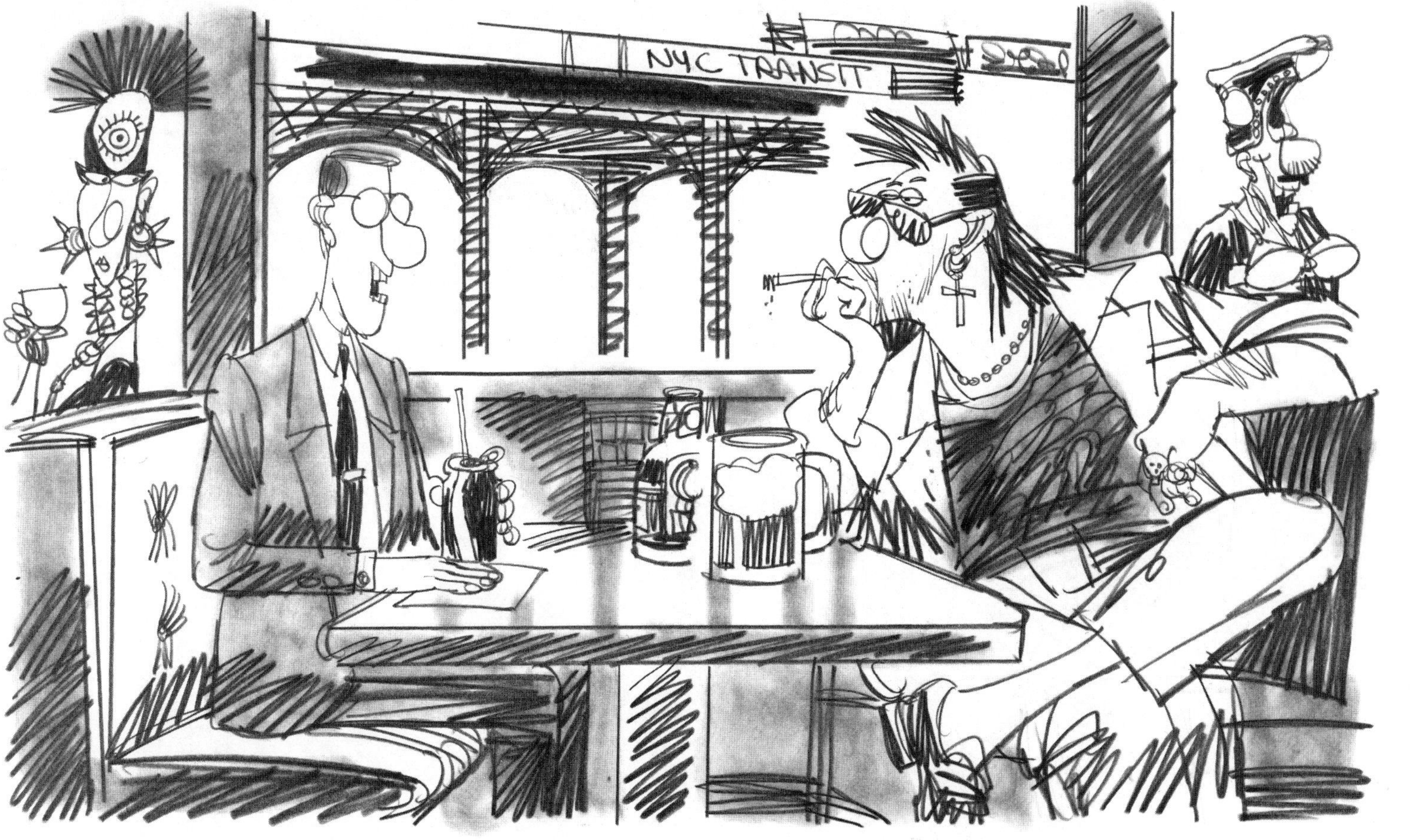
NYC TRANSIT

"I had to leave Utah because I was too much of a radical—
the way I dressed, my hairstyle, my favorite soft drink."

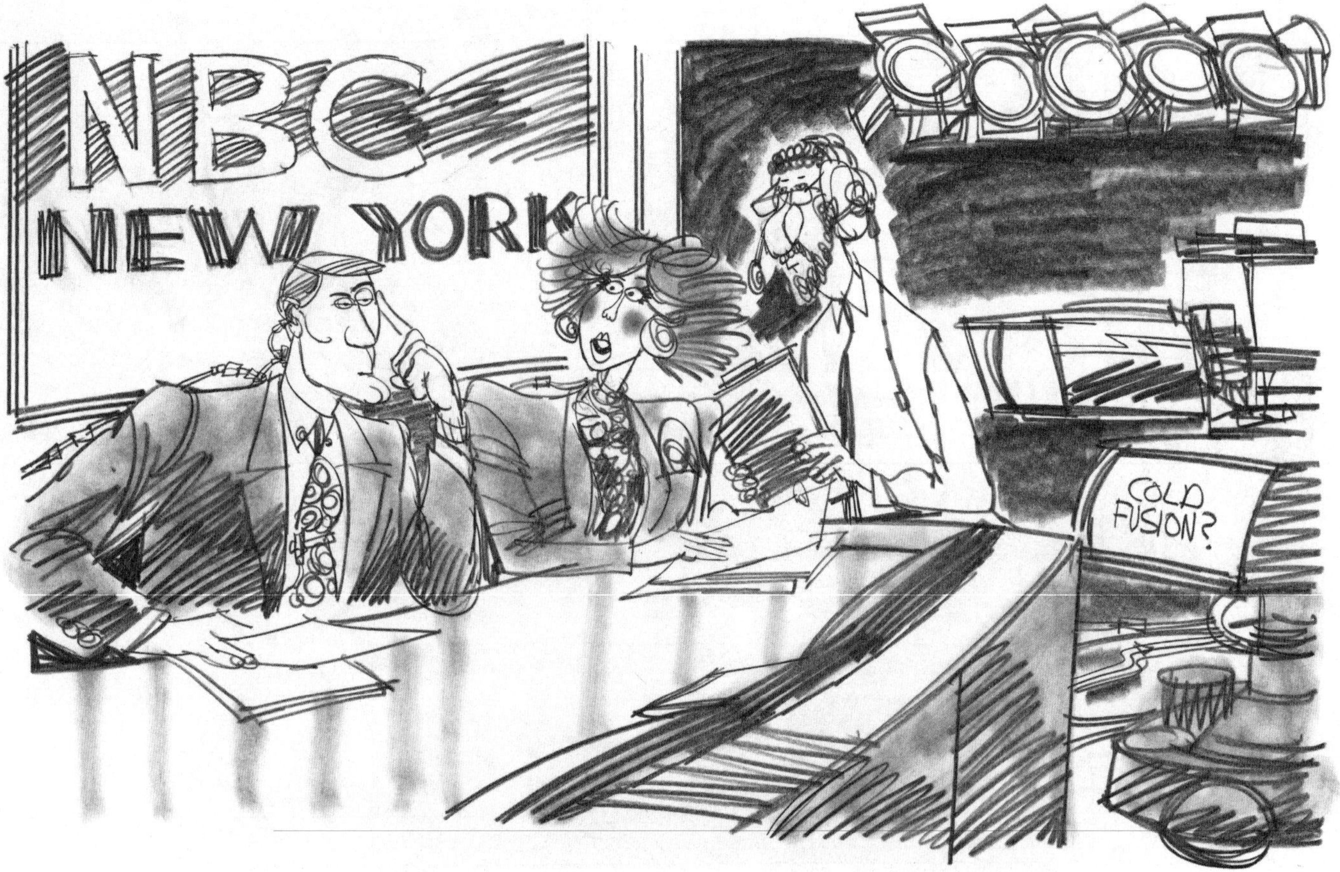
NBC
NEW YORK
COLD FUSION?

"Utah . . . you remember. You were a nightly news anchor there."

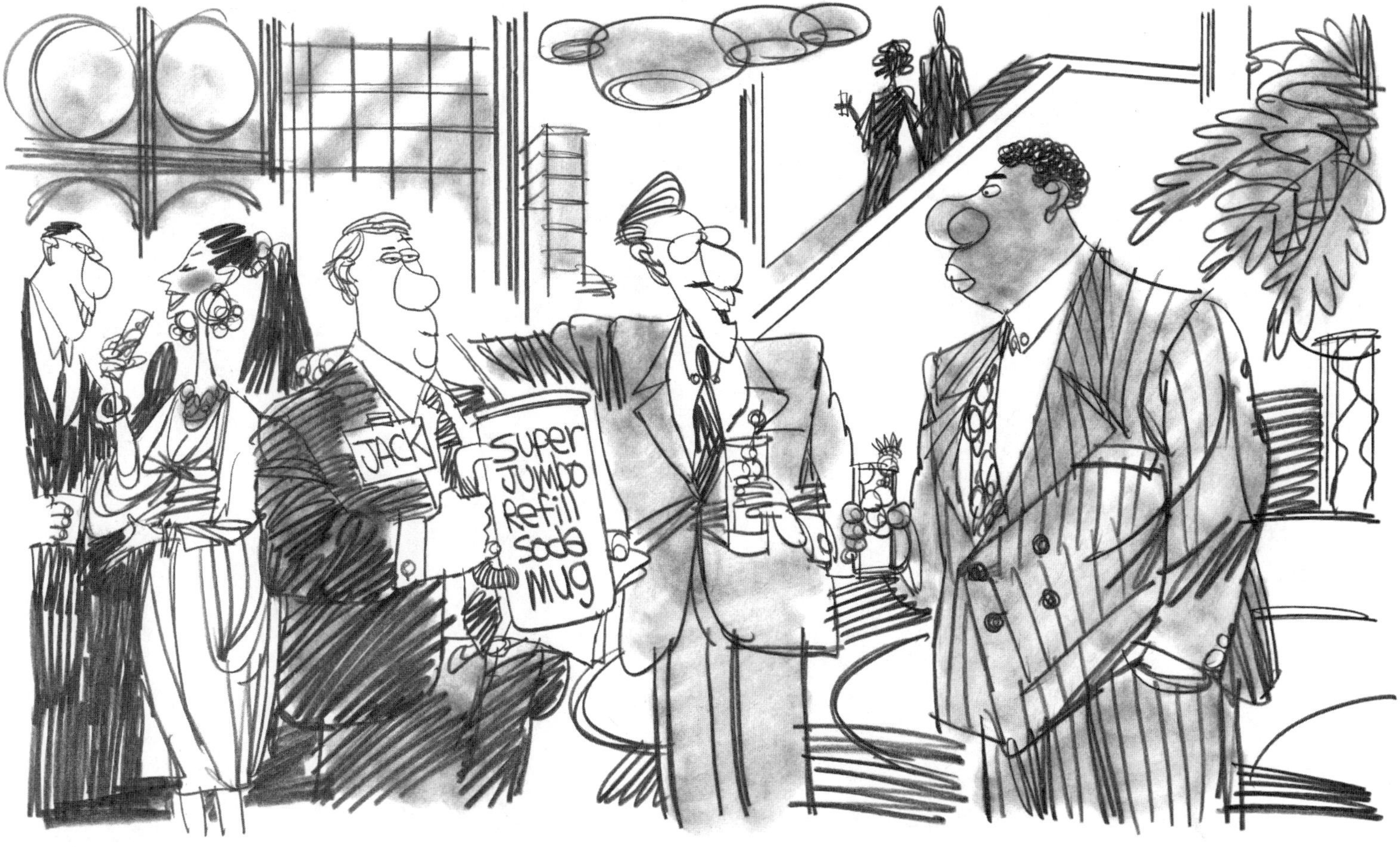
JACK
Super JUMBO Refill Soda Mug

"Jack here is our sales rep in Utah."

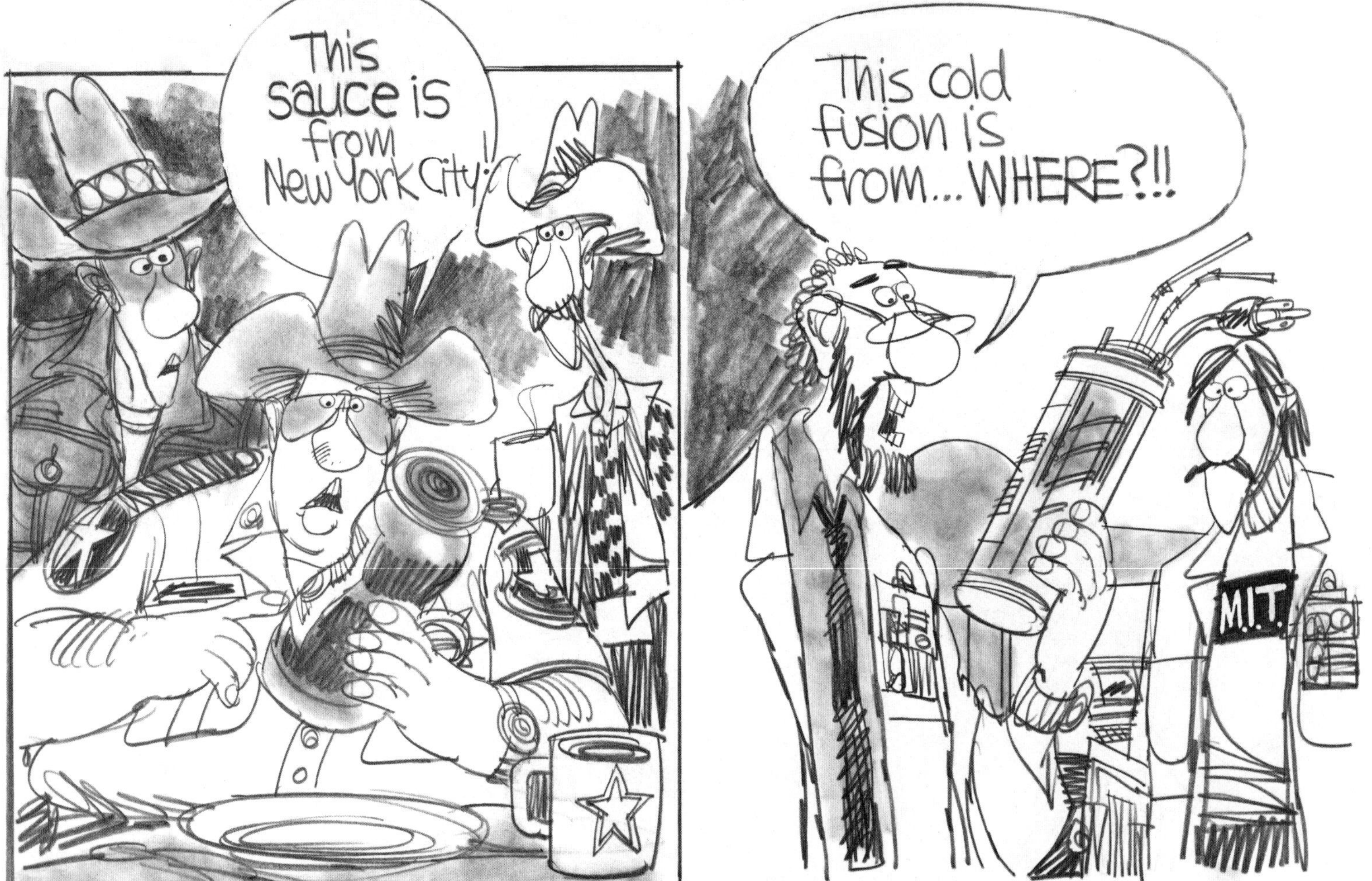
This sauce is from New York City!
This cold fusion is from... WHERE?!!
M.I.T.

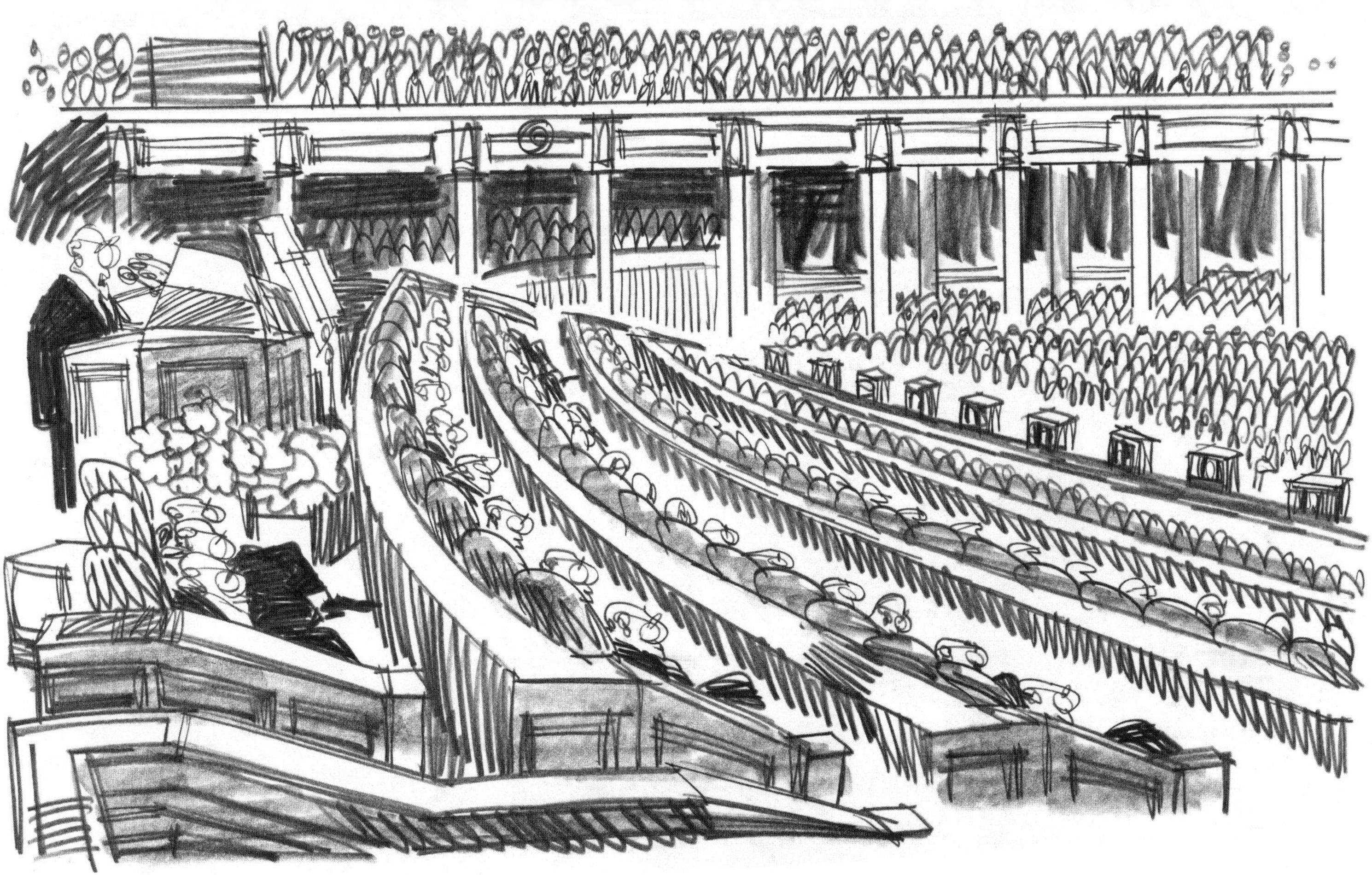

"After which we'll rise and sing from our new hymn books, 'The Spirit of God Like Fusion is Burning.' "

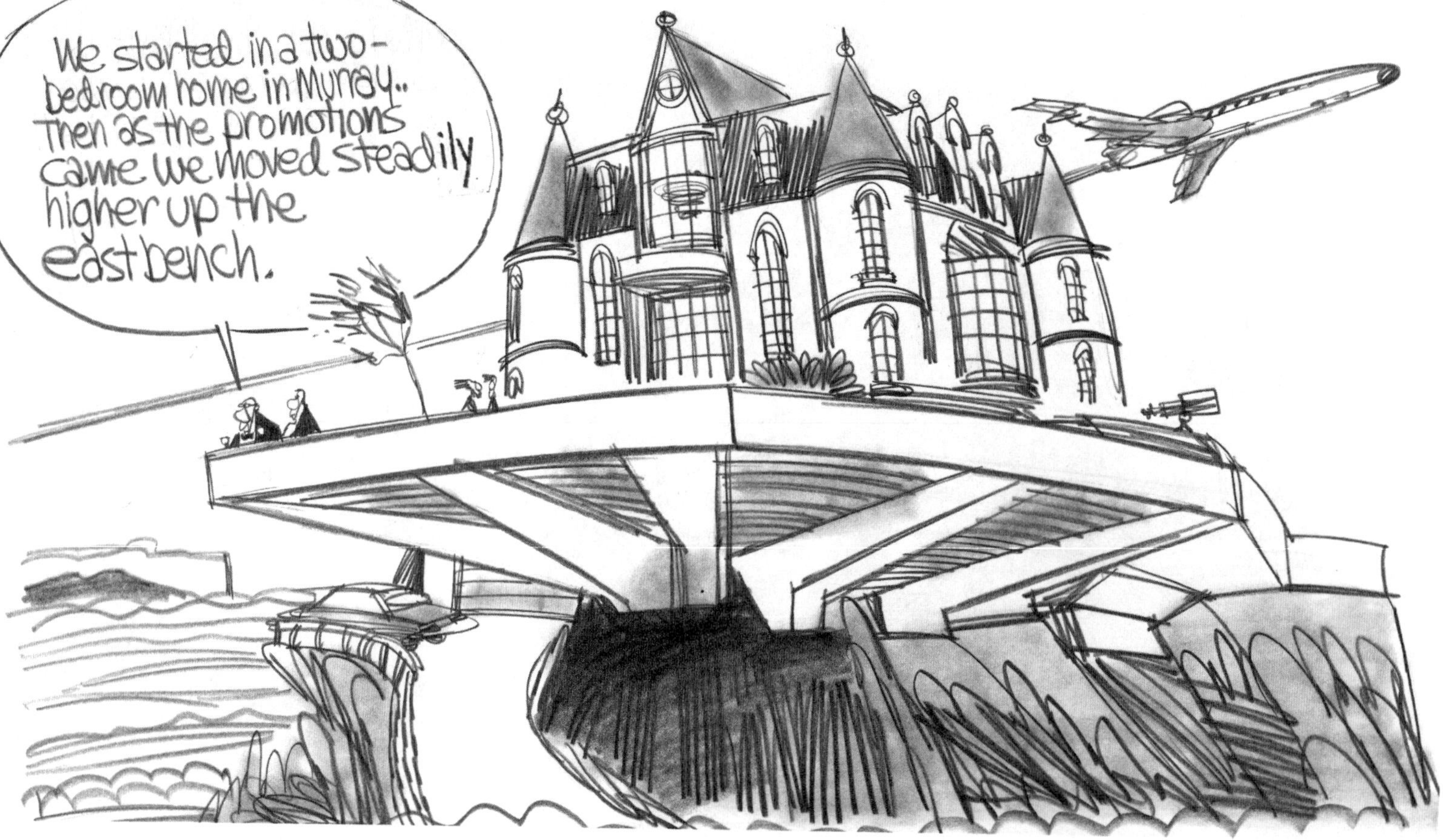
We started in a two-bedroom home in Murray.. Then as the promotions came we moved steadily higher up the east bench.

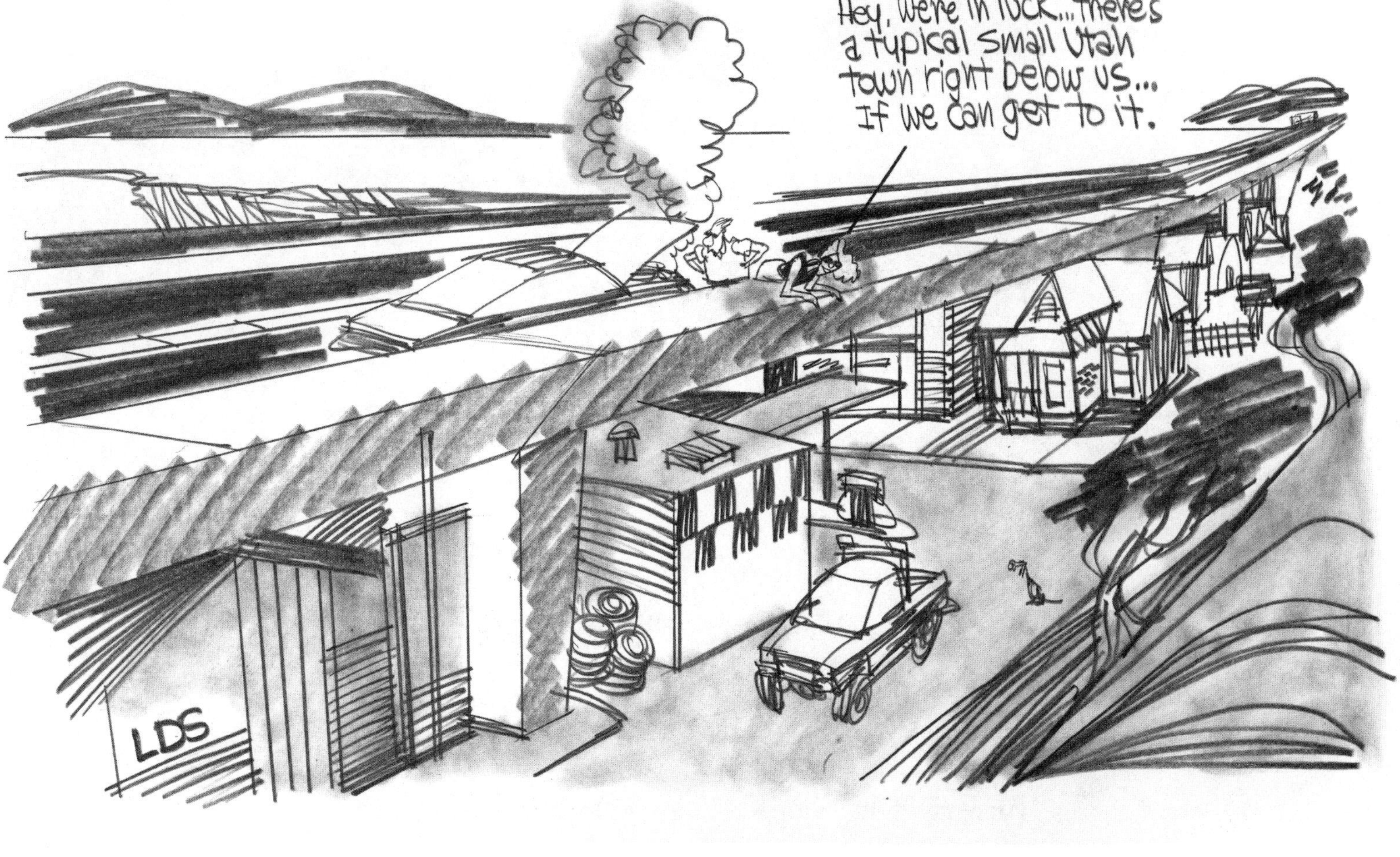
Hey, we're in luck... there's a typical small Utah town right below us... If we can get to it.
LDS

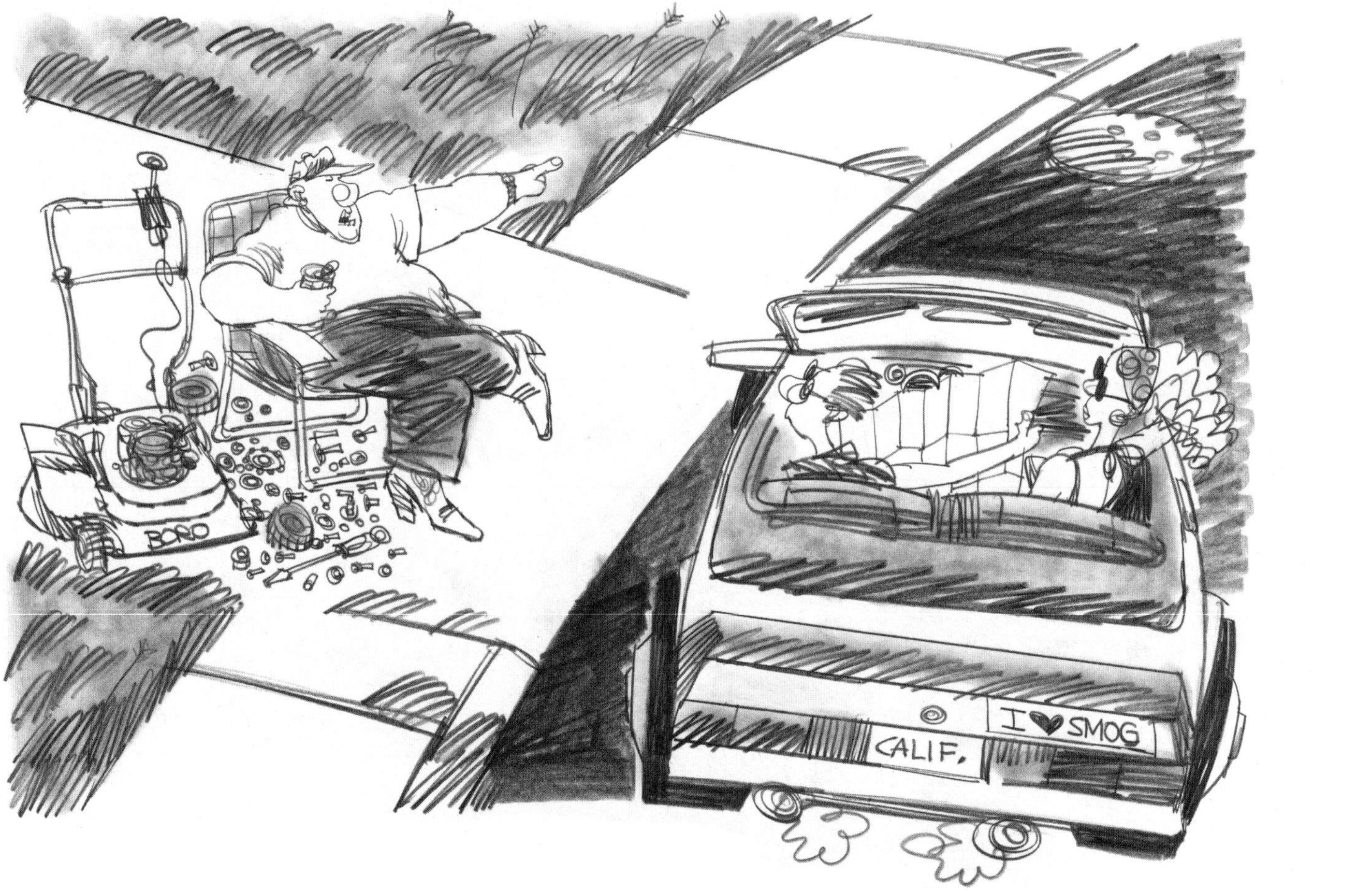
BORO
CALIF.
I ♥ SMOG

"Turn right at ShopKo, then left at Fred Meyer's, past Pic-N-Save, right at K-Mart, and a left at Food-for-Less—right across from Price Savers. You can't miss it."

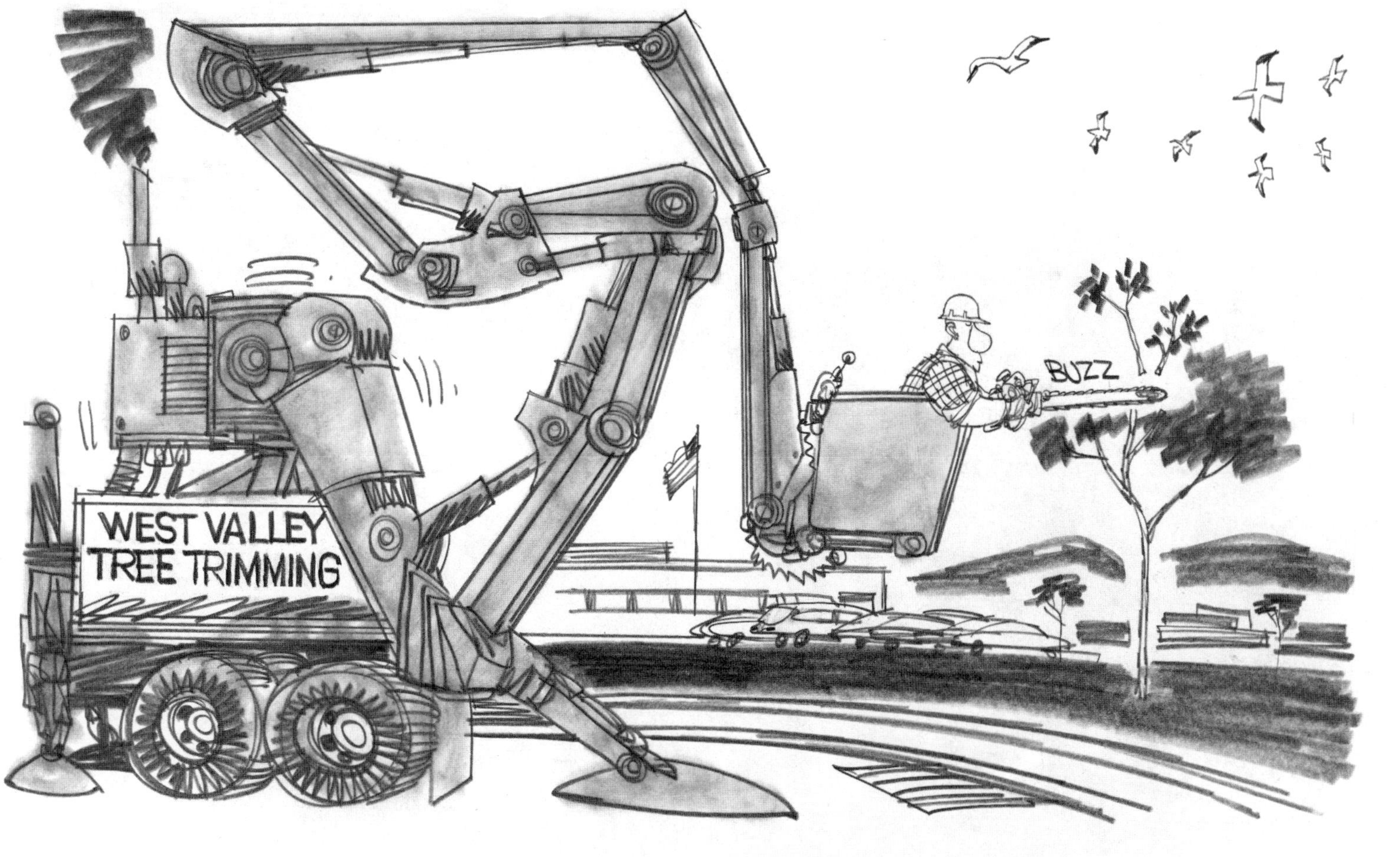
WEST VALLEY
TREE TRIMMING
BUZZ

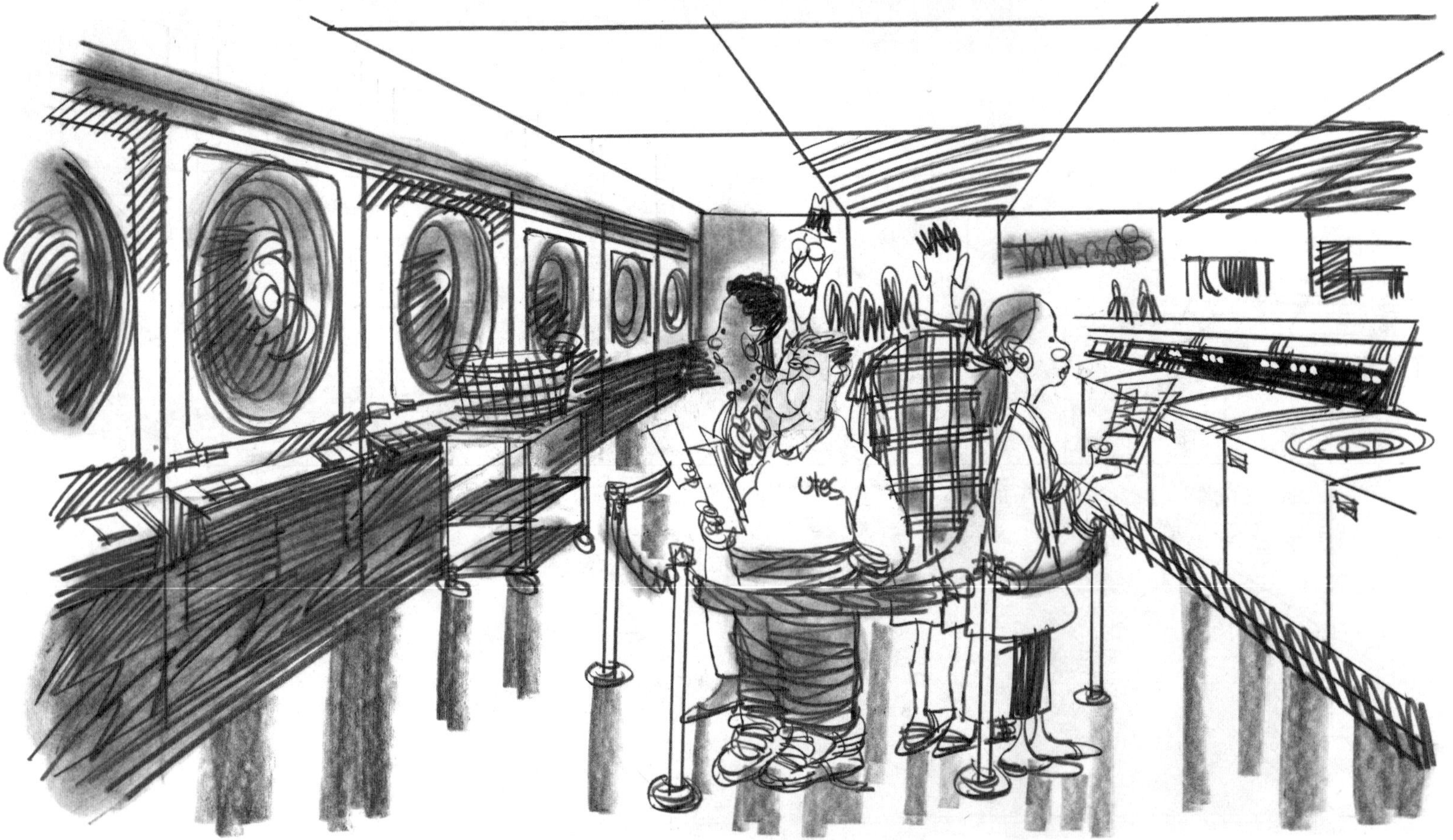
Utes

For the apartment dweller—
Utah's Parade of Laundromats

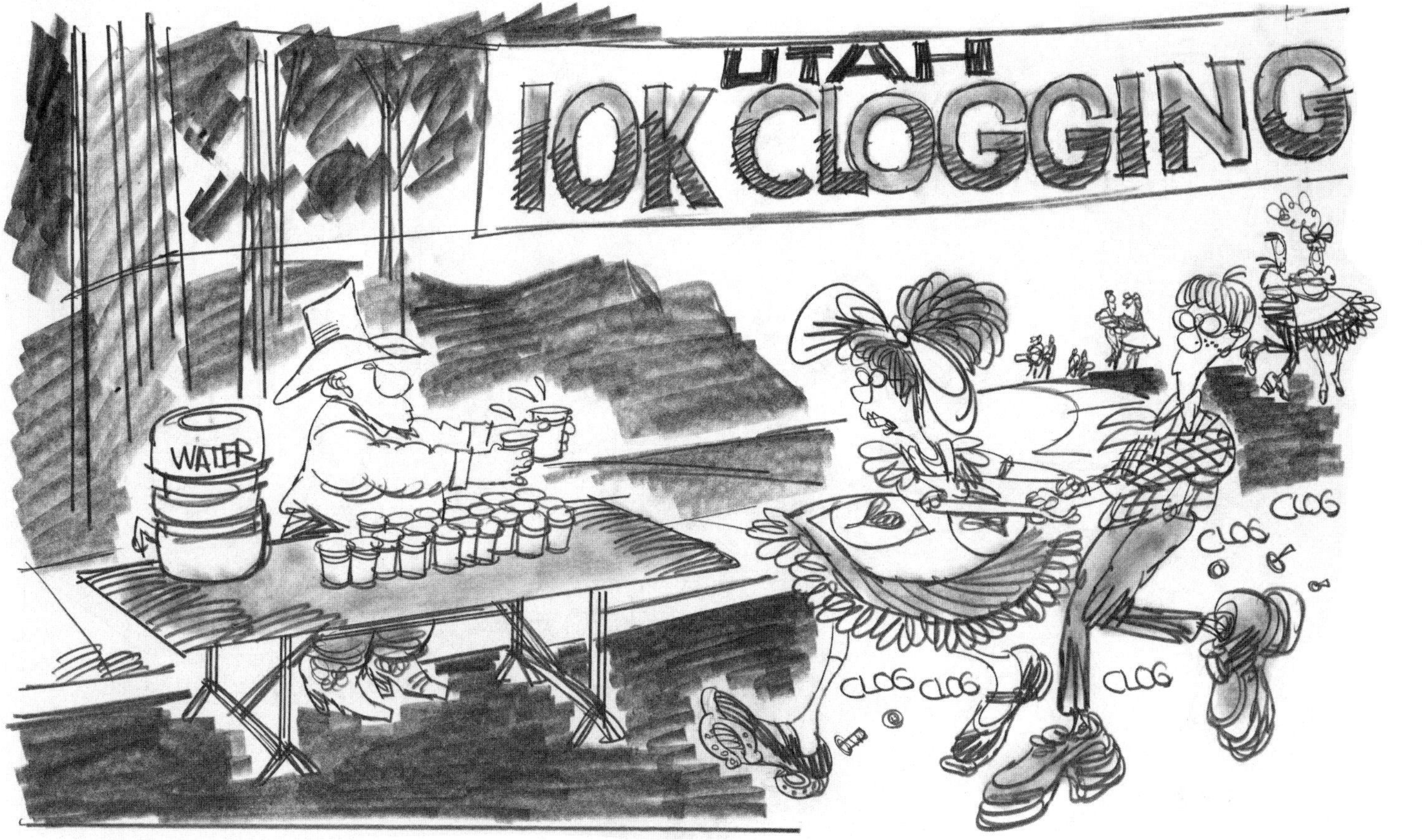
UTAH
10K CLOGGING
WATER
CLOG CLOG
CLOG CLOG
CLOG

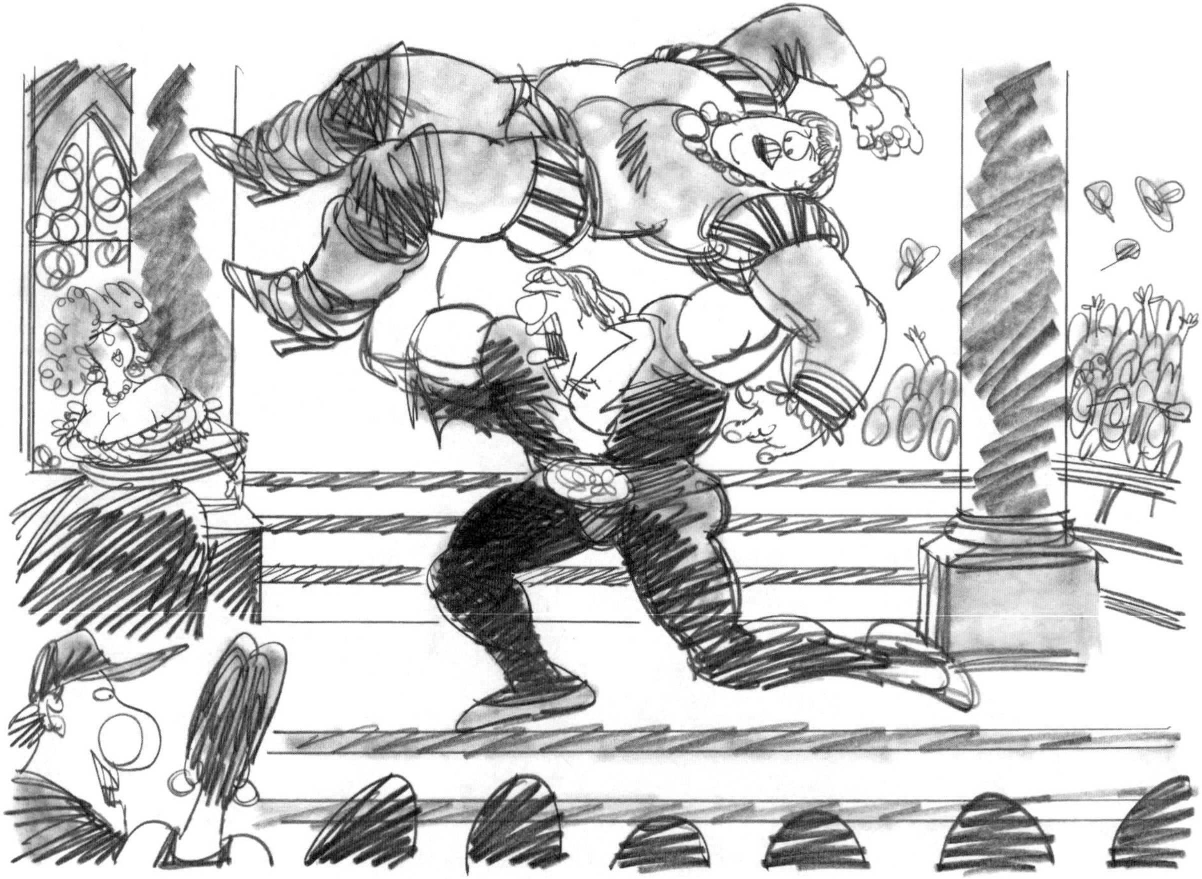

" 'Hulk Hamlet' . . . Finally Cedar City puts on a play I can understand!"

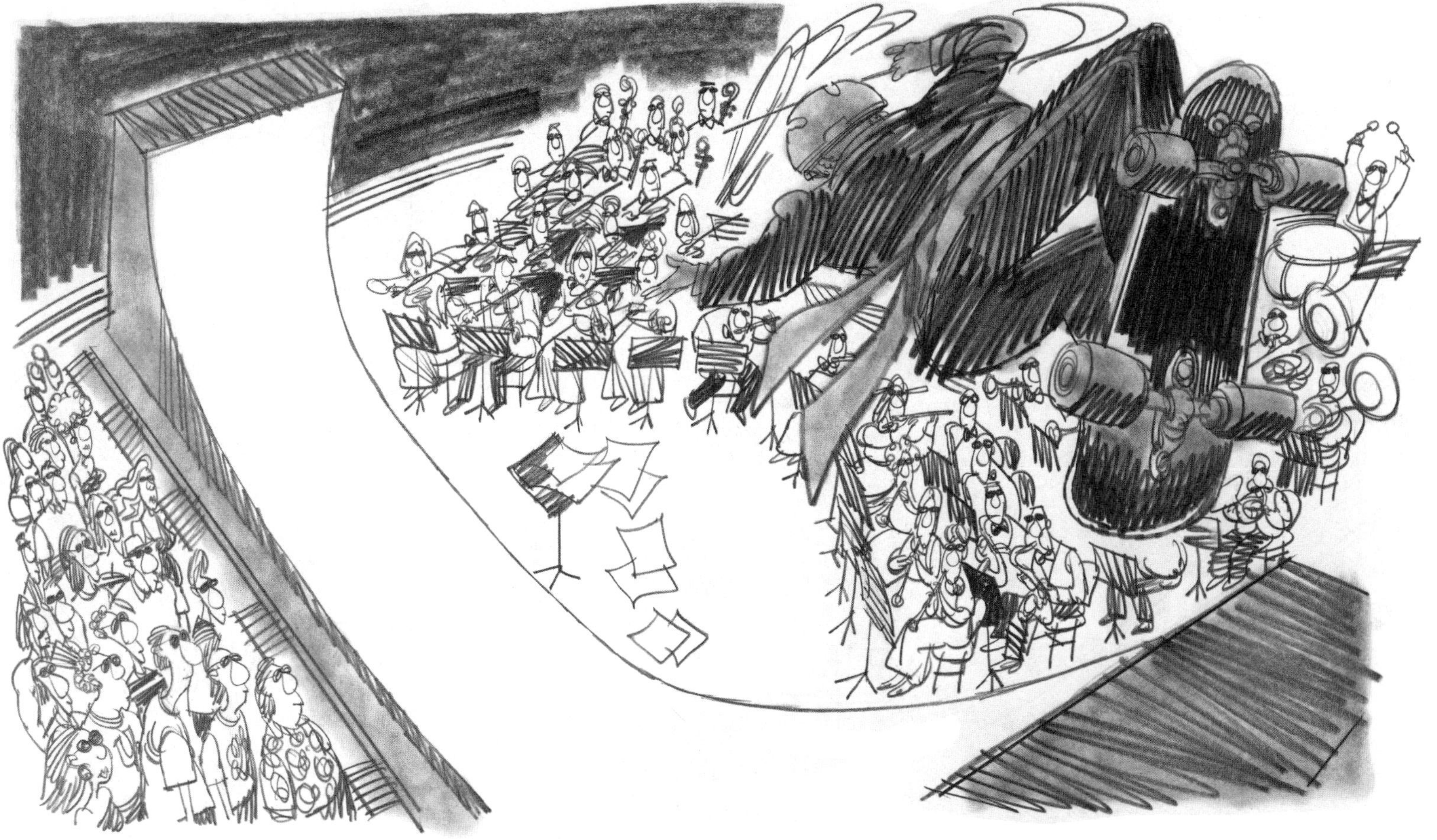

THE UTAH SYMPHONY'S
ANYTHING-TO-DRAW-A-CROWD SUMMER CONCERT SERIES

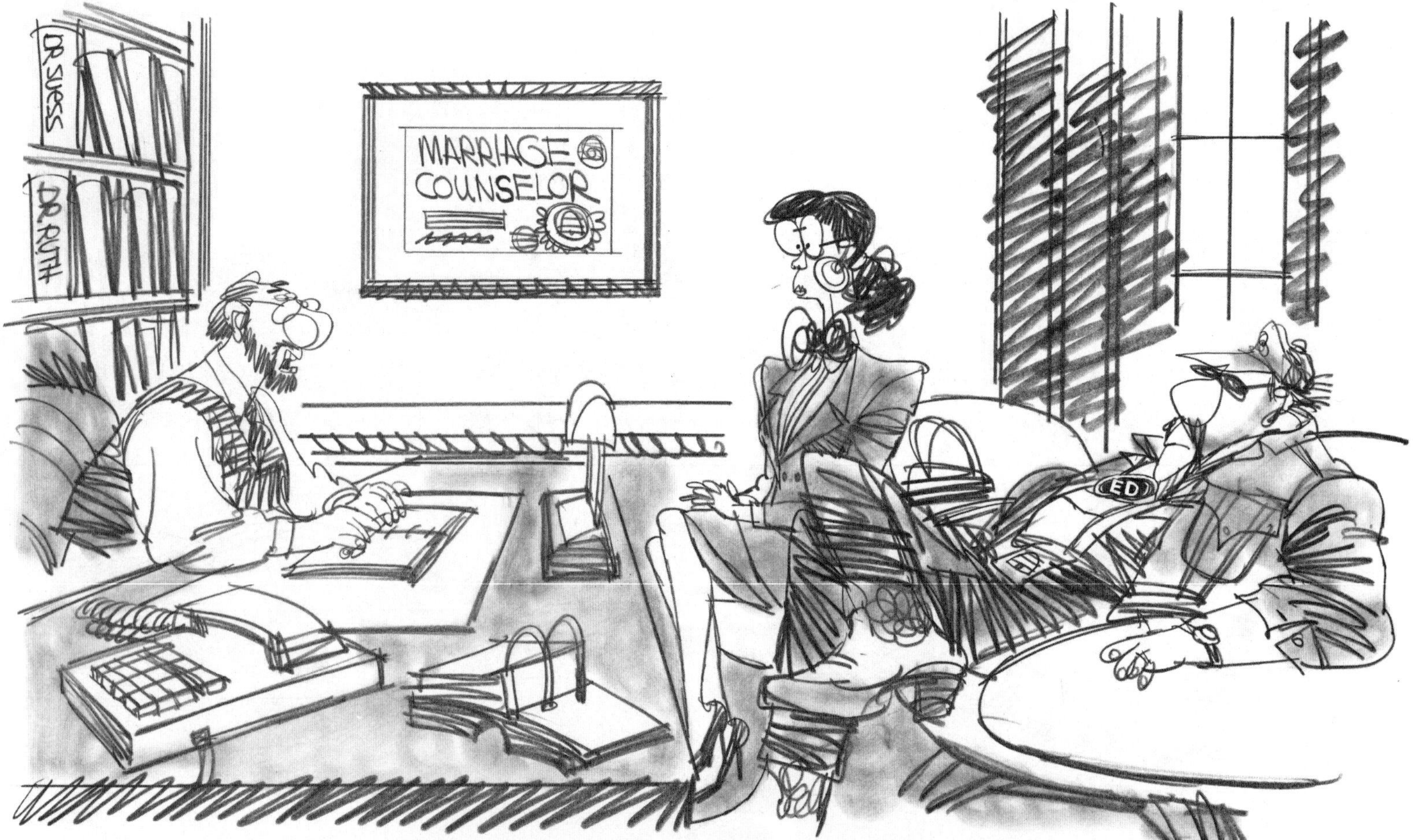
DR SUESS
DR. RUTH
MARRIAGE
COUNSELOR
ED

“Then why not Ballet West one weekend and monster trucks at the Salt Palace the next?”

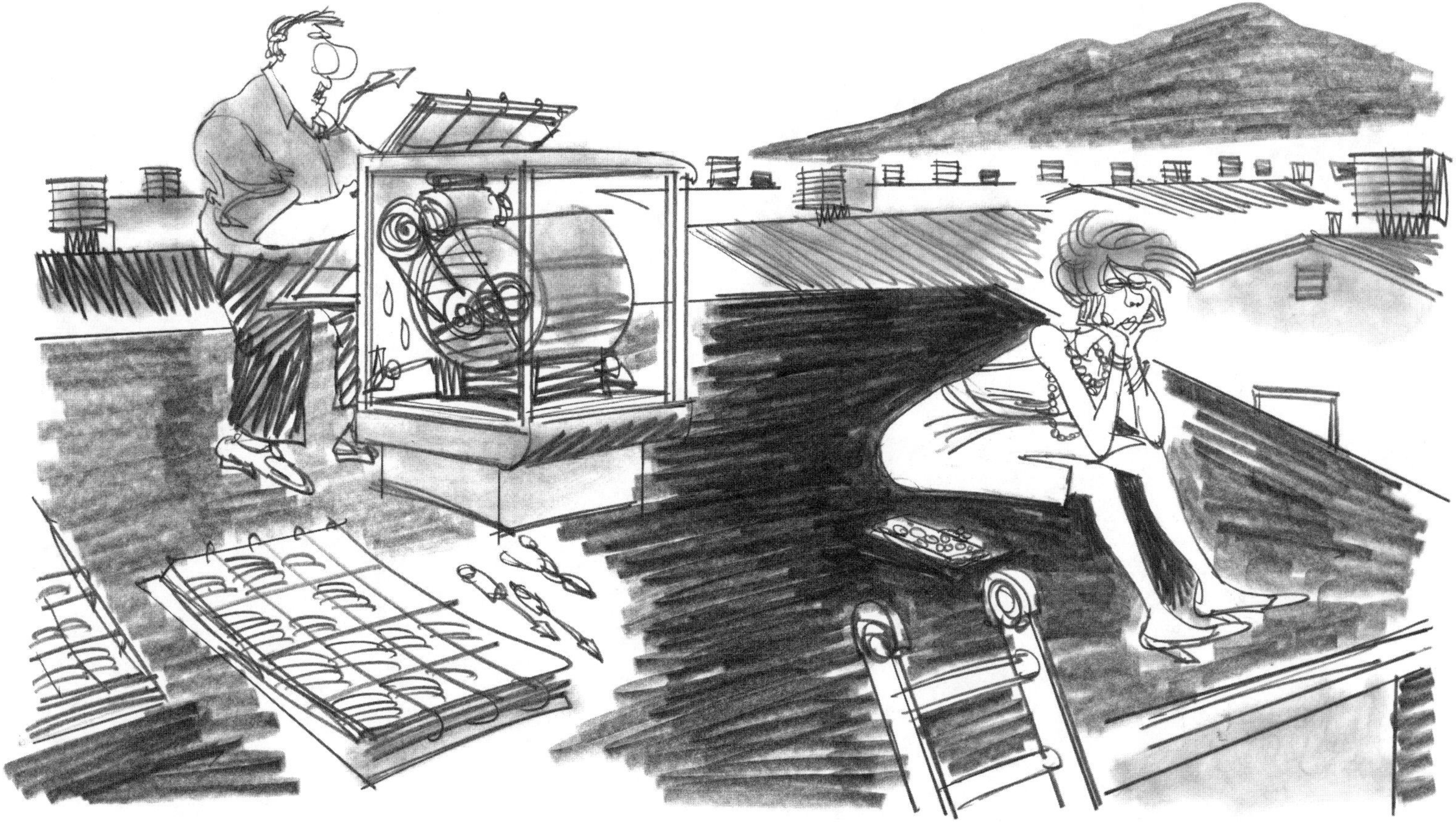

"Well, you said you wanted to get out of the house and spend more time together."

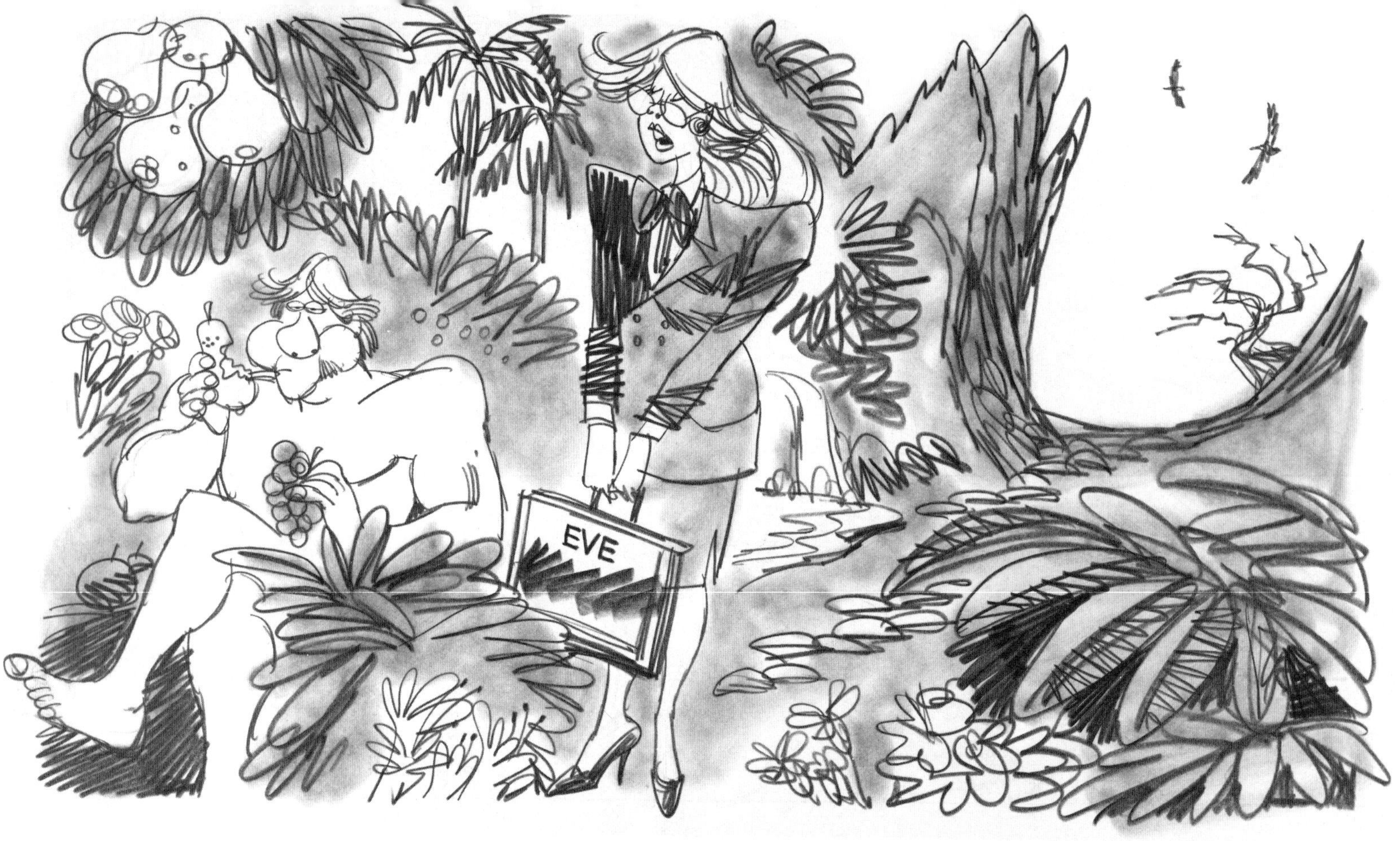
EVE

"The serpent beguiled me, and I went out and got a job . . .
I suggest you do, too."

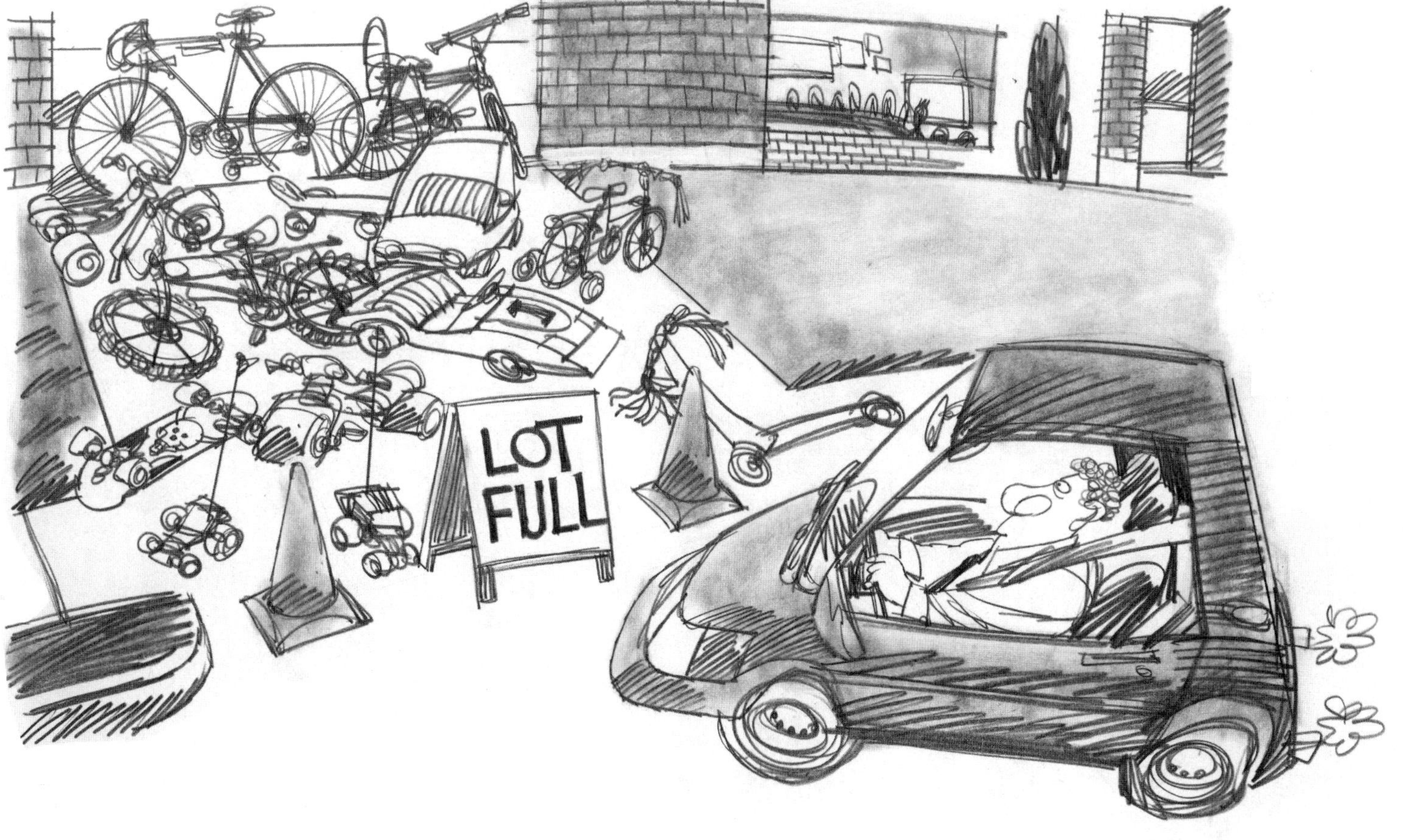
LOT
FULL

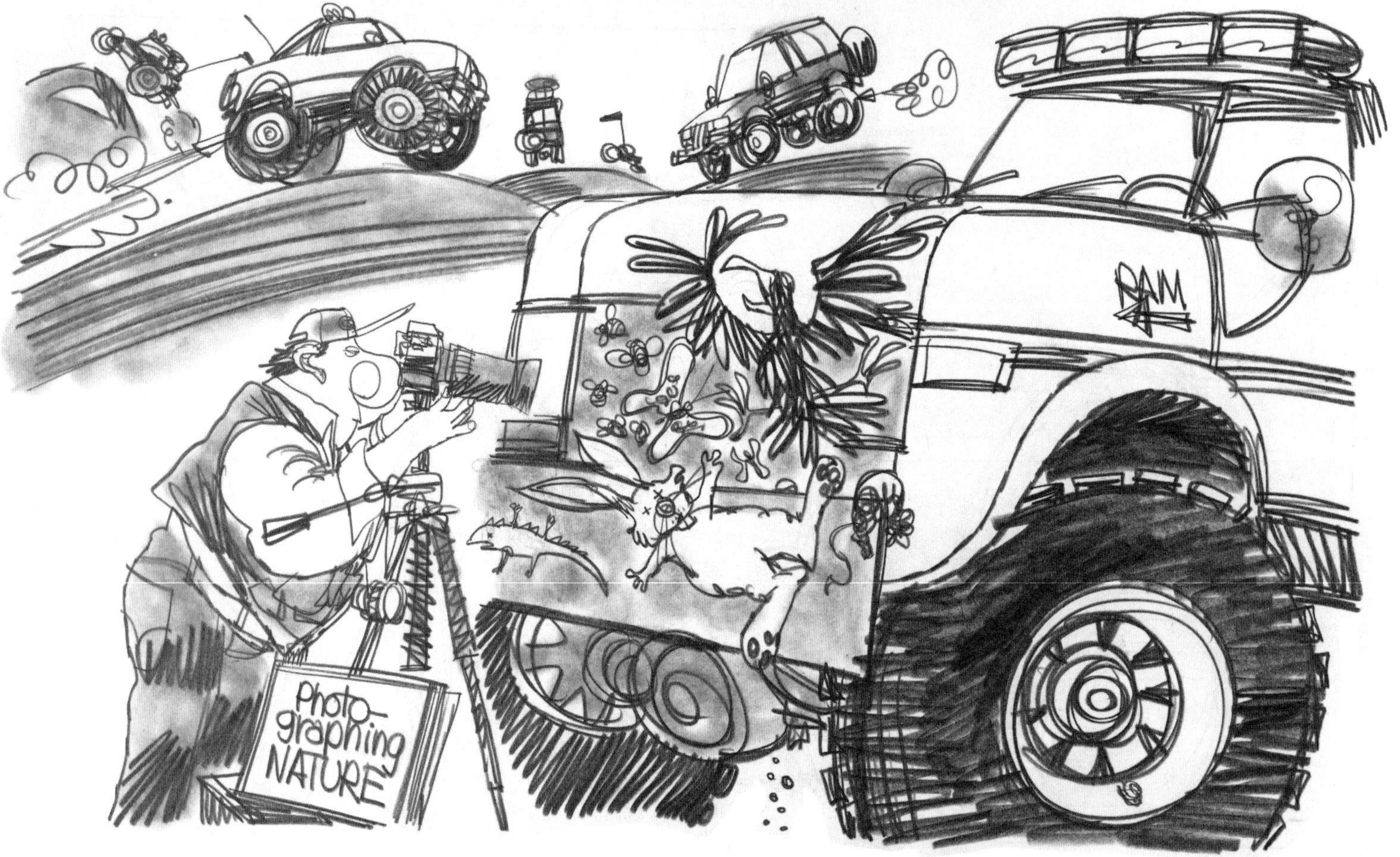
Photo-
graphing
NATURE
RAM

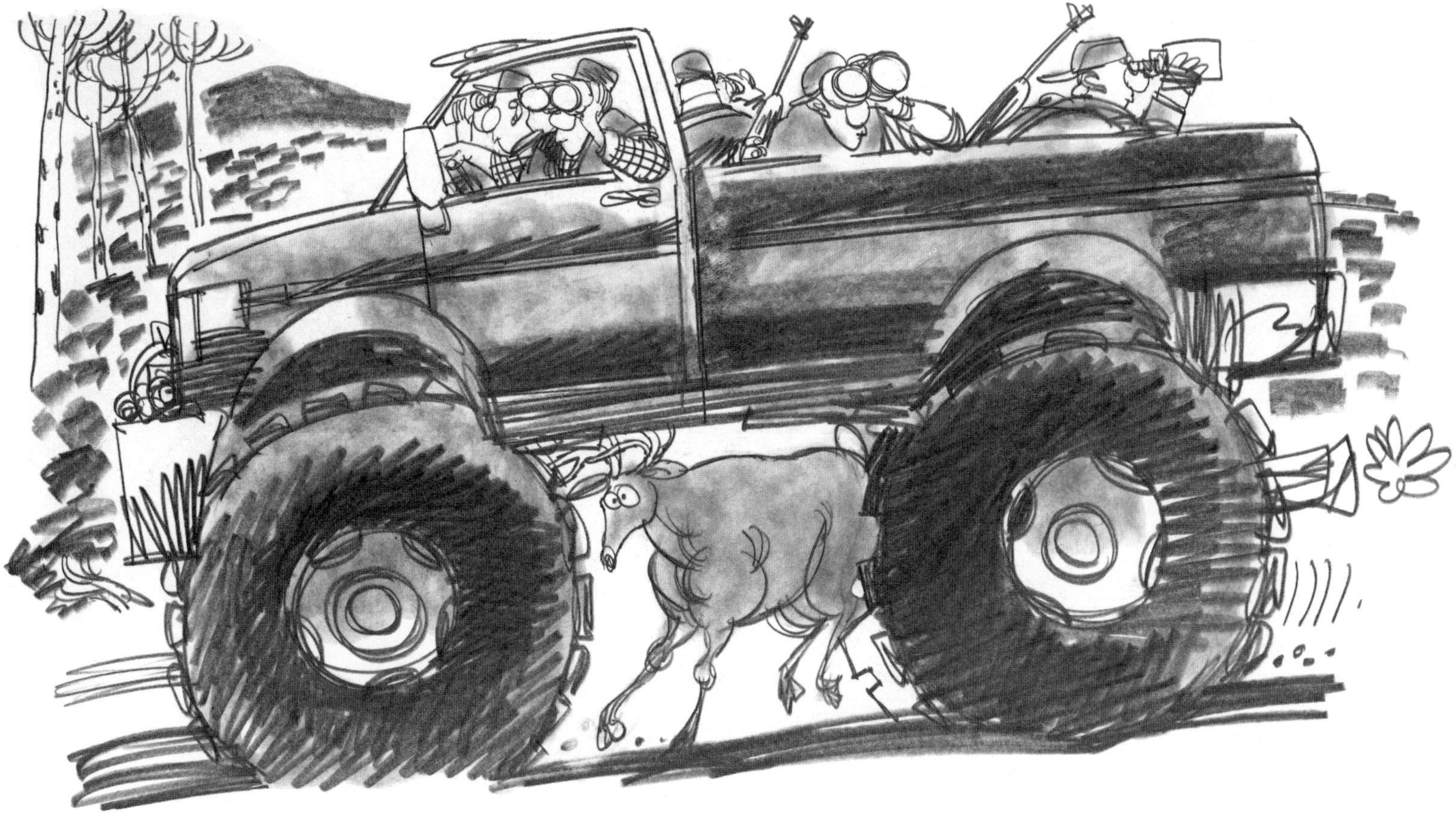

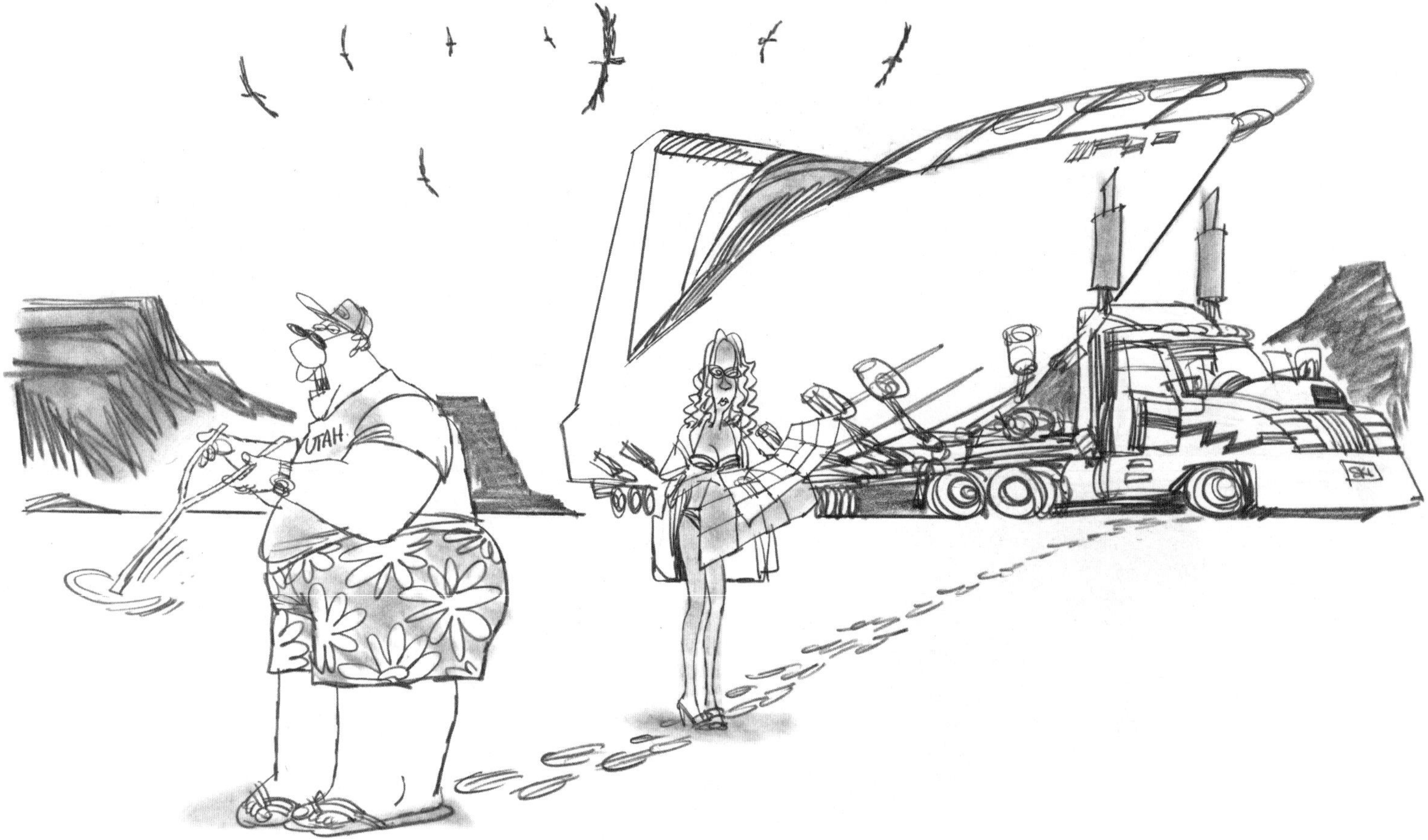
UTAH

"Lost? Hey, there's got to be a reservoir around here somewhere!"

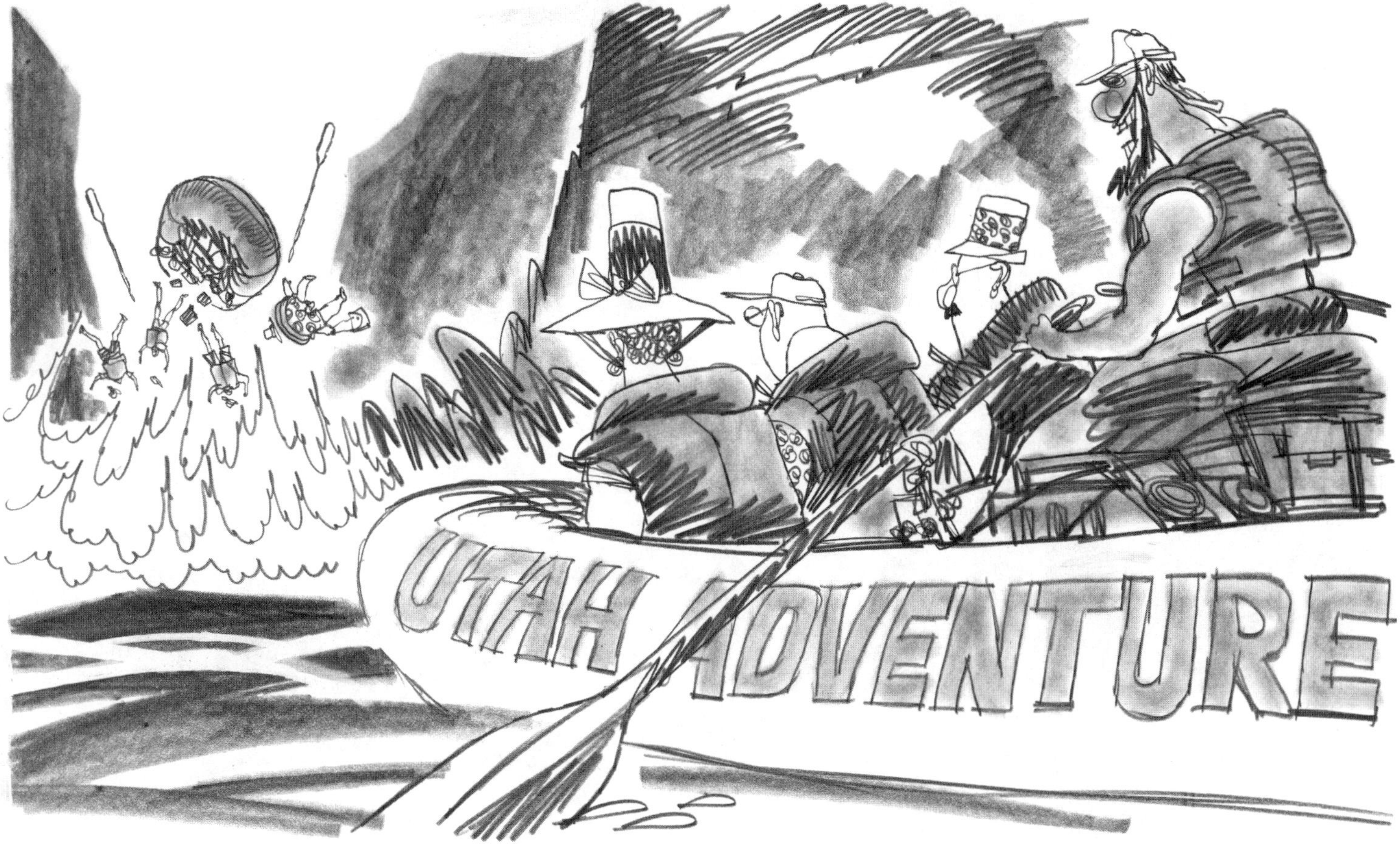
UTAH ADVENTURE

"Hang on everyone. This is going to be fun!"

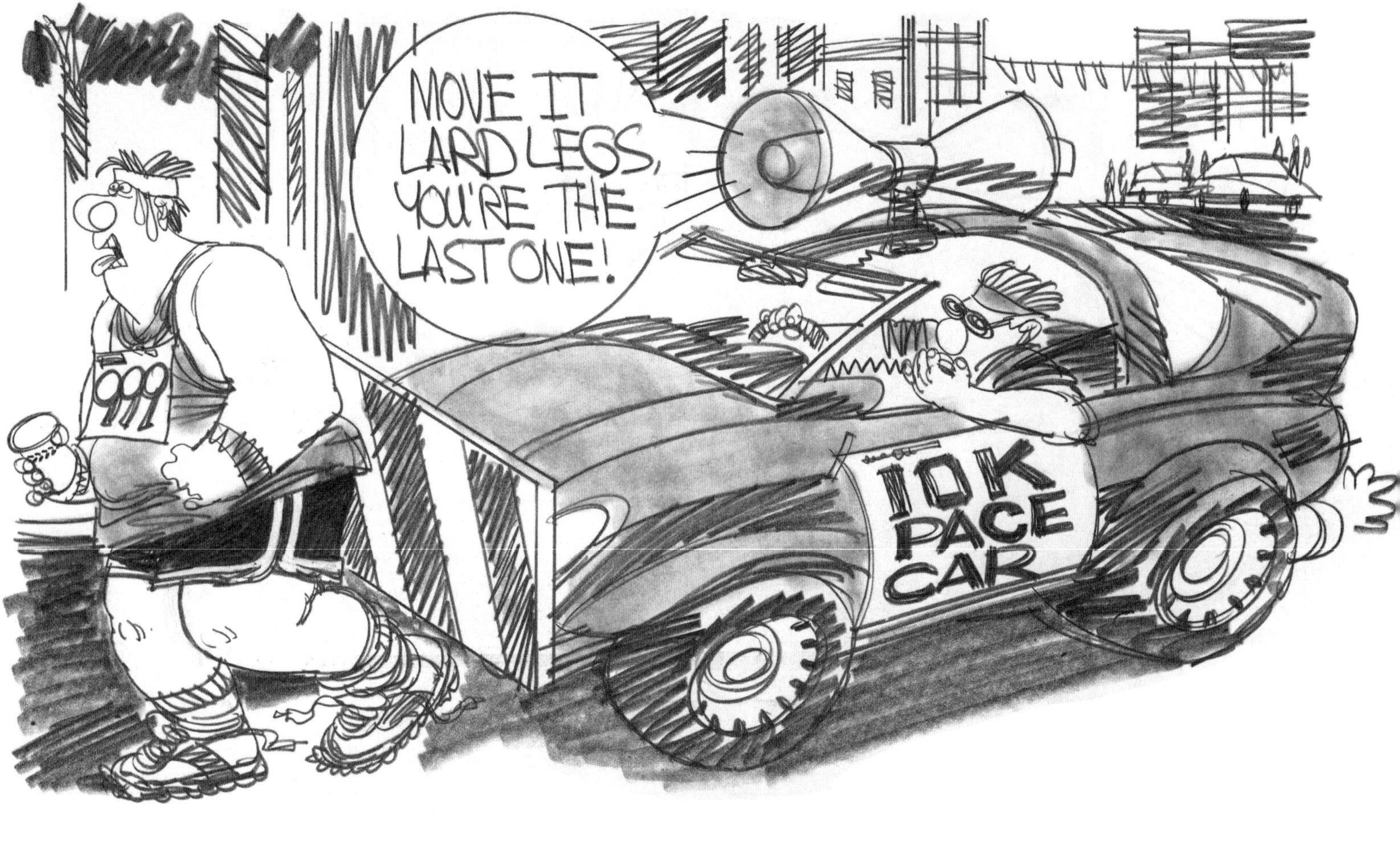
MOVE IT LARD LEGS, YOU'RE THE LAST ONE!
999
10K PACE CAR

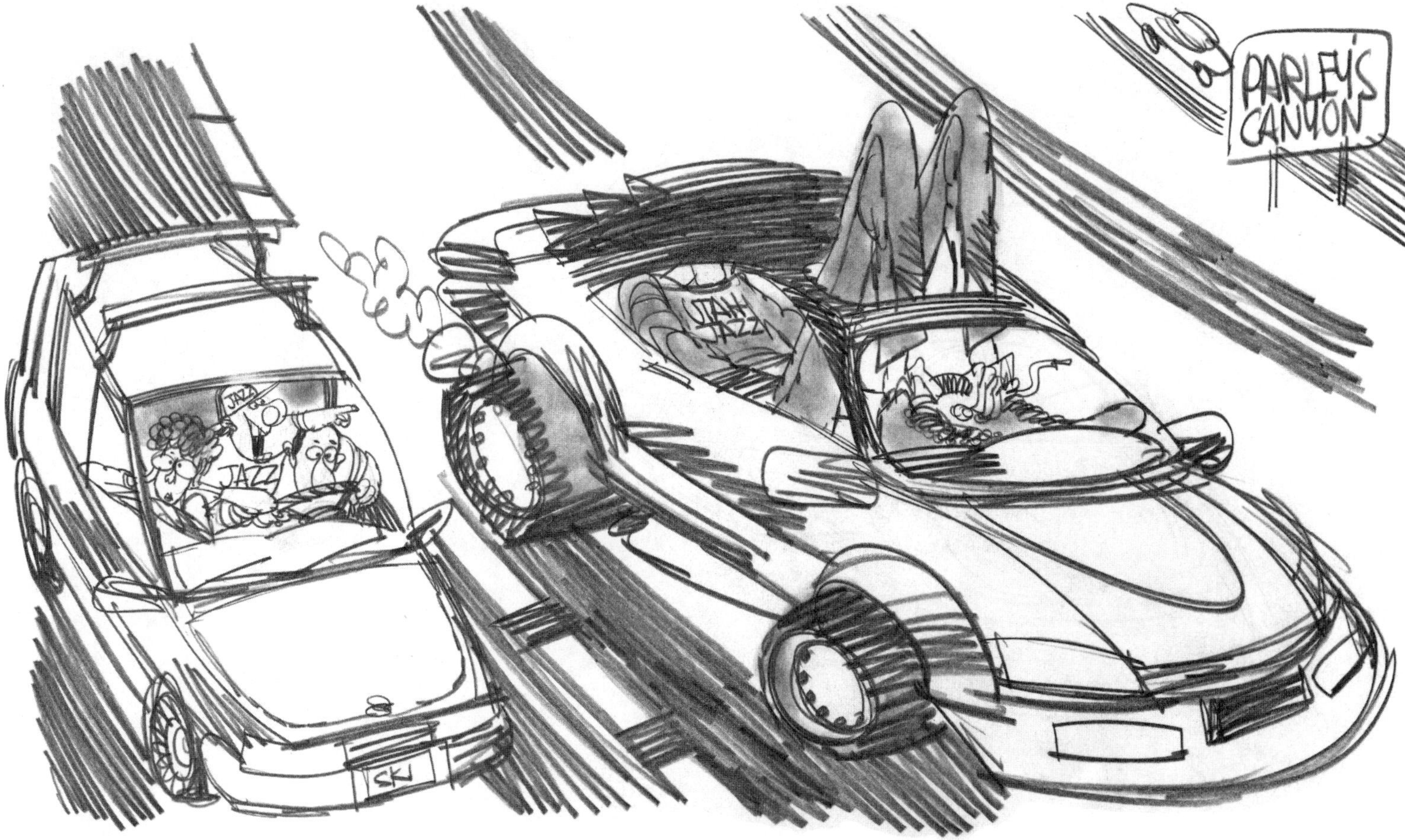
PARLEY'S CANYON
UTAH JAZZ
JAZZ
JAZZ
SKI

"Mom! Dad! . . . It's Mark Eaton's knees!"

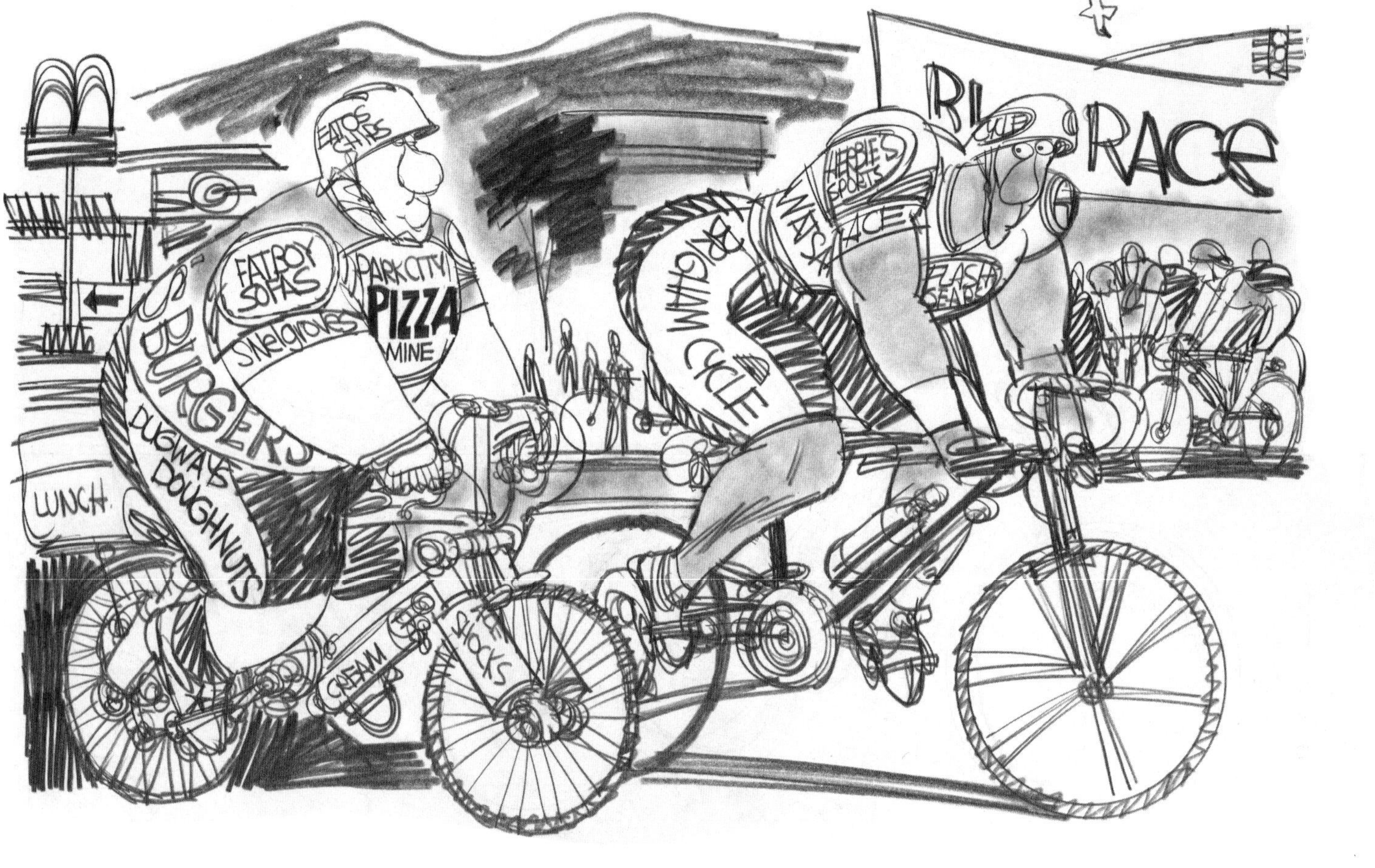
RACE
FATBOY SOFAS
PARK CITY PIZZA MINE
Snelgroves
BURGERS
DUGWAYS DOUGHNUTS
LUNCH.
CREAM
SHOCKS
HERBIE'S SPORTS
BRIGHAM CYCLE

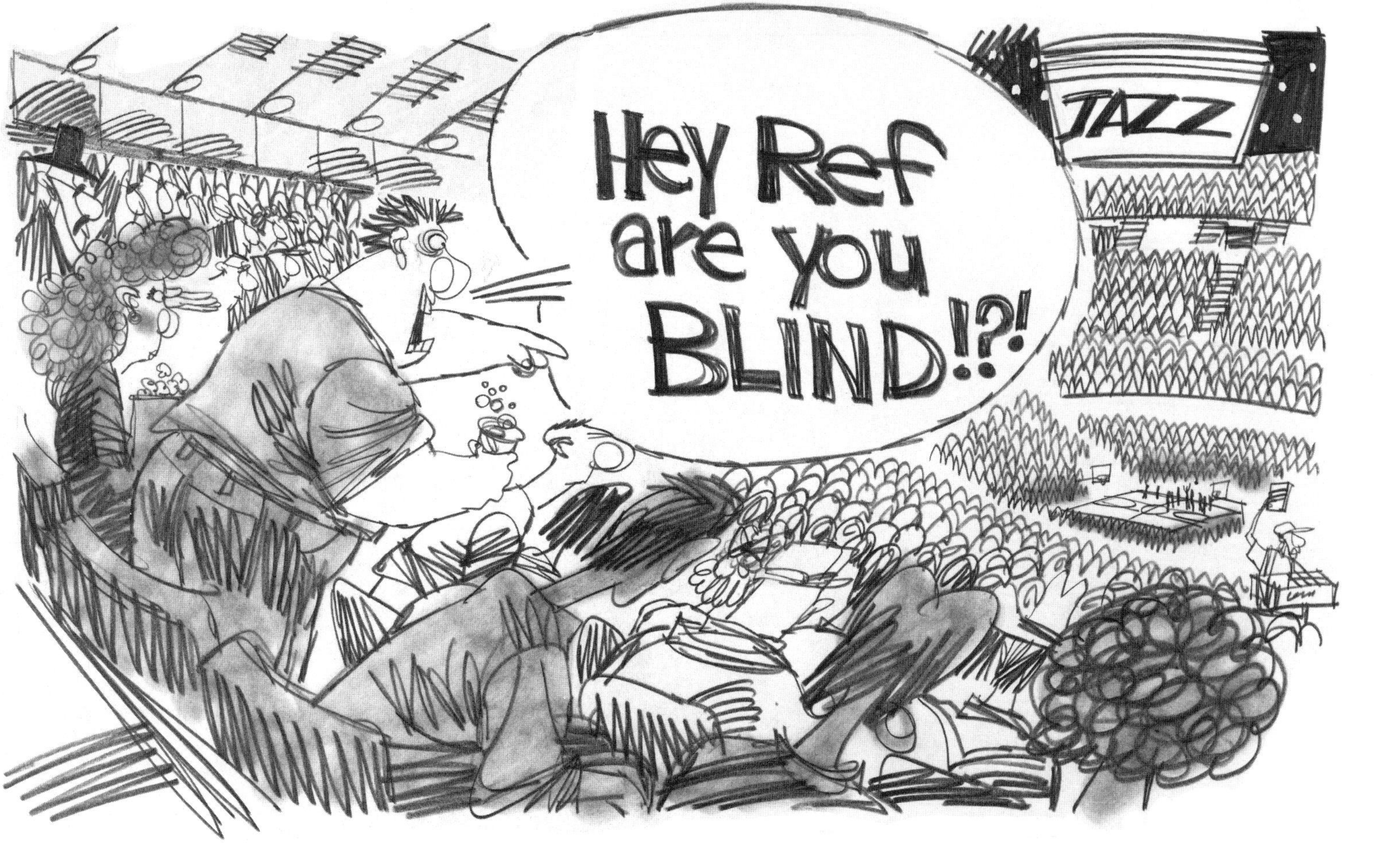
Hey Ref are you BLIND!?!
JAZZ

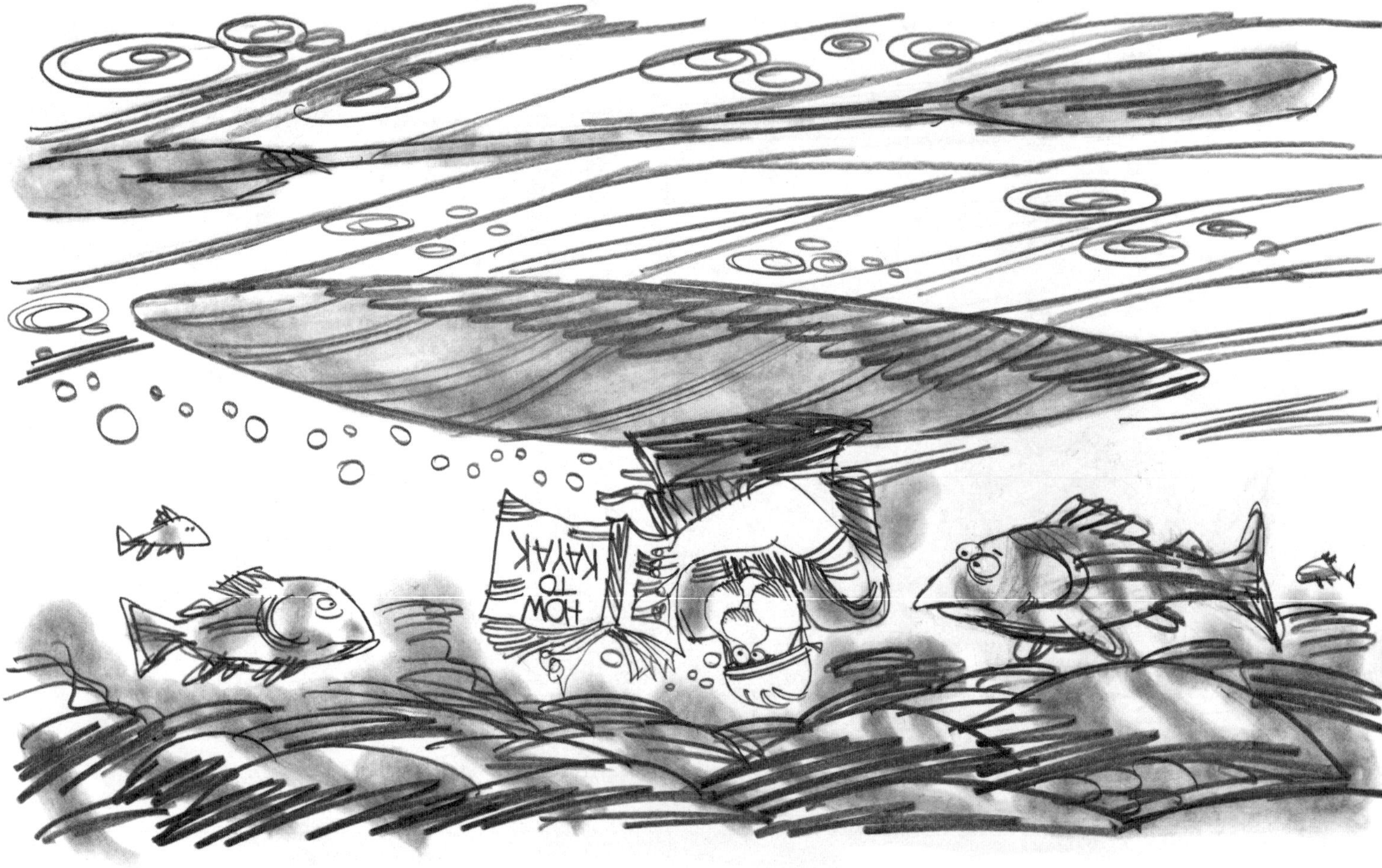
HOW TO KAYAK

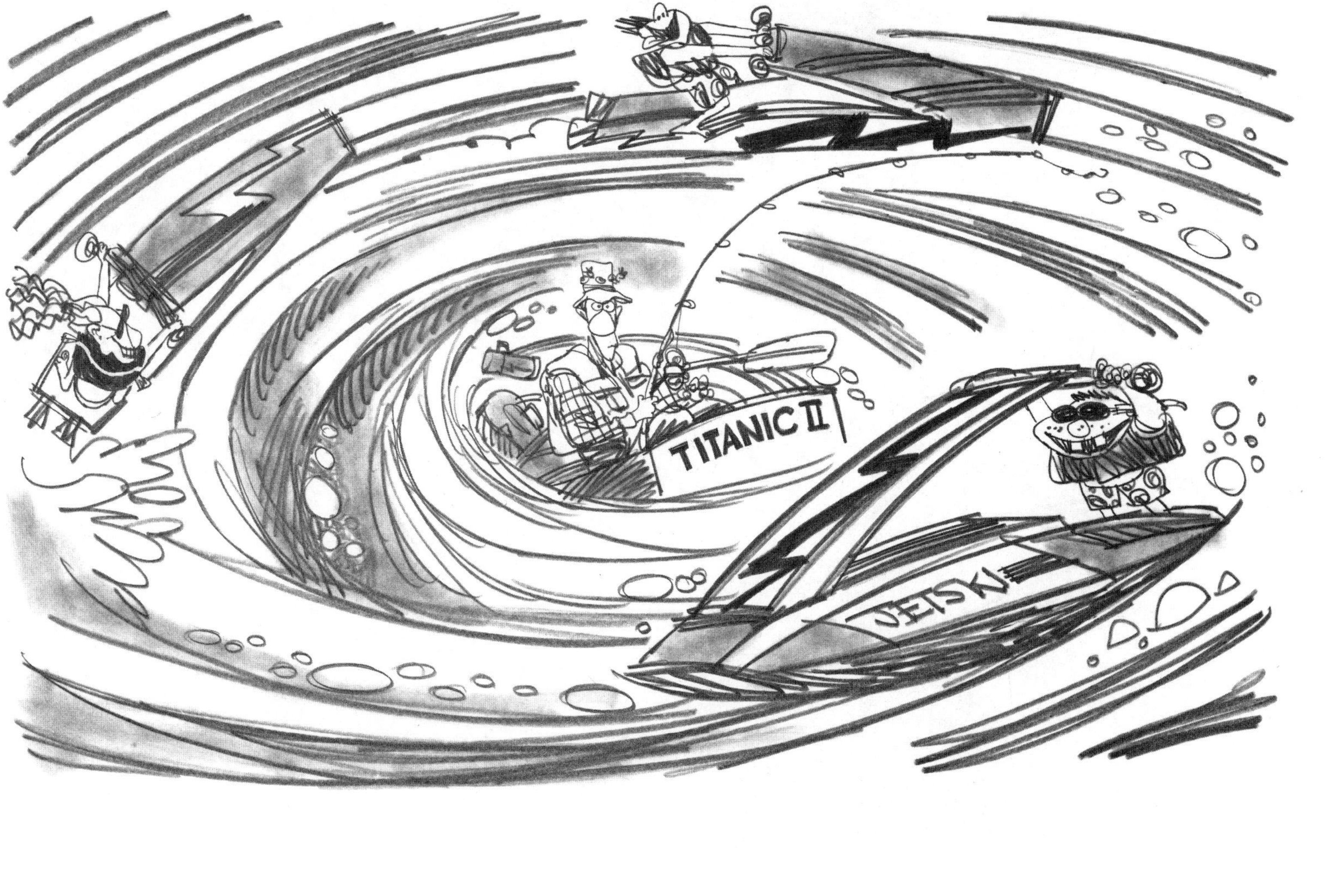
TITANIC II
JETSKI

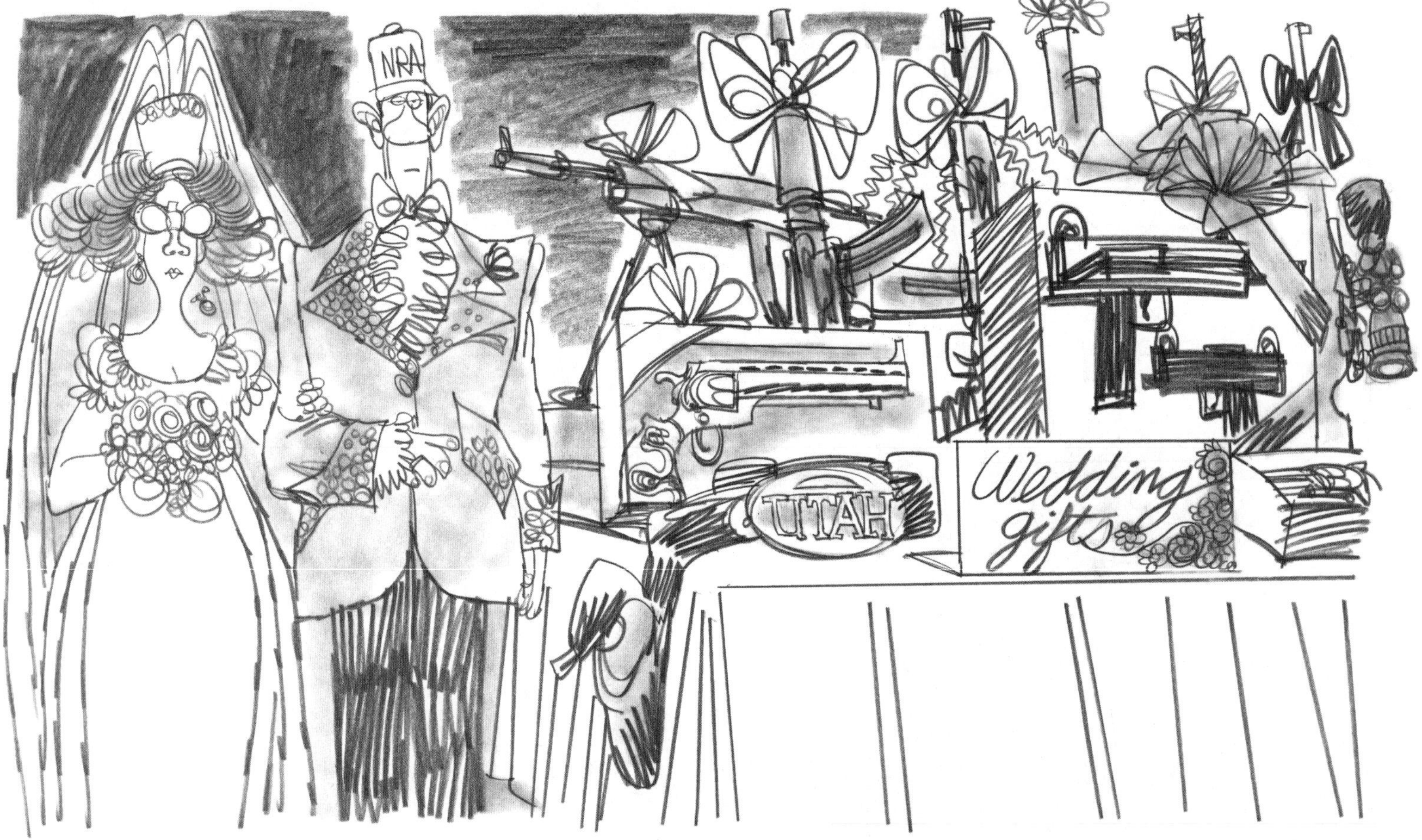
NRA
UTAH
Wedding gifts

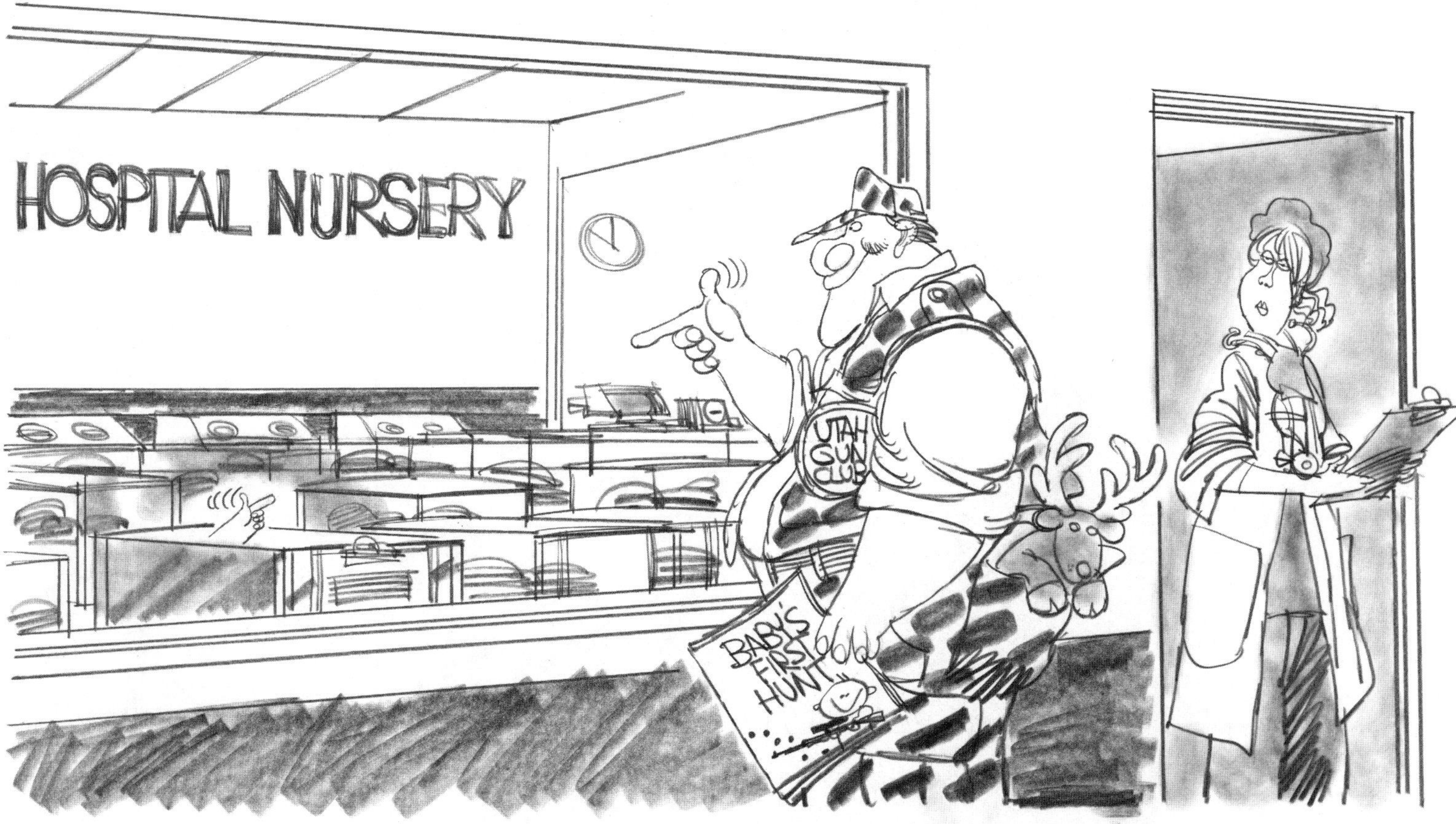
HOSPITAL NURSERY
UTAH GUN CLUB
BABY'S FIRST HUNT

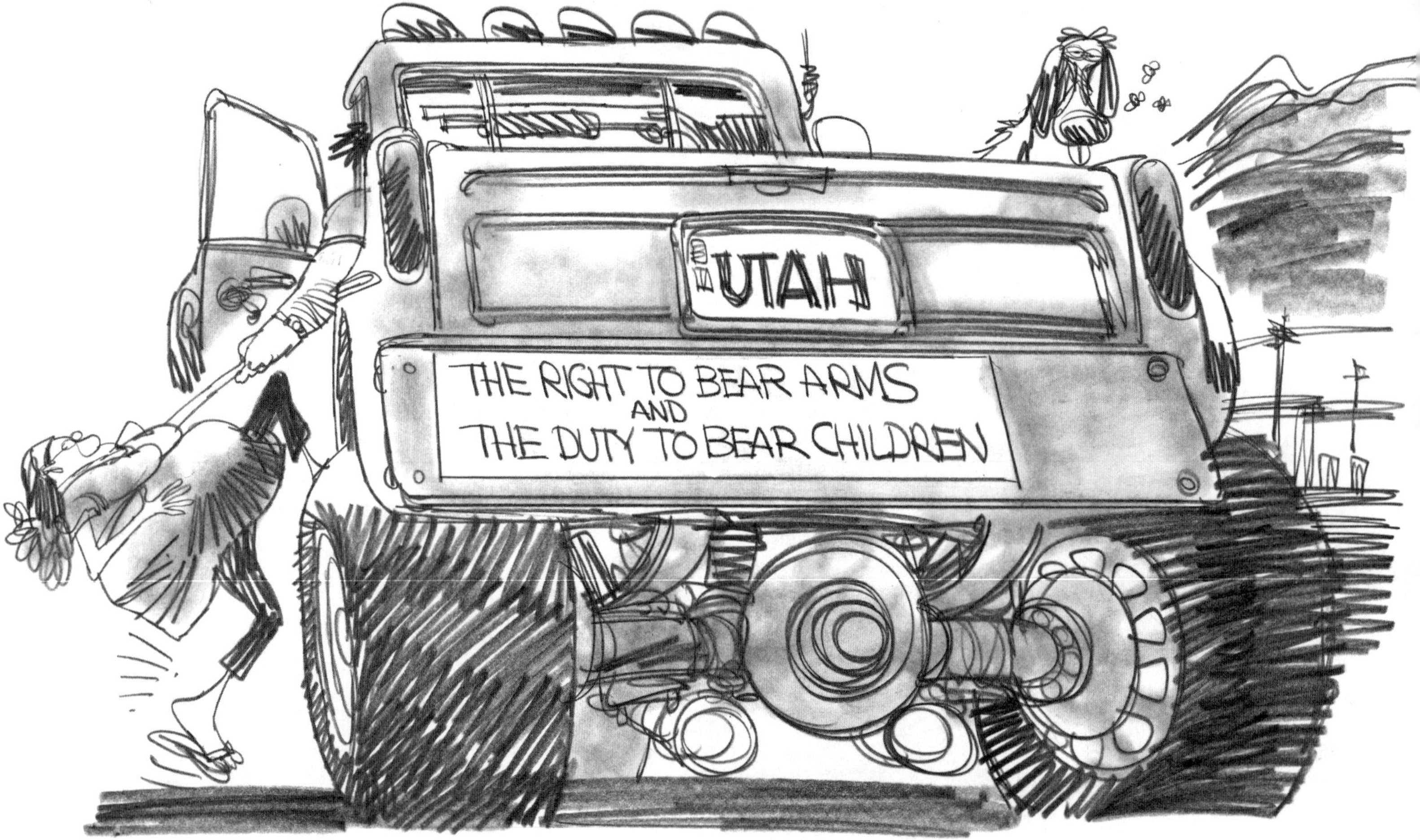
UTAH
THE RIGHT TO BEAR ARMS
AND
THE DUTY TO BEAR CHILDREN

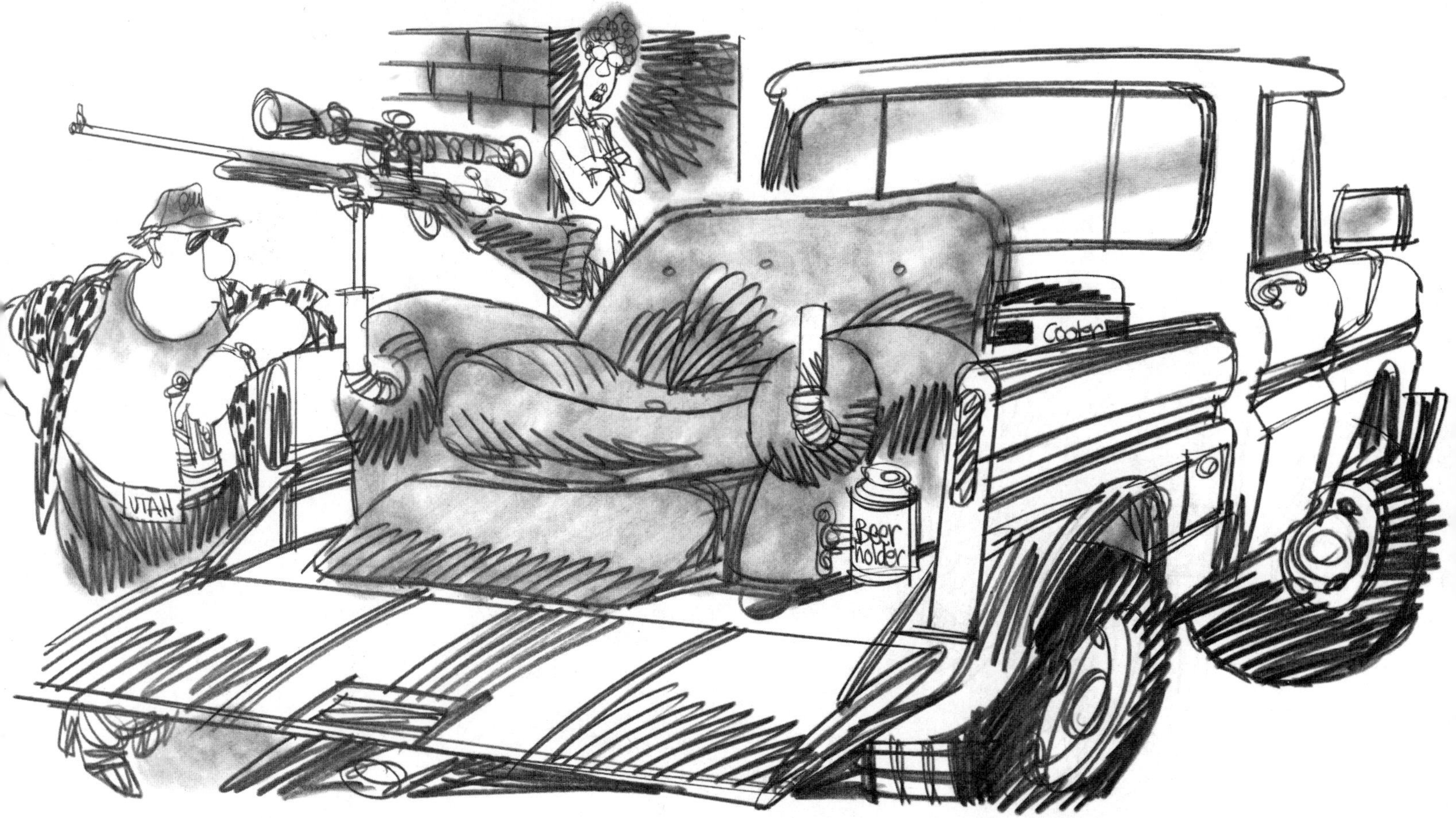
UTAH
Cooler
Beer holder
"Well, it looks like you're about ready for the deer hunt."

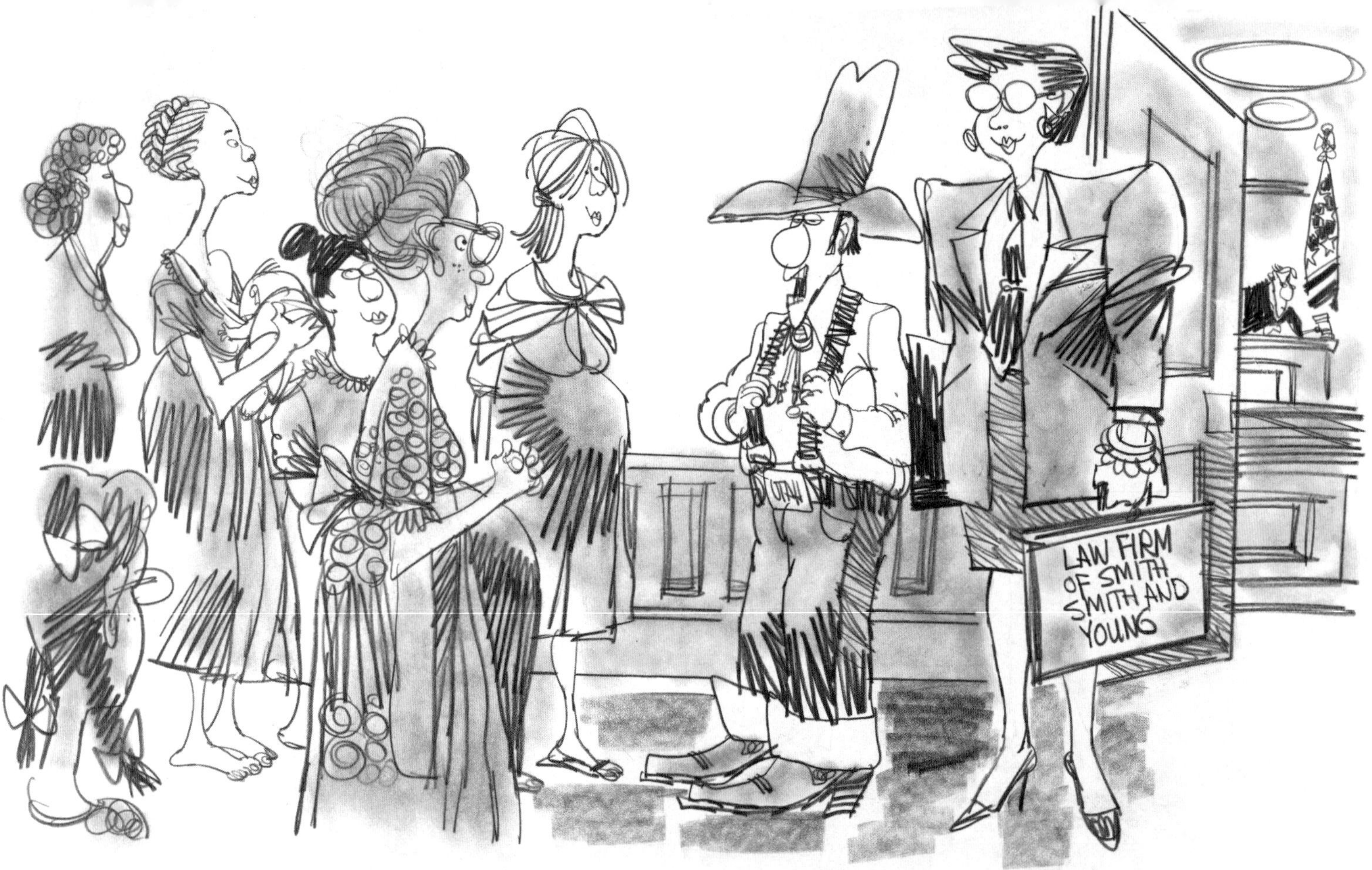
UTAH
LAW FIRM
OF SMITH
SMITH AND
YOUNG

"I got off the polygamy charge thanks to wife number fourteen here."

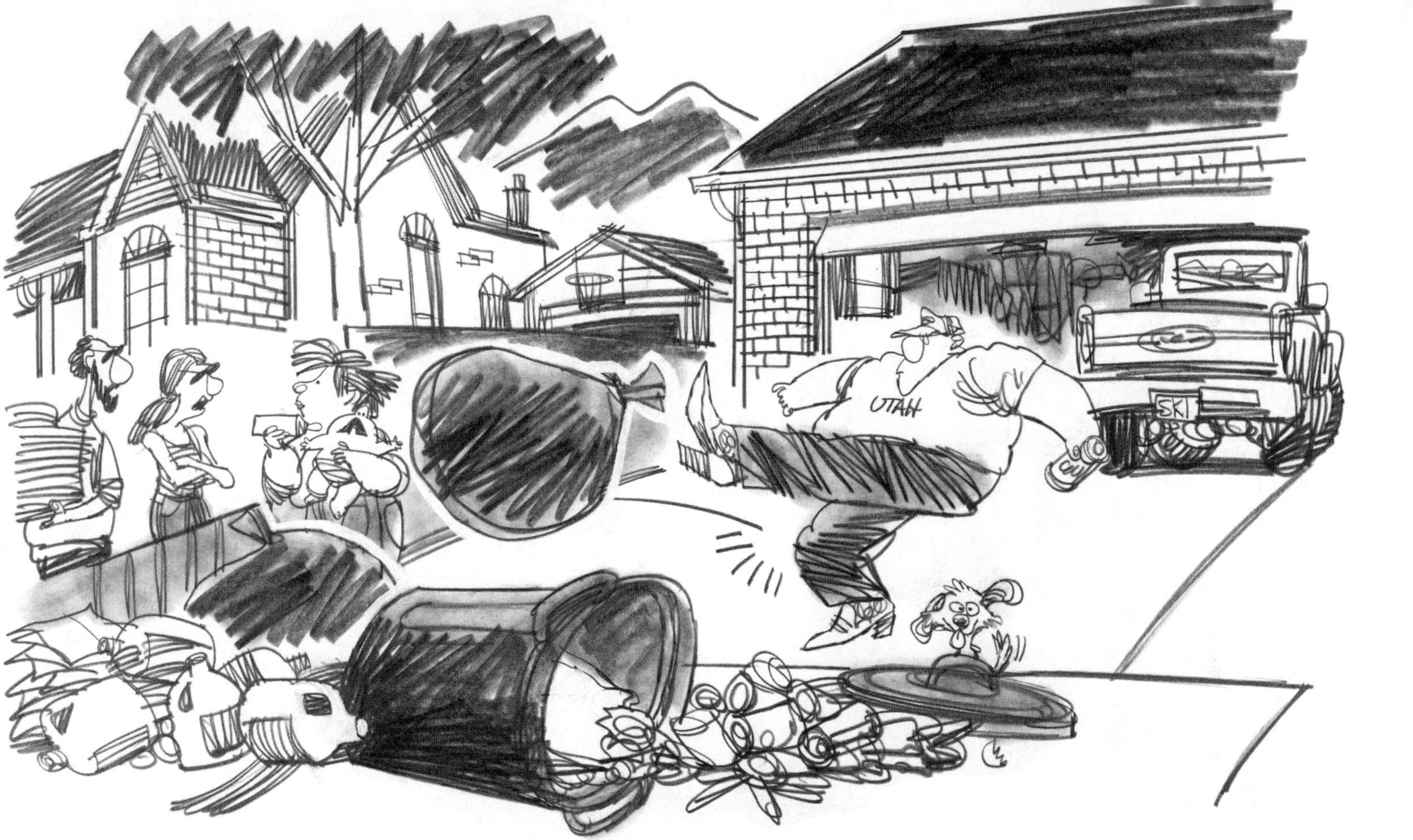
UTAH
SKI

"We just moved here from the Northwest.
I see this state doesn't share Oregon's enthusiasm for recycling."

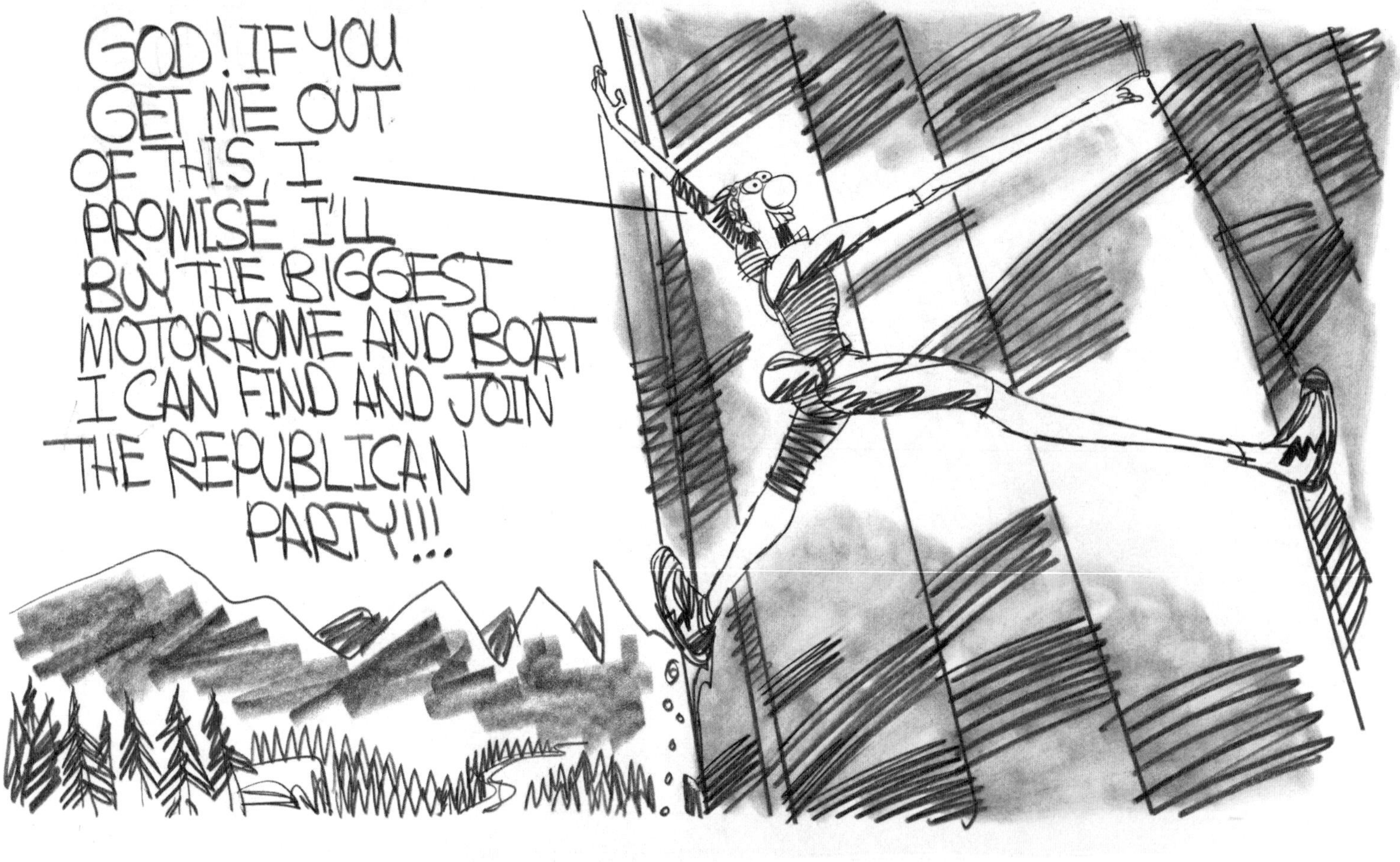
GOD! IF YOU GET ME OUT OF THIS, I PROMISE I'LL BUY THE BIGGEST MOTORHOME AND BOAT I CAN FIND AND JOIN THE REPUBLICAN PARTY!!!...

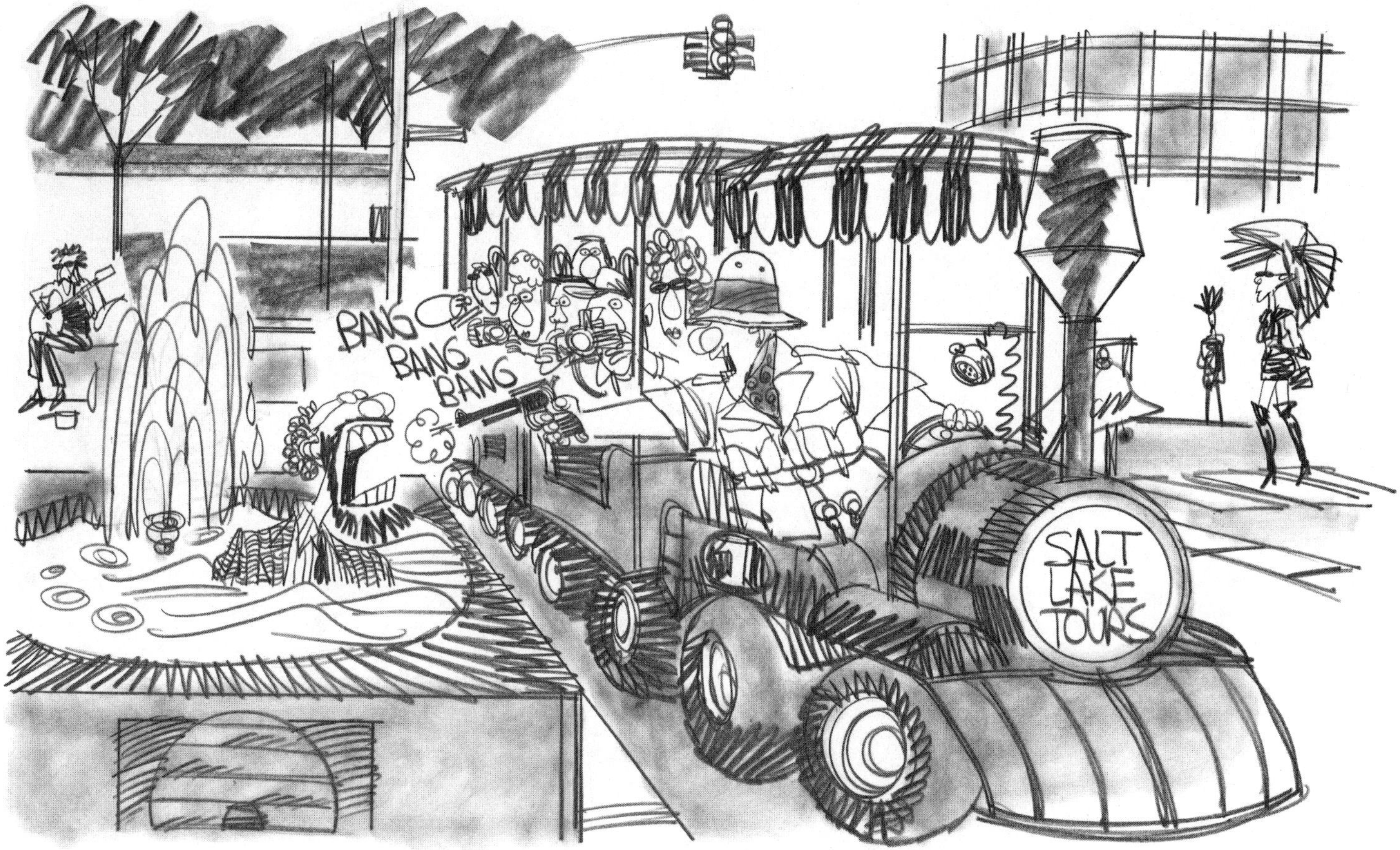
BANG
BANG
BANG
SALT LAKE TOURS

"Watch out folks! It's a liberal Democrat!"

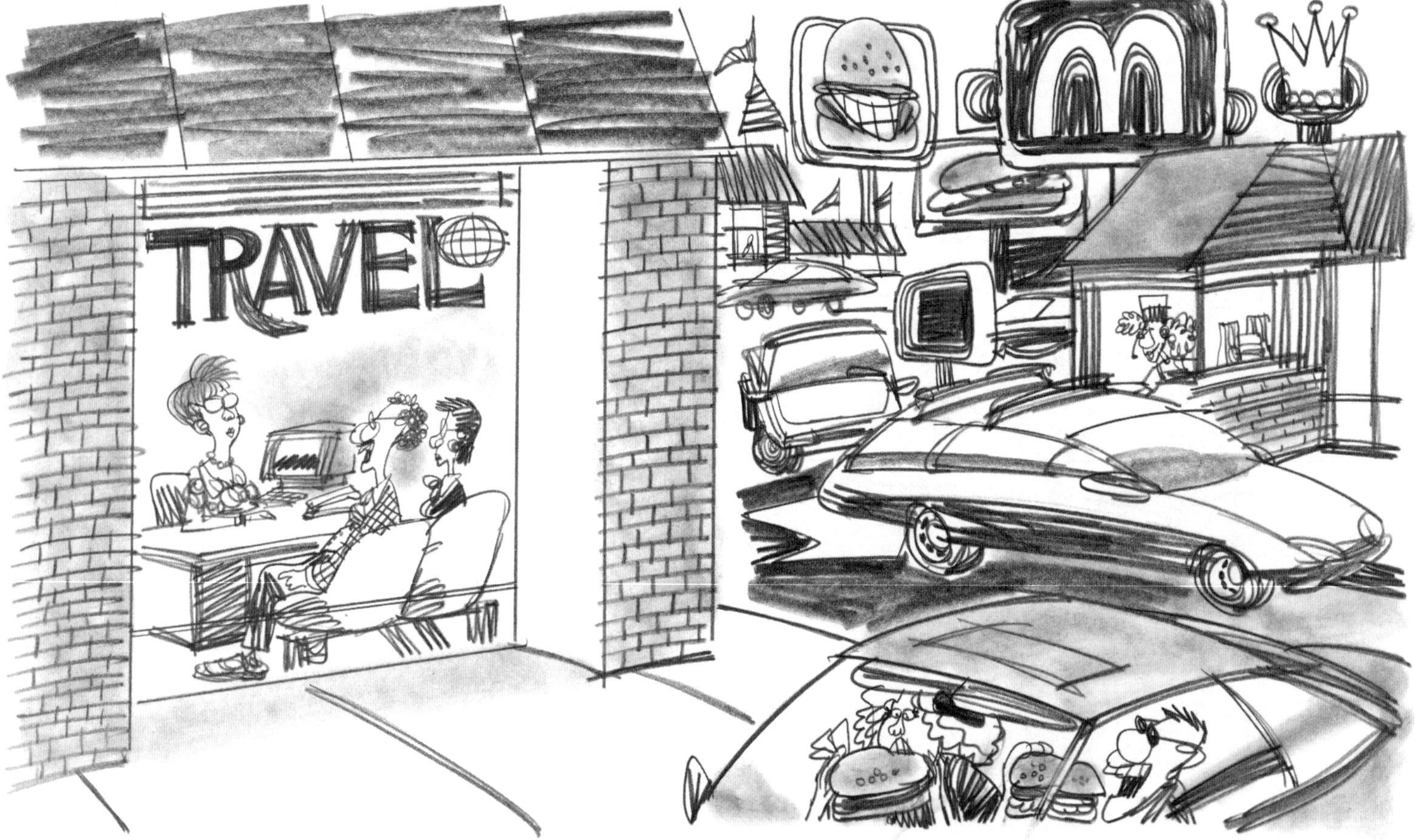
TRAVEL

"Anyplace where the restaurants don't have take-out windows."

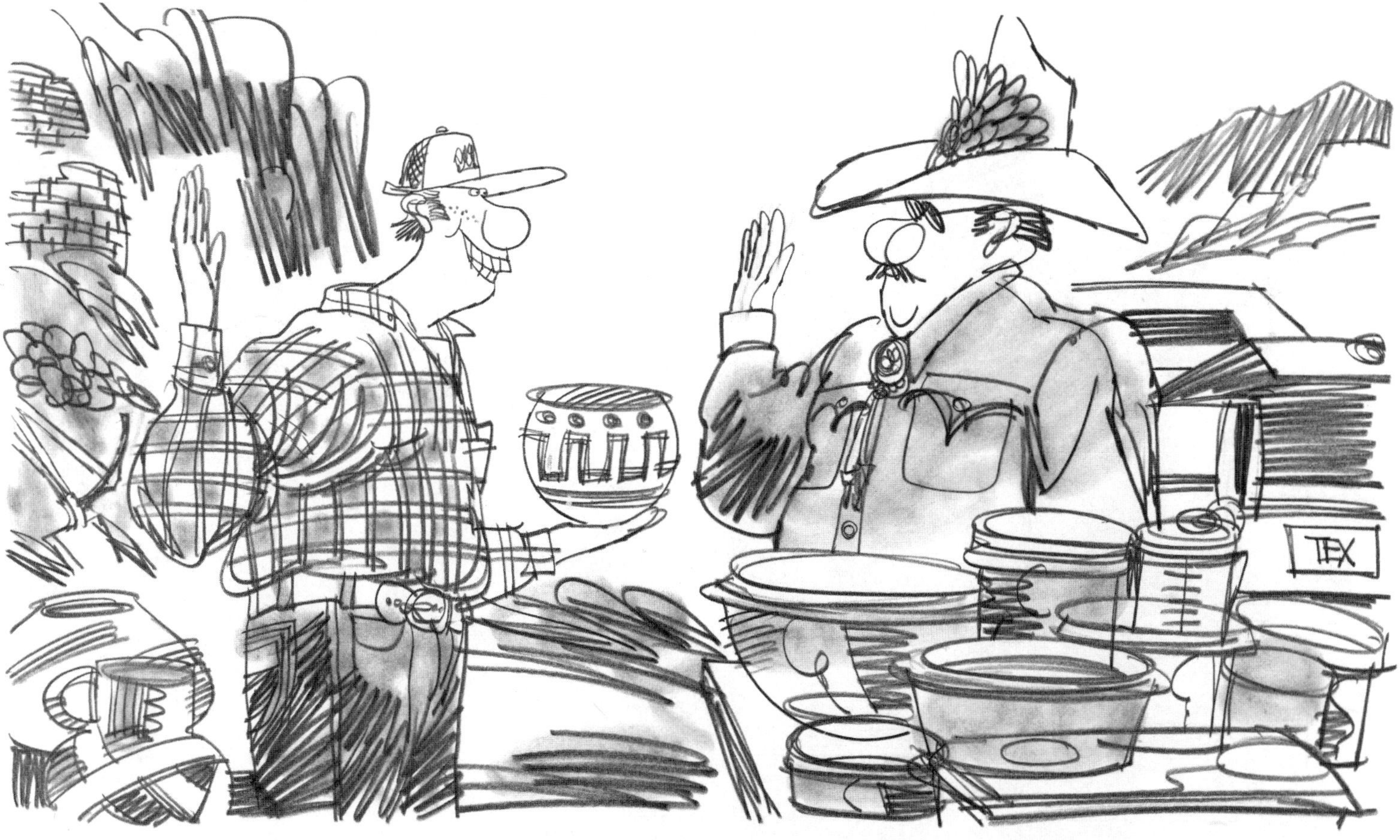
TEX

SOUTHERN UTAH POT HUNTER TRADING FOR WHITE MAN'S TUPPERWARE

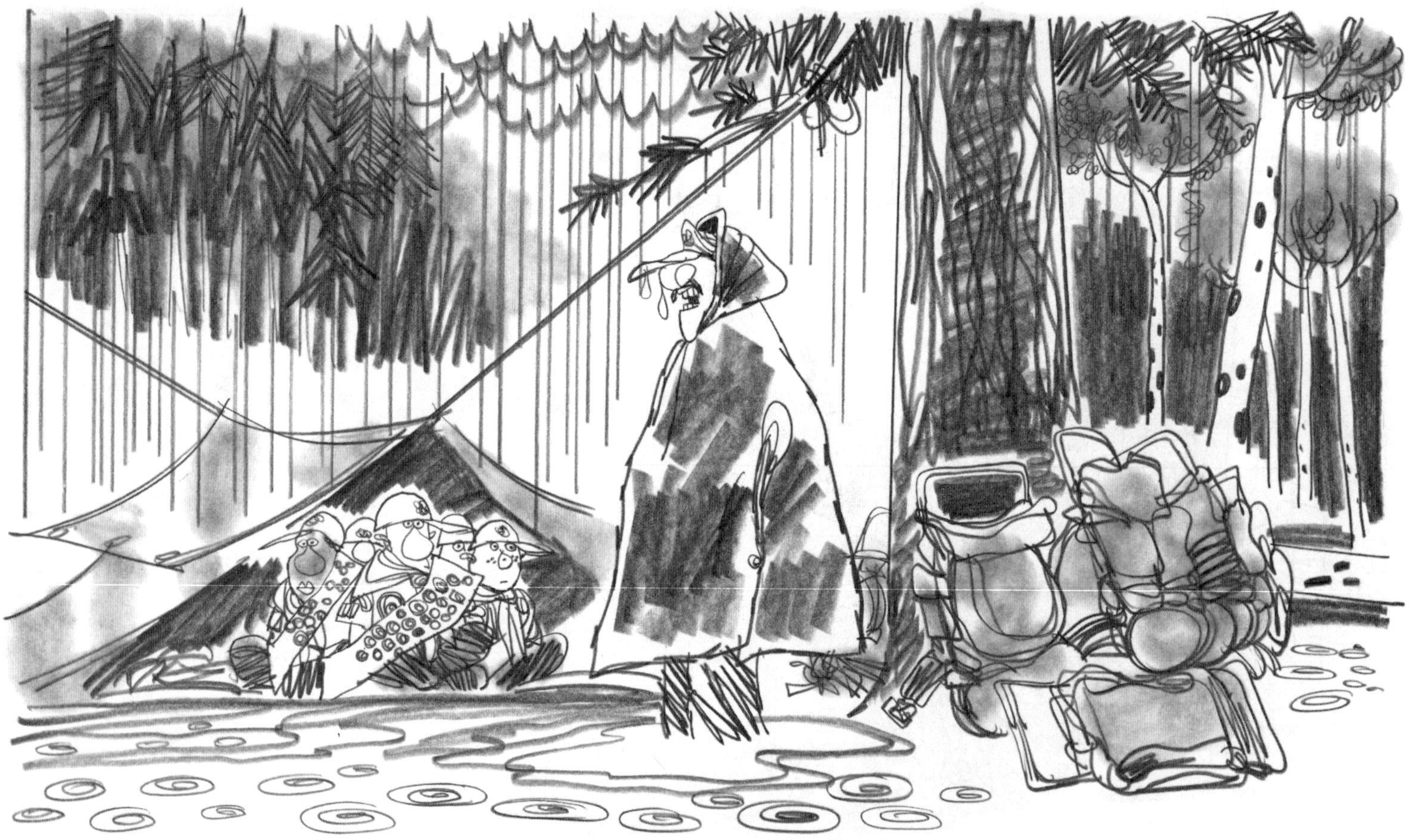

"Are we sure that there's not a merit badge
for watching T.V. in a motel room?"

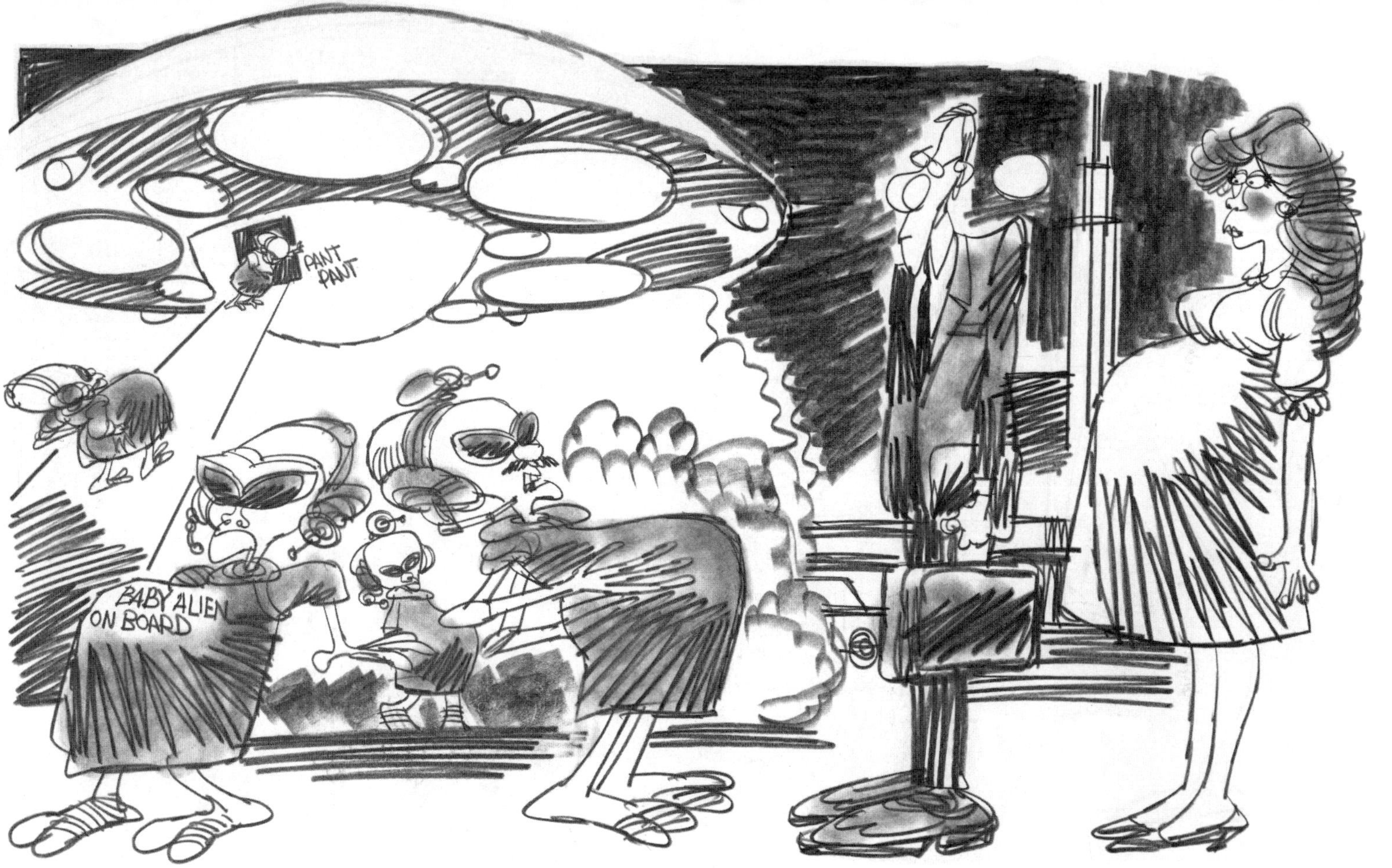
PANT
PANT
BABY ALIEN
ON BOARD

"No wonder you have big families here . . .
It's your females that get pregnant!"

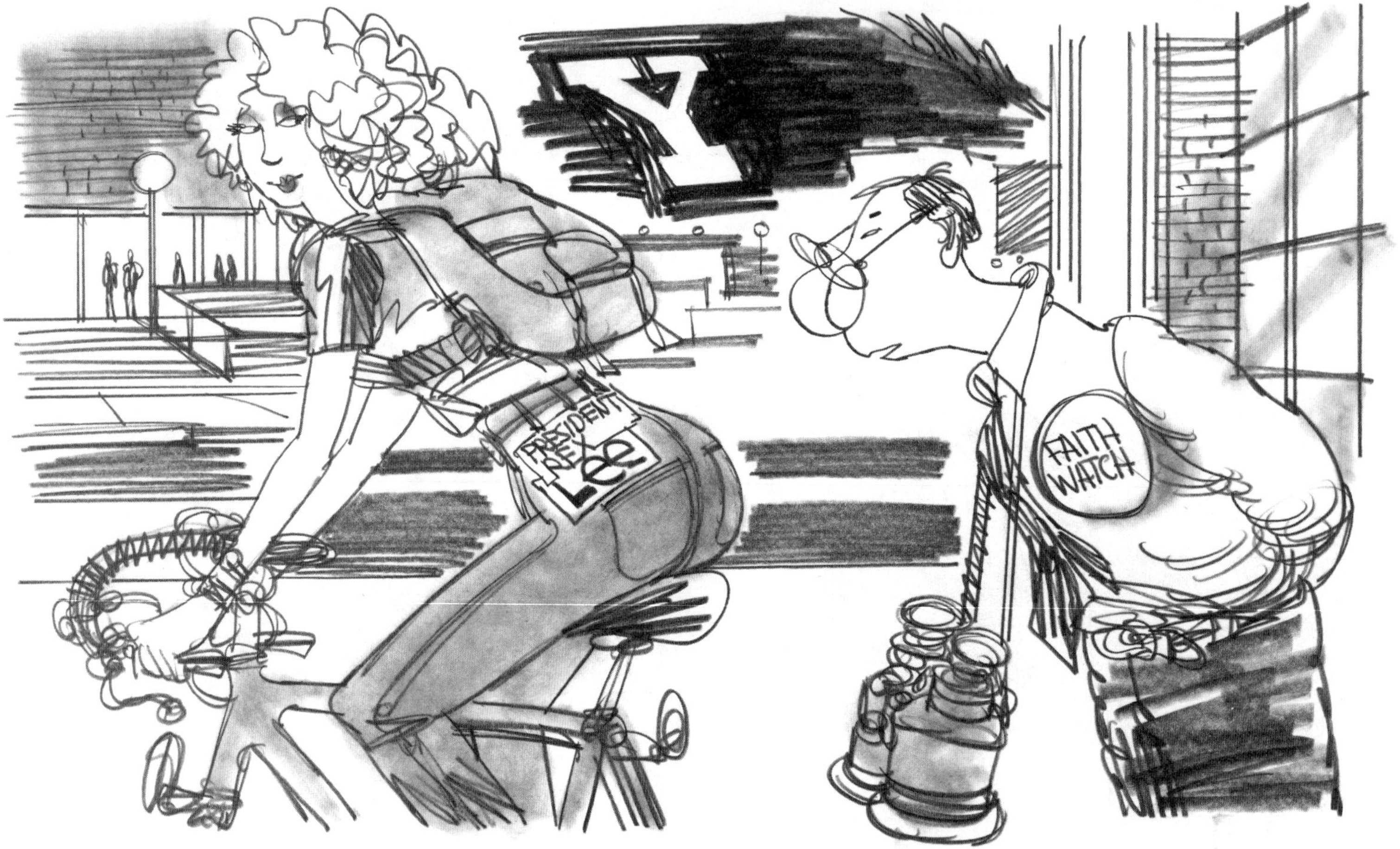
Y
PRESIDENT
REX
Lee
FAITH
WATCH

"Then these jeans *do* conform to the dress code?"

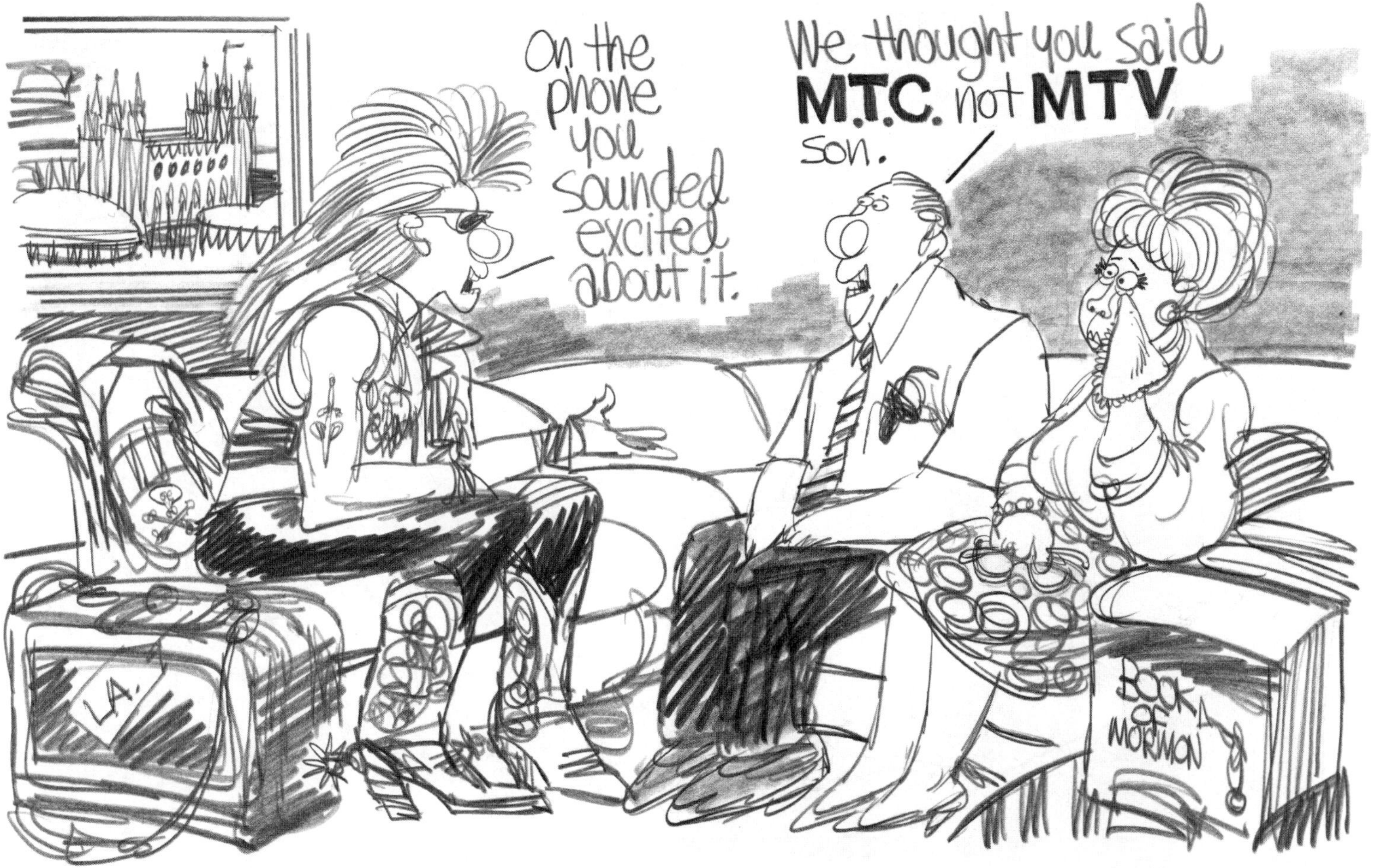
On the phone you sounded excited about it.
We thought you said M.T.C. not MTV, son.
L.A.
BOOK OF MORMON

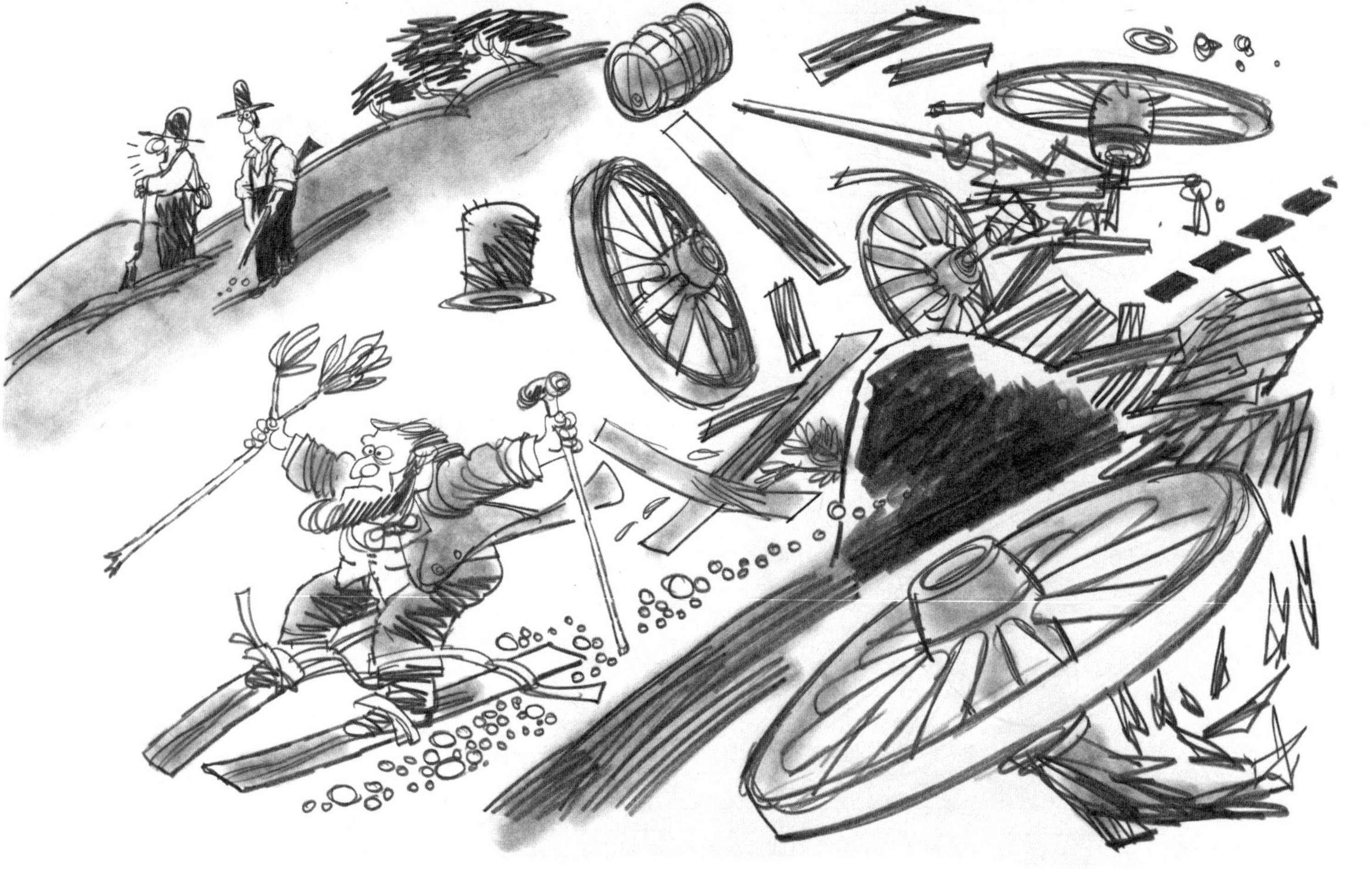

"*This* is the place?
And just how does the Lord expect us to make a living here?"

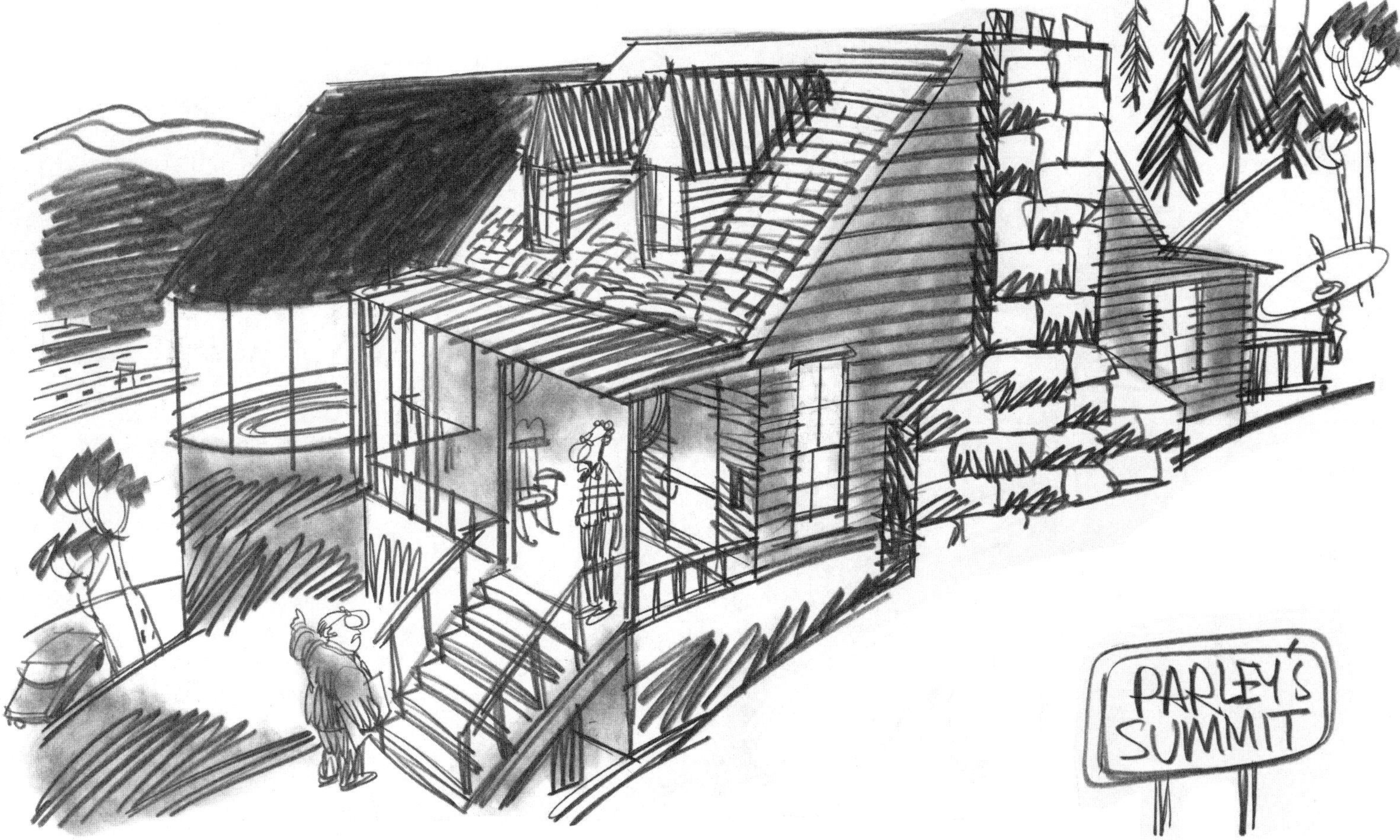
PARLEY'S
SUMMIT

"Excuse me, but we need to build an Olympic luge-run through your hot tub."

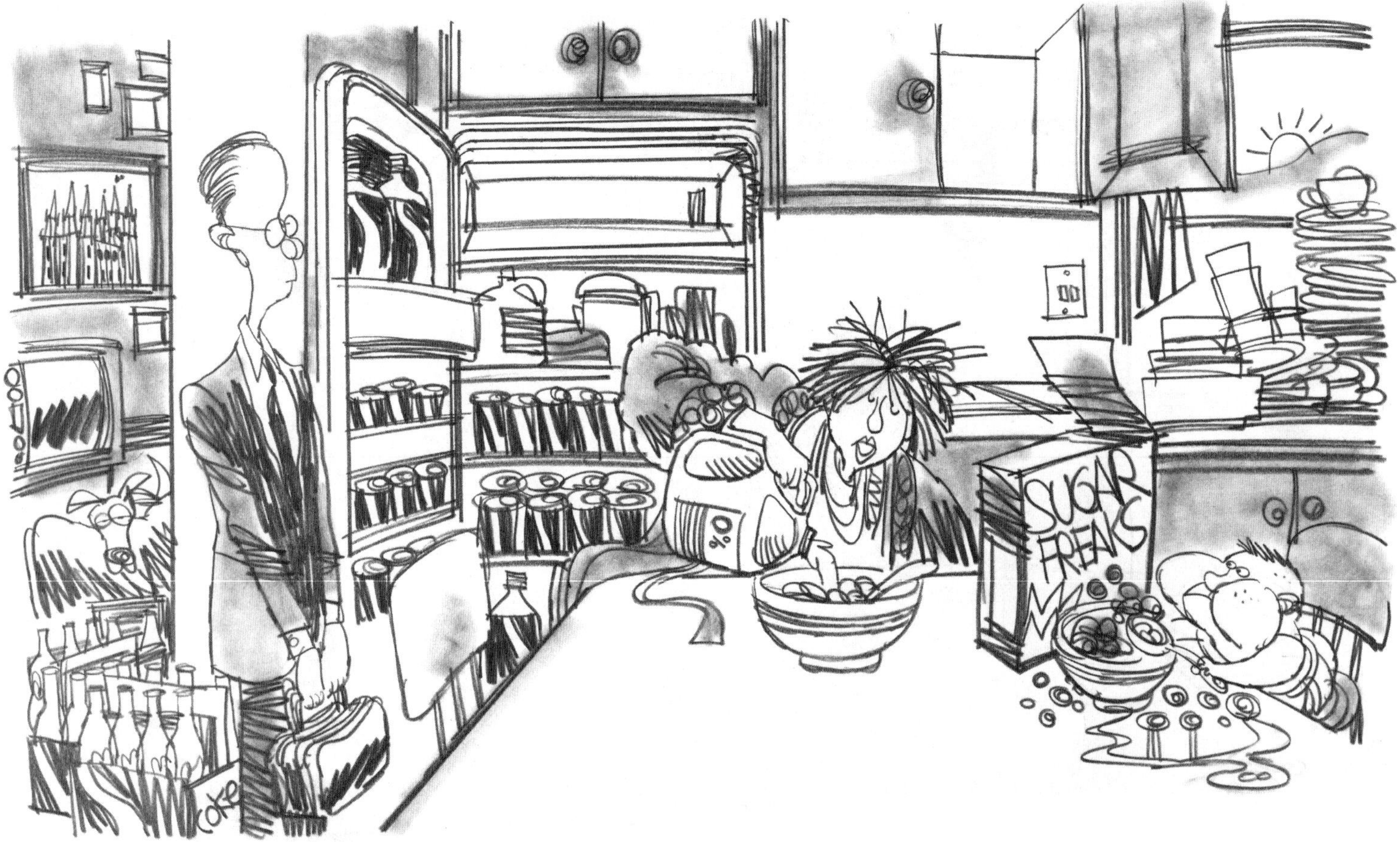

SUGAR FREAKS
COKE

“Hey, going without Coke Classic for two meals *is* fasting.”

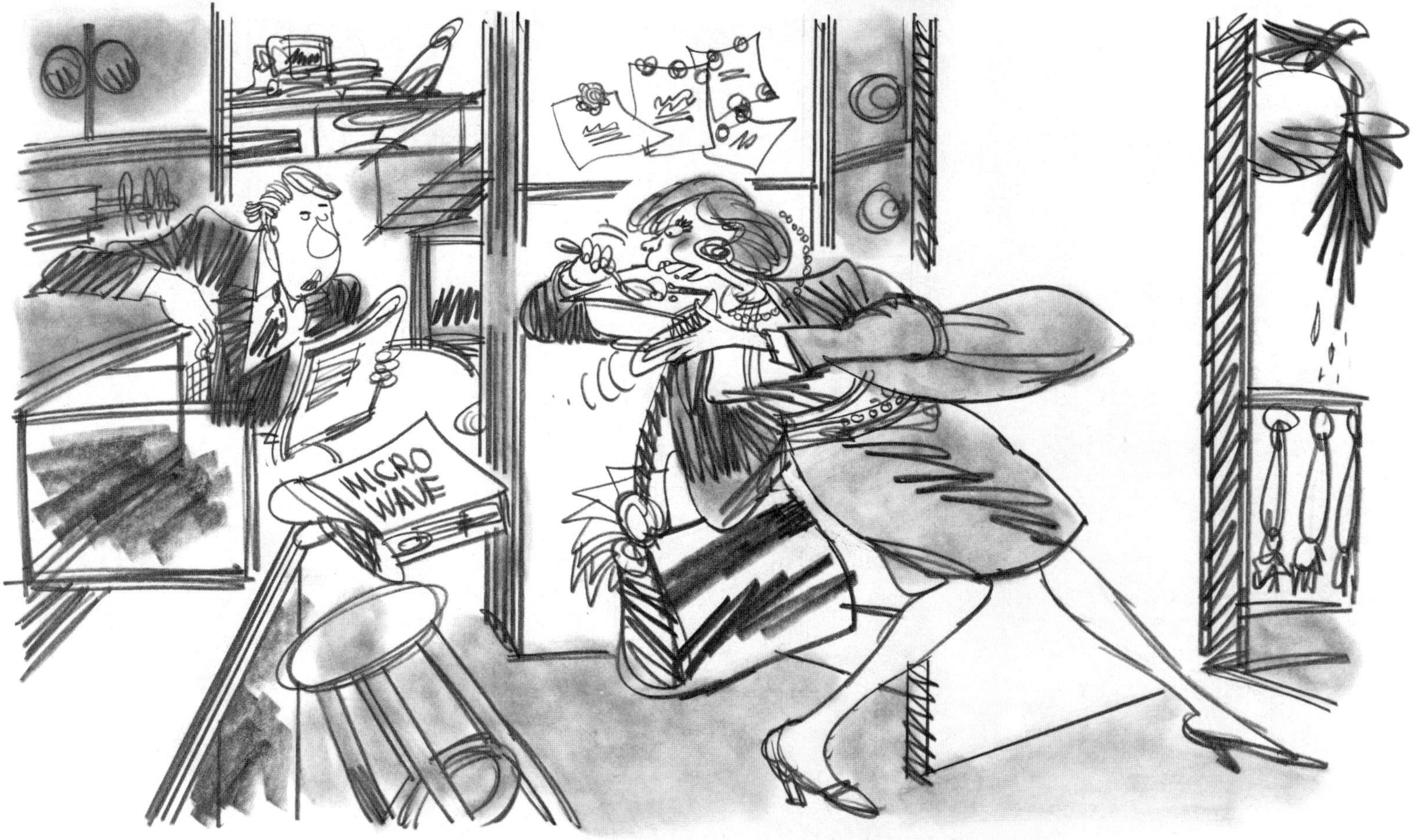
MICRO WAVE

"The *Ensign* has suggested blessings on the food that can be said in a microsecond."

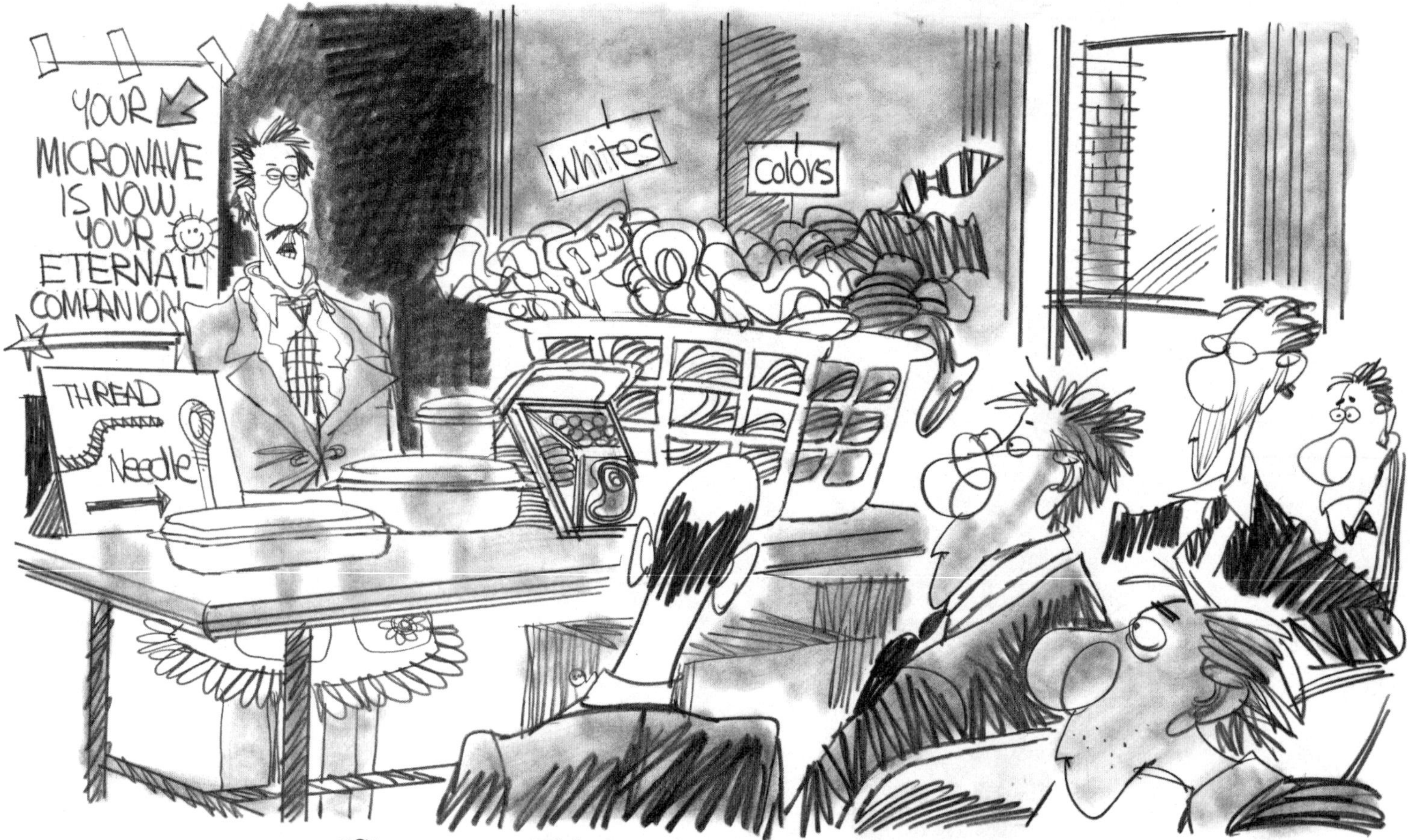
YOUR MICROWAVE IS NOW YOUR ETERNAL COMPANION
THREAD
Needle
Whites
Colors

"Since every Elder in the quorum is now divorced, we'll be having a homemaking lesson each month."

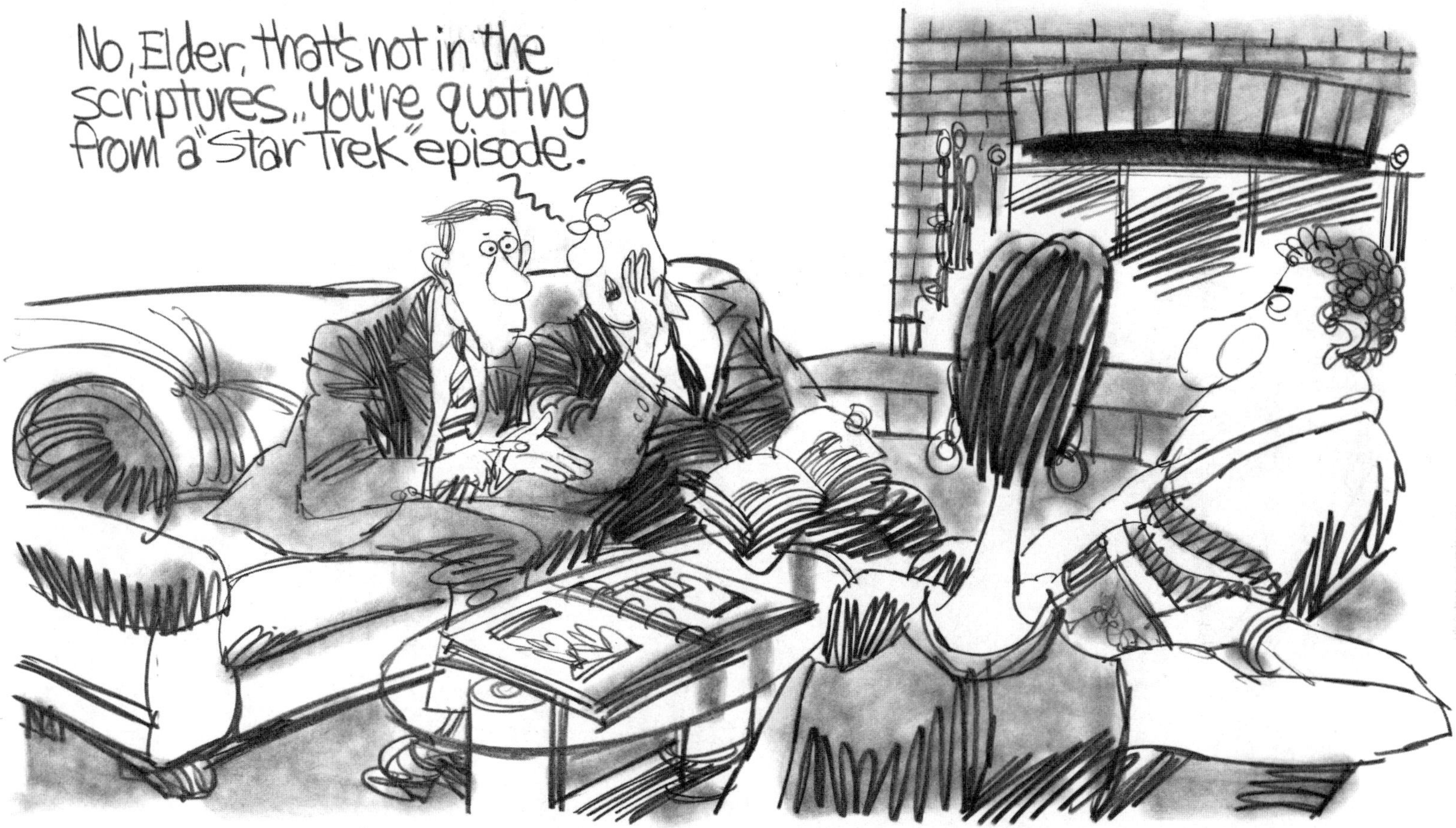
No, Elder, that's not in the scriptures... You're quoting from a "Star Trek" episode.

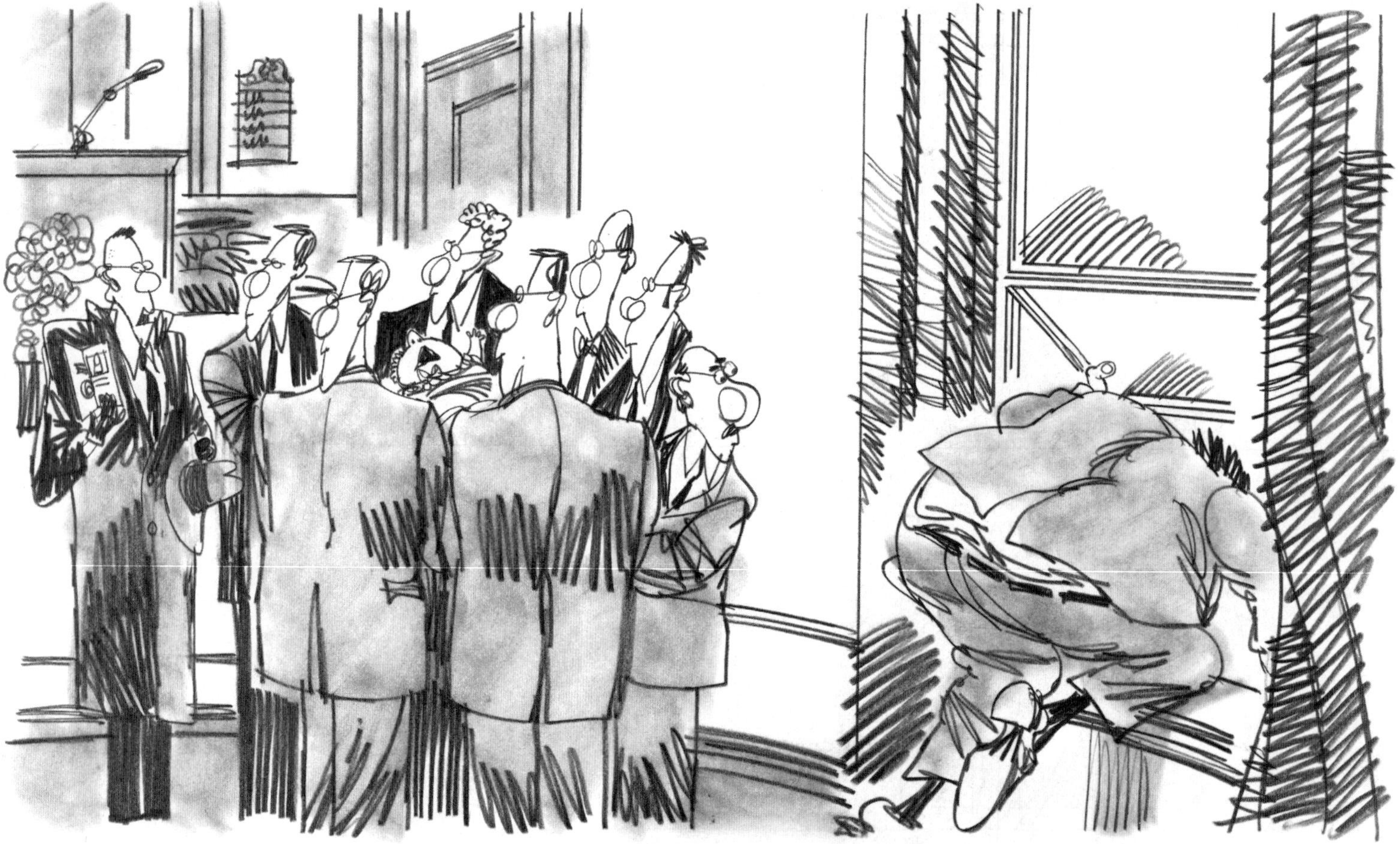

“Only worthy males can now bless an infant.
Everyone will please show me their papers.”

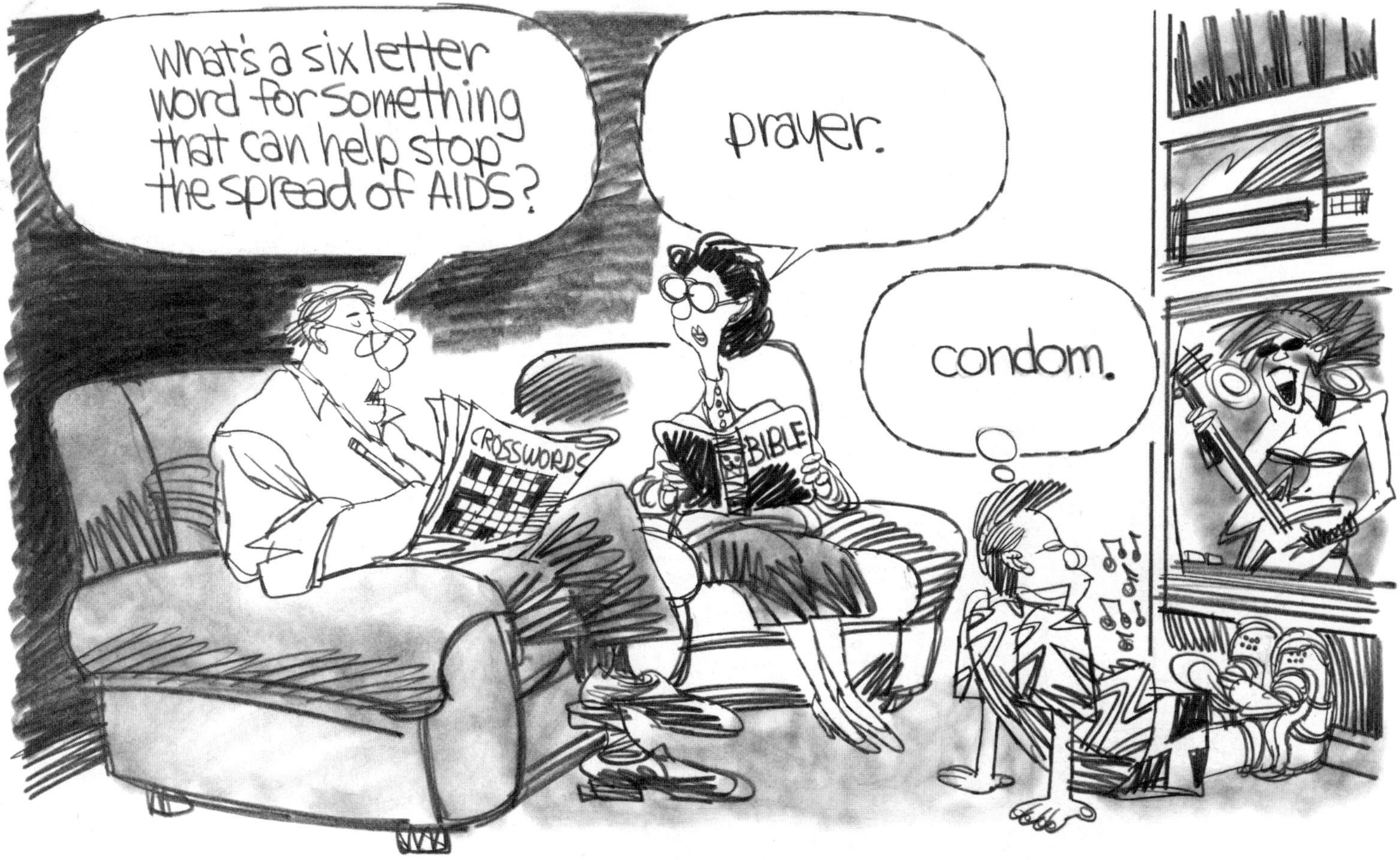
What's a six letter word for something that can help stop the spread of AIDS?
prayer.
condom.
CROSSWORDS
BIBLE

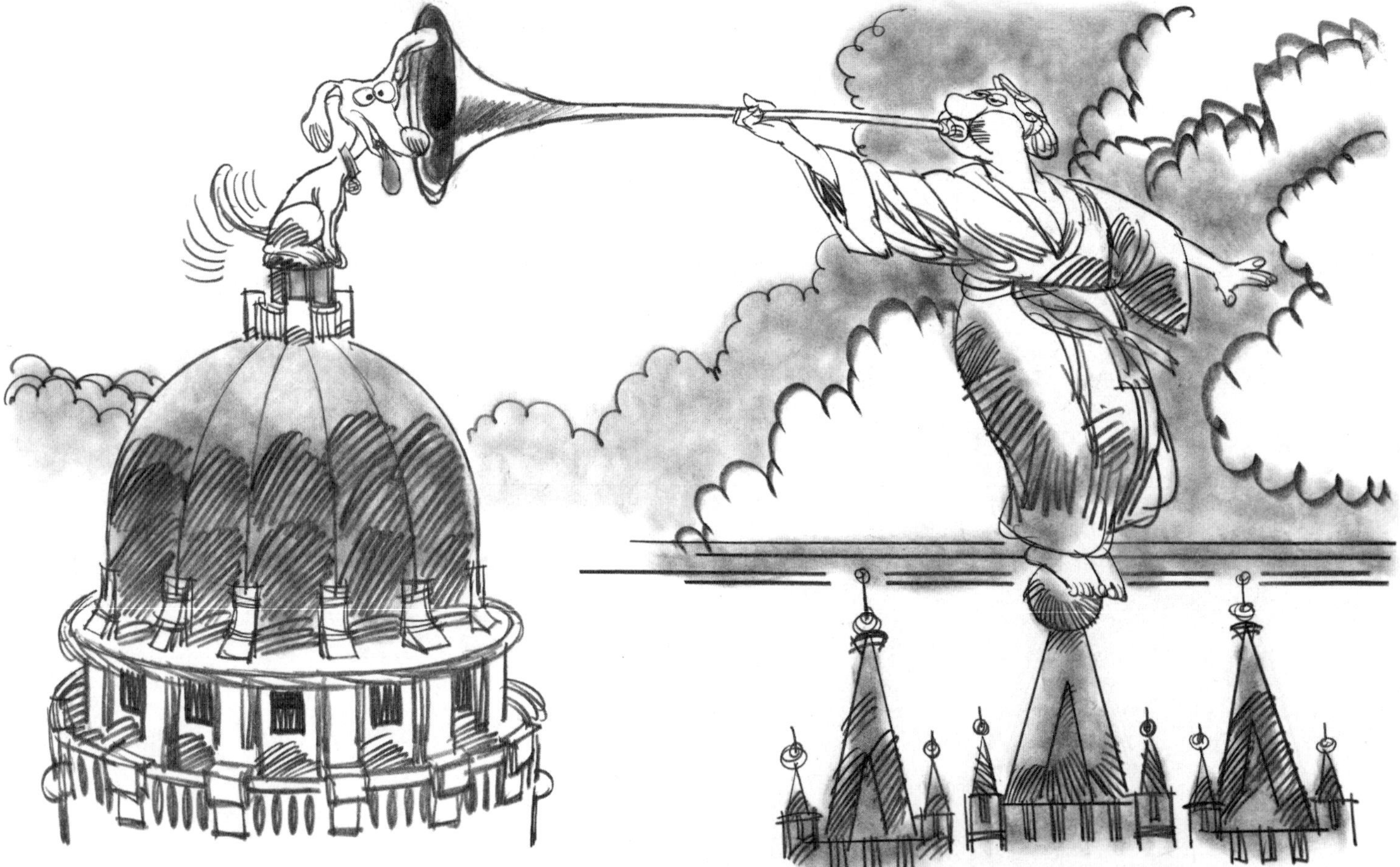

HIS MASTER'S VOICE

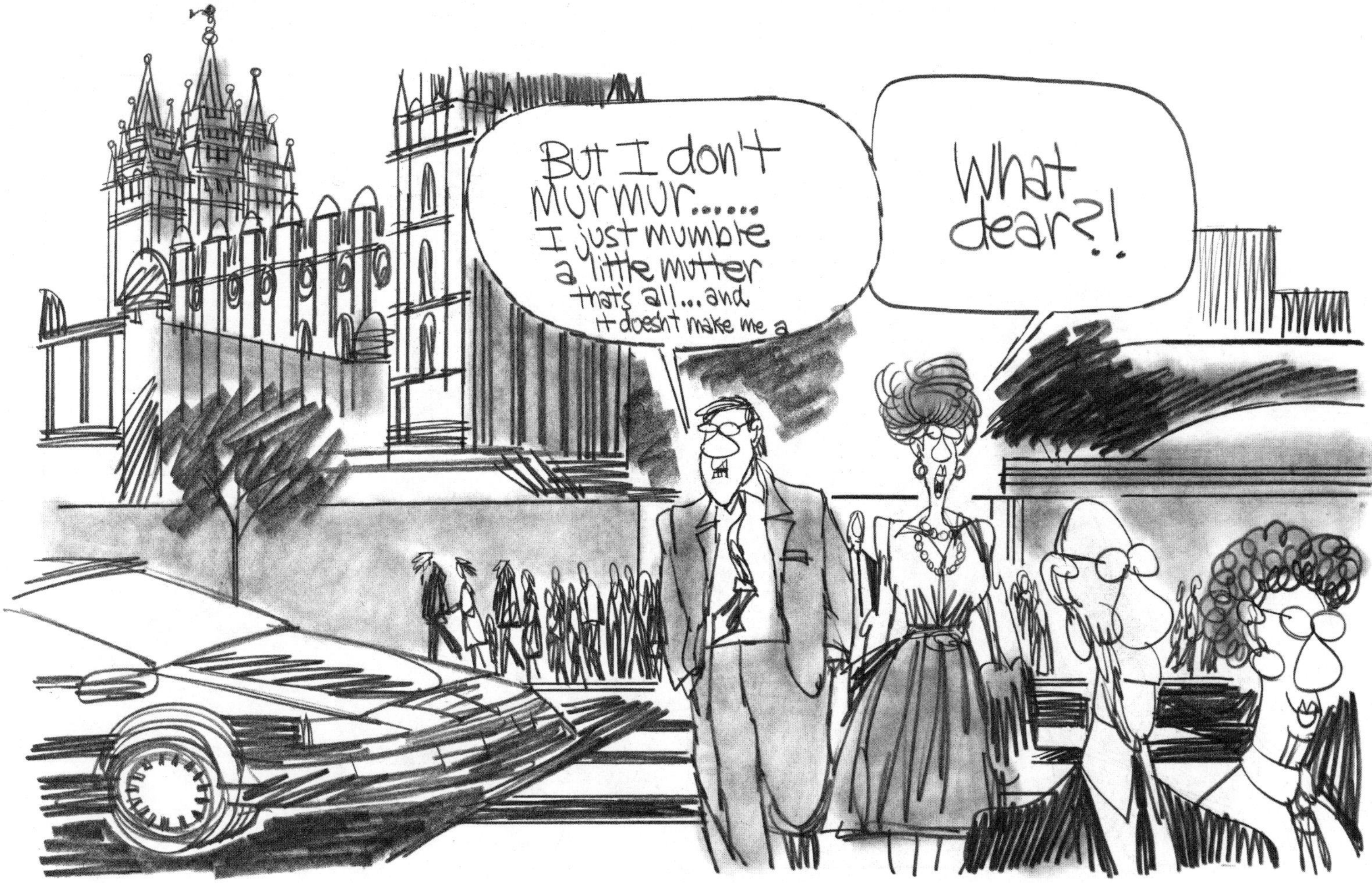
But I don't murmur....... I just mumble a little mutter that's all... and it doesn't make me a
What dear?!

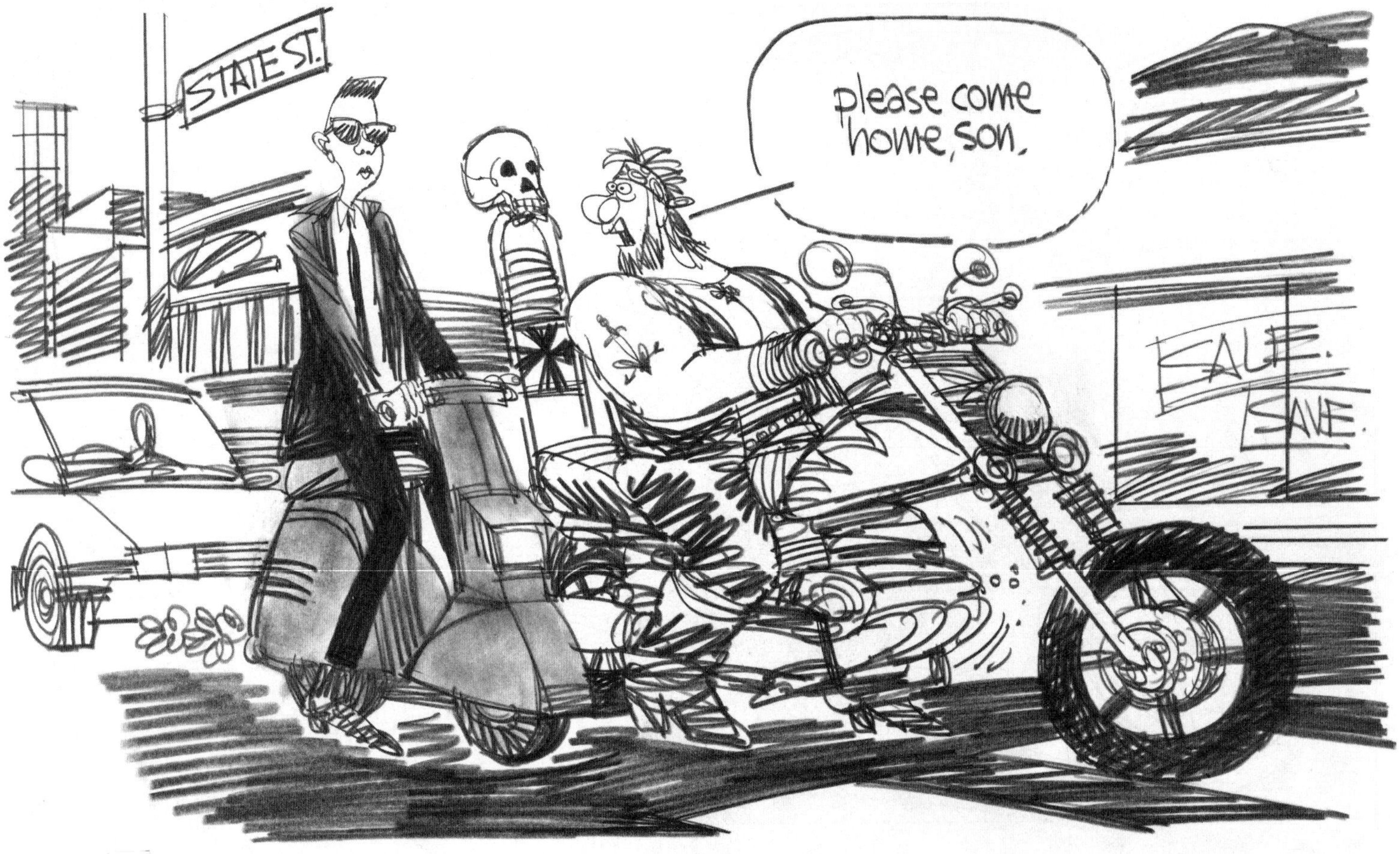
STATE ST.
please come home, son.
SALE
SAVE

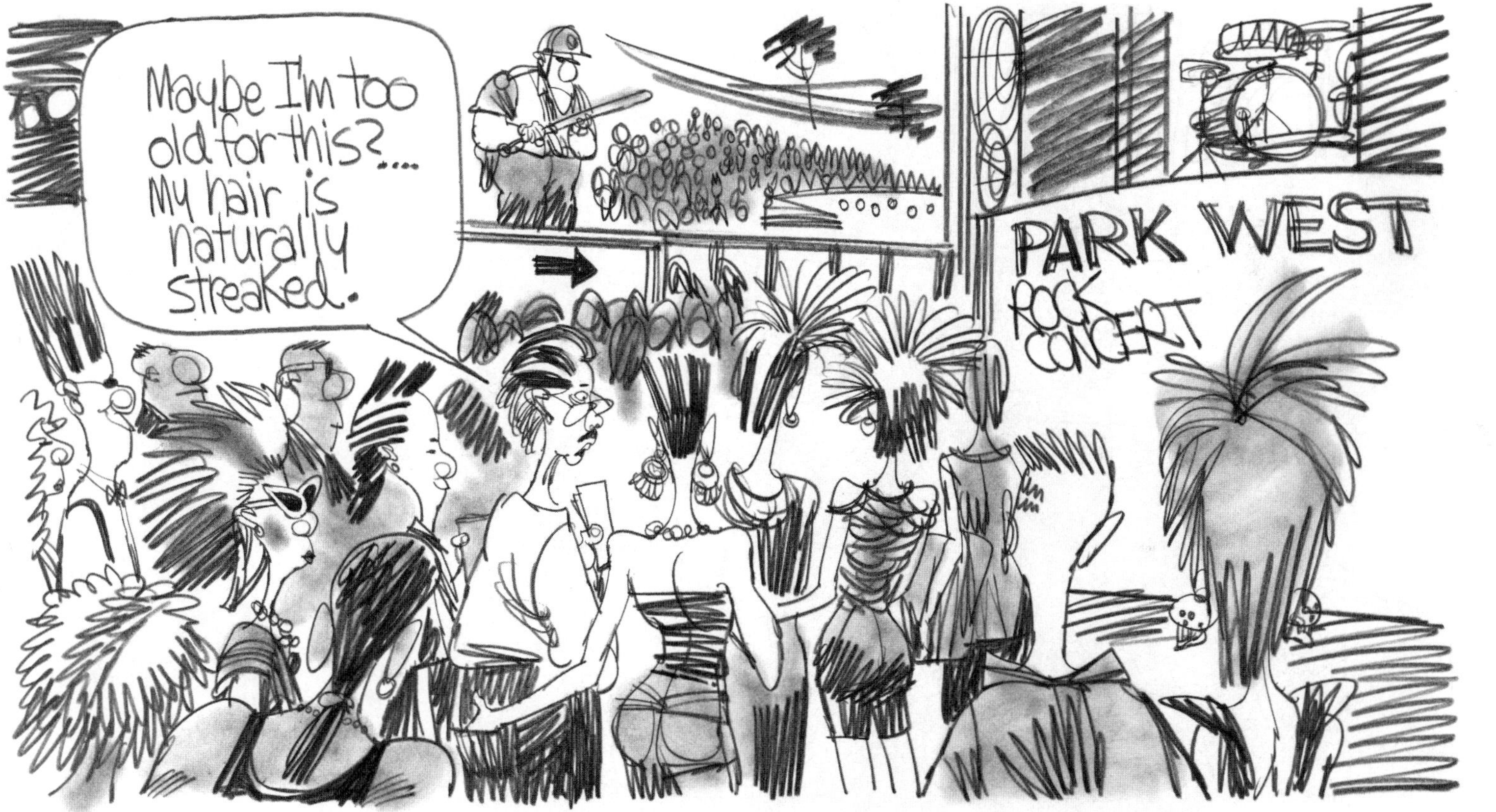
Maybe I'm too old for this?.... My hair is naturally streaked.
PARK WEST
ROCK CONCERT

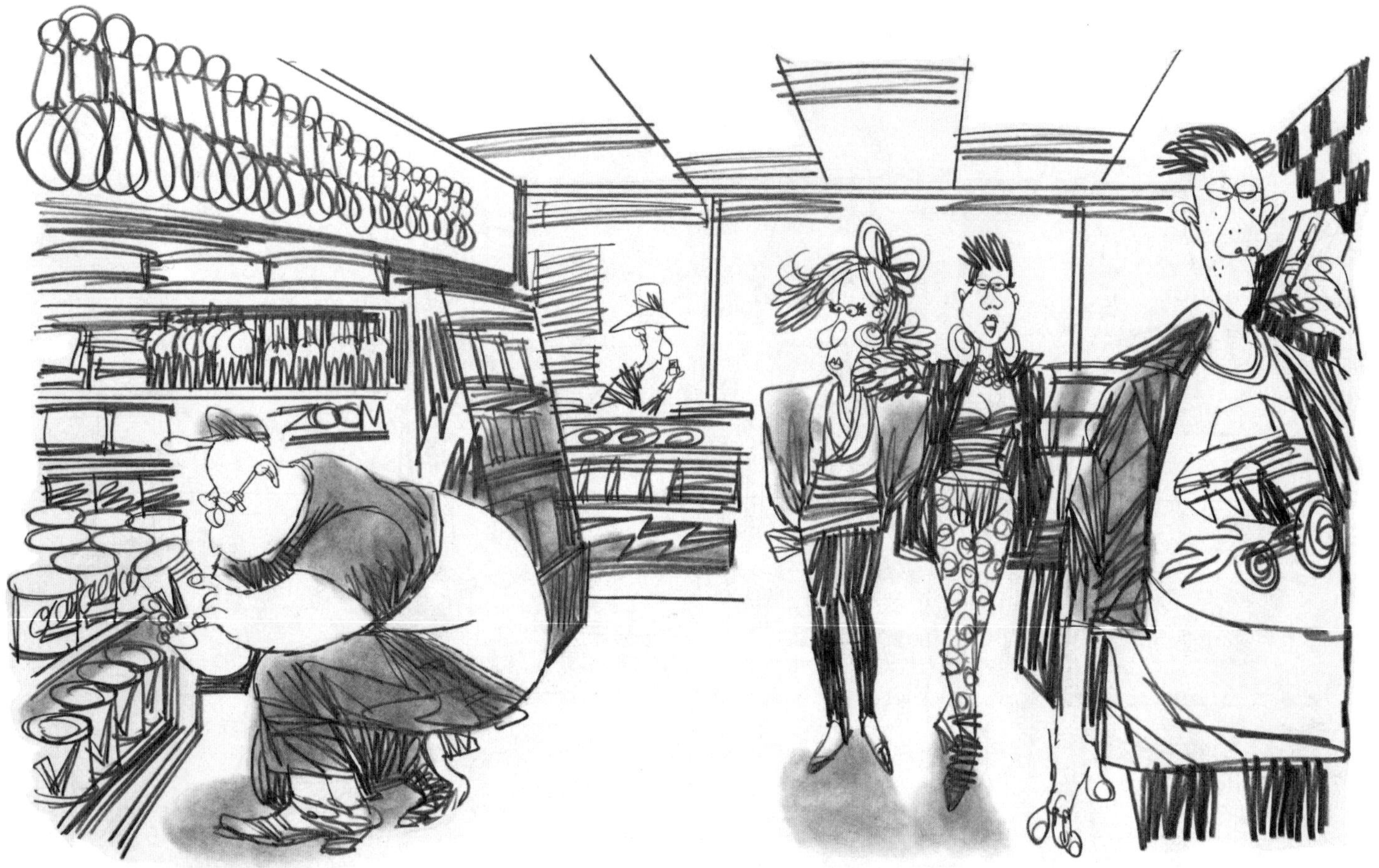
ZOOM

"Patience . . . an auto parts store is the best place in Utah to meet single men."

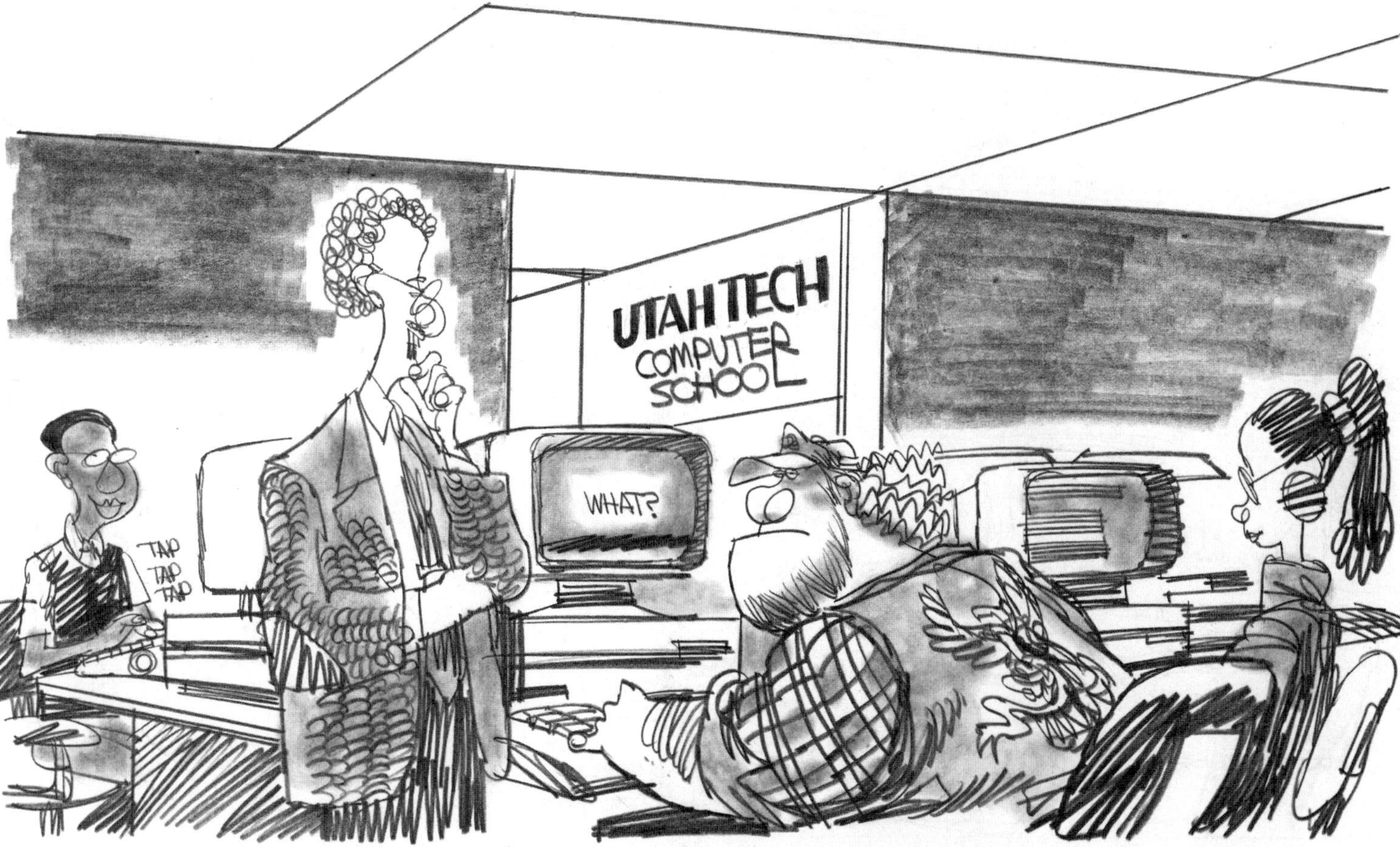
UTAH TECH
COMPUTER
SCHOOL
WHAT?
TAP
TAP
TAP

"Maybe we should start with the difference between a computer chip and a potato chip."

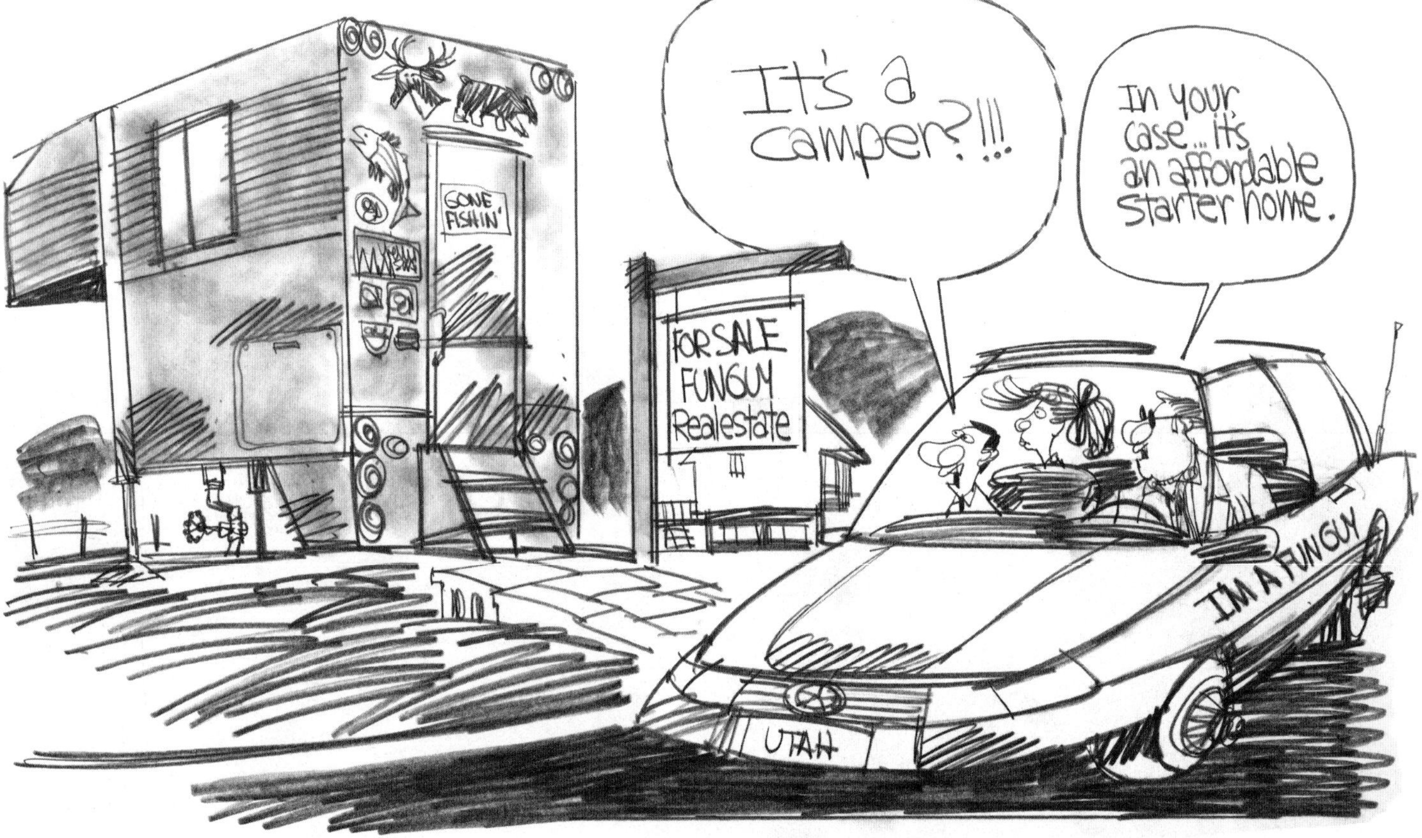
It's a camper?!!!
In your case... it's an affordable starter home.
GONE FISHIN'
FOR SALE FUNGUY Realestate
I'M A FUNGUY
UTAH

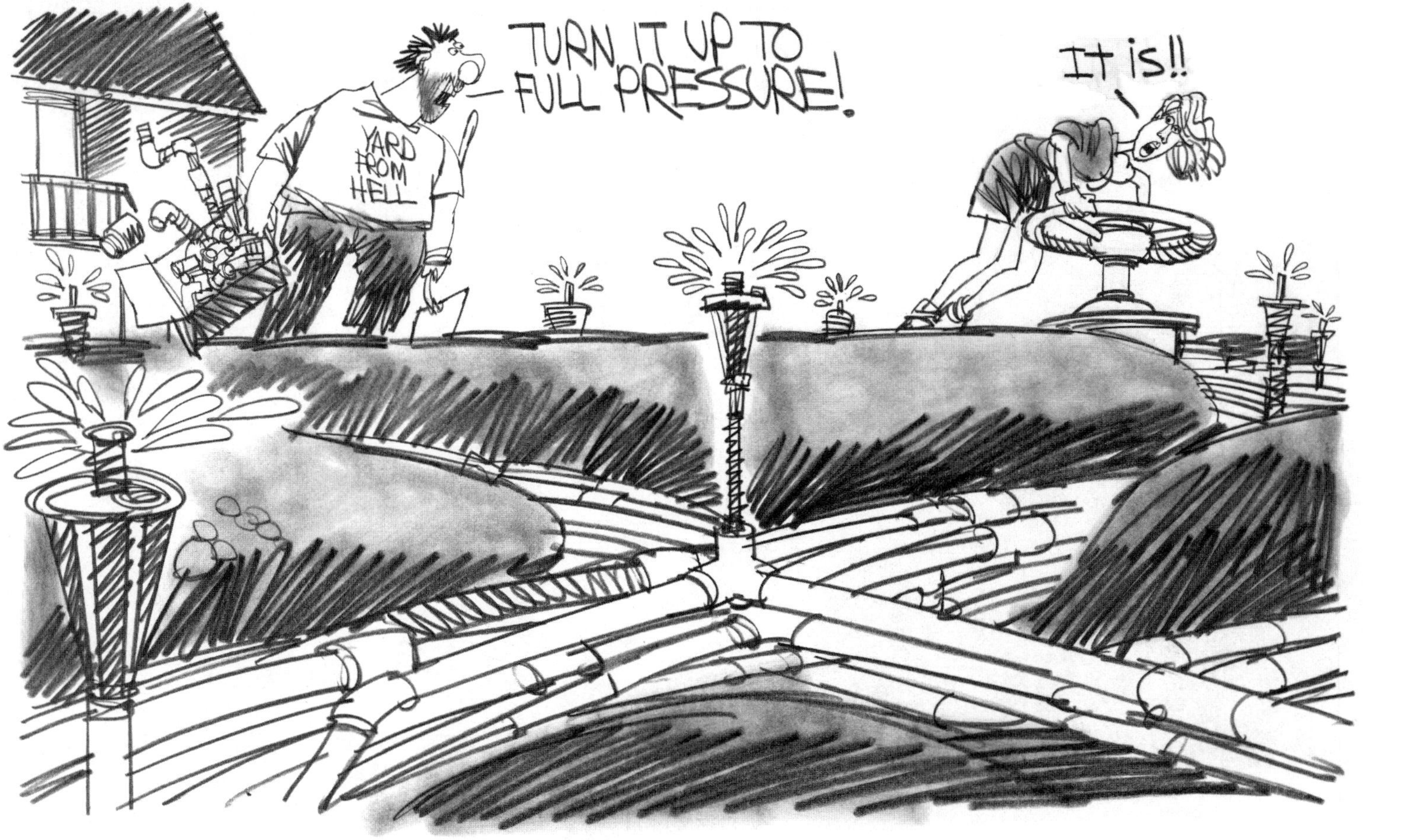
TURN IT UP TO FULL PRESSURE!
YARD FROM HELL
It is!!

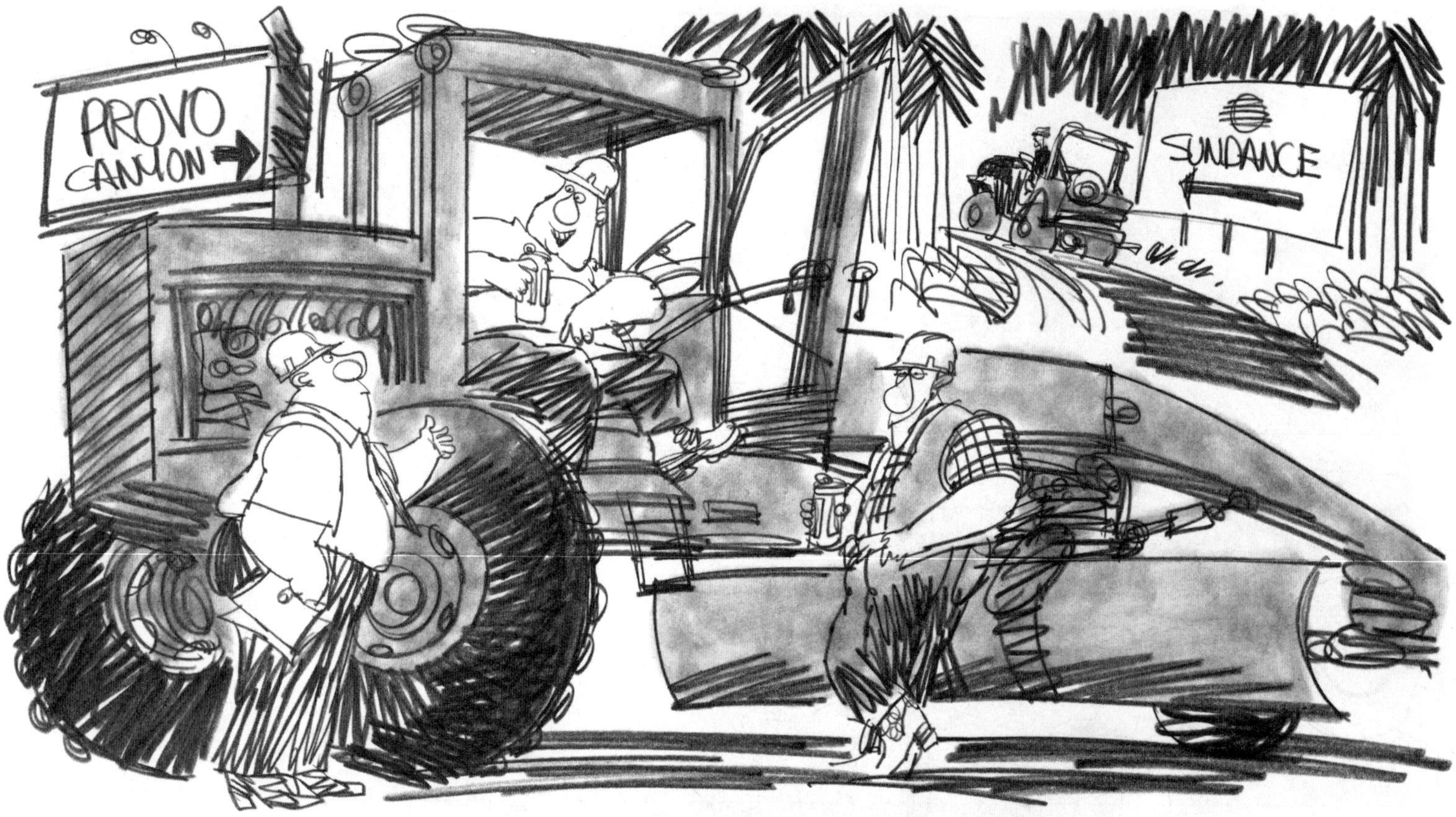
PROVO
CANYON
SUNDANCE

"He said that if we didn't widen the highway we'd all get to be big shot Hollywood stars in his next movie."

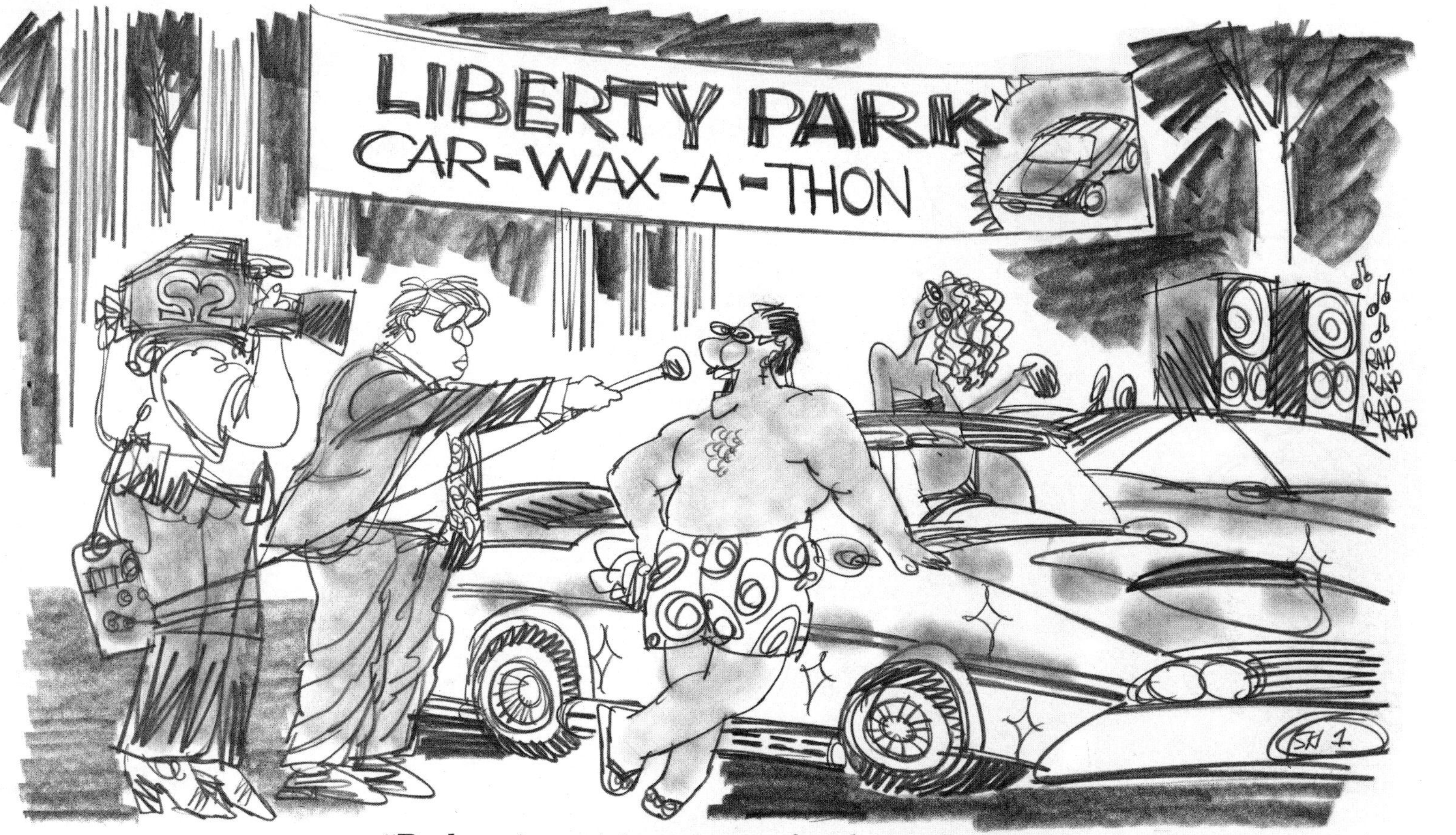
LIBERTY PARK
CAR-WAX-A-THON
S2
RAP
RAP
RAP
RAP

"Rod, we're raising money for the unfortunate who cannot afford tanning beds."

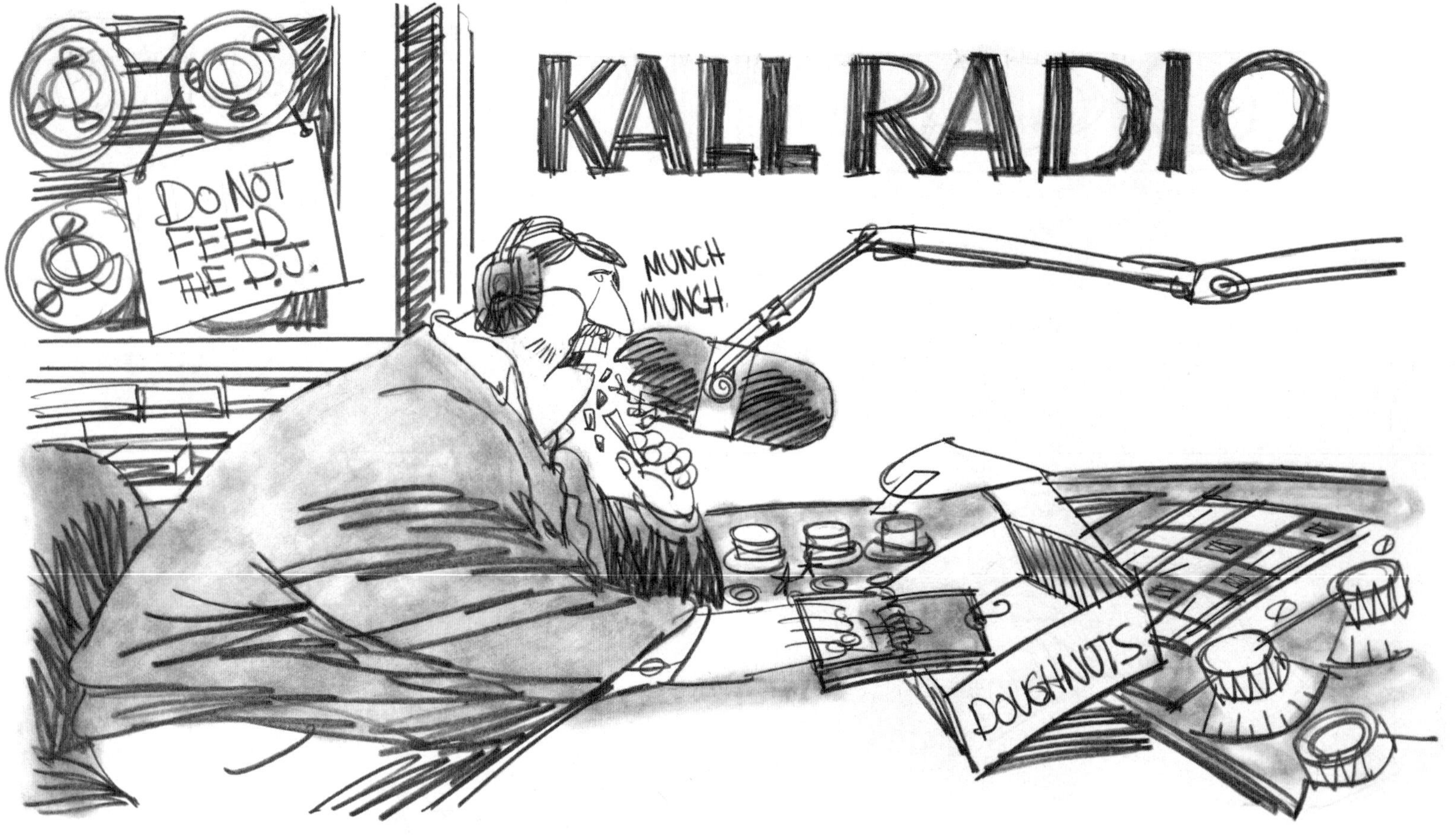
KALL RADIO
DO NOT FEED THE D.J.
MUNCH
MUNCH
DOUGHNUTS

"This is Tom Blueberry . . .
and I'm now on my third week with Nutron Systems weightloss program."

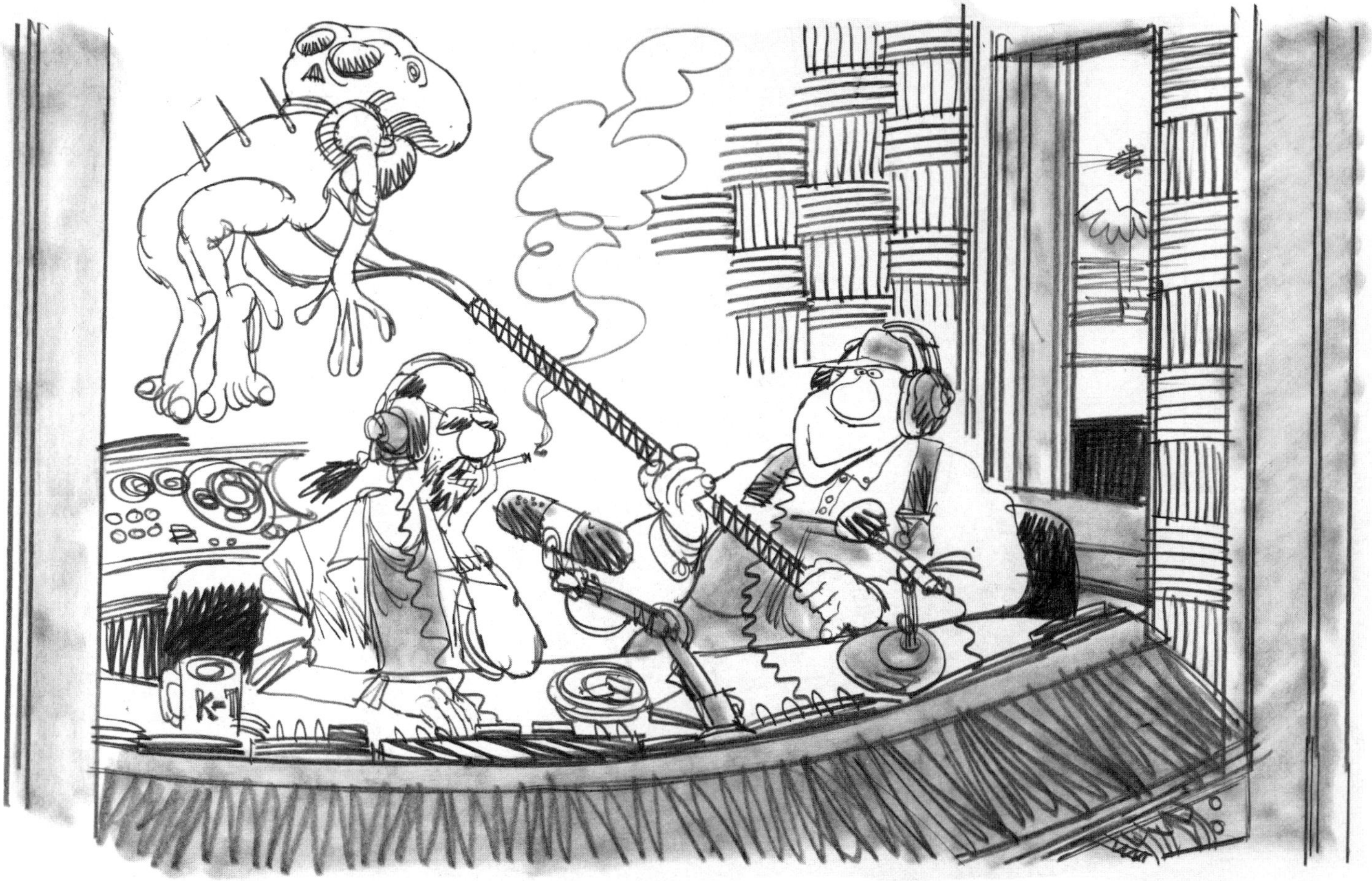
K-T

“My guest is an alien hunter from Tooele . . .
We welcome your calls.”

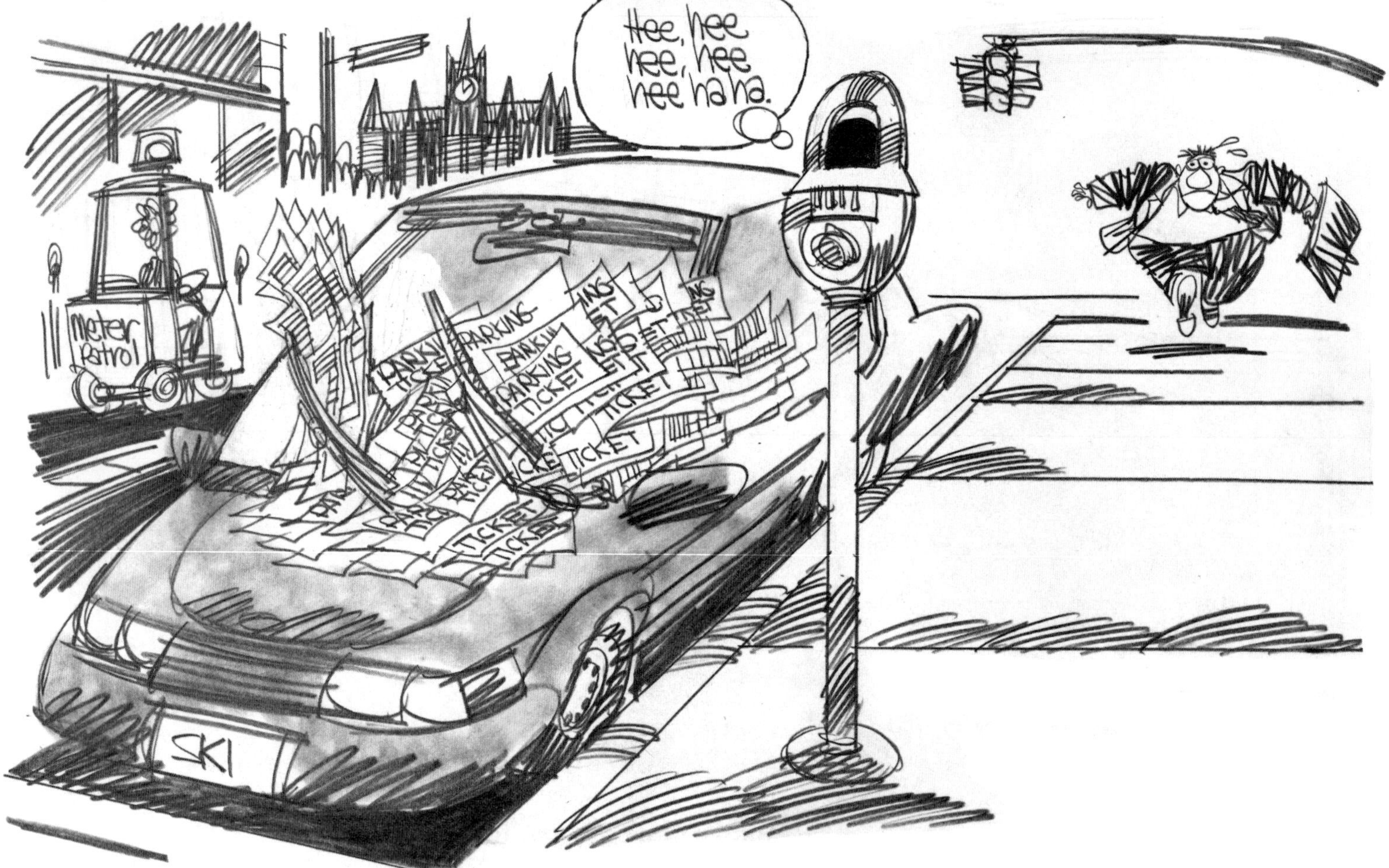
Hee, hee hee, hee hee ha ha.
meter patrol
PARKING TICKET
SKI

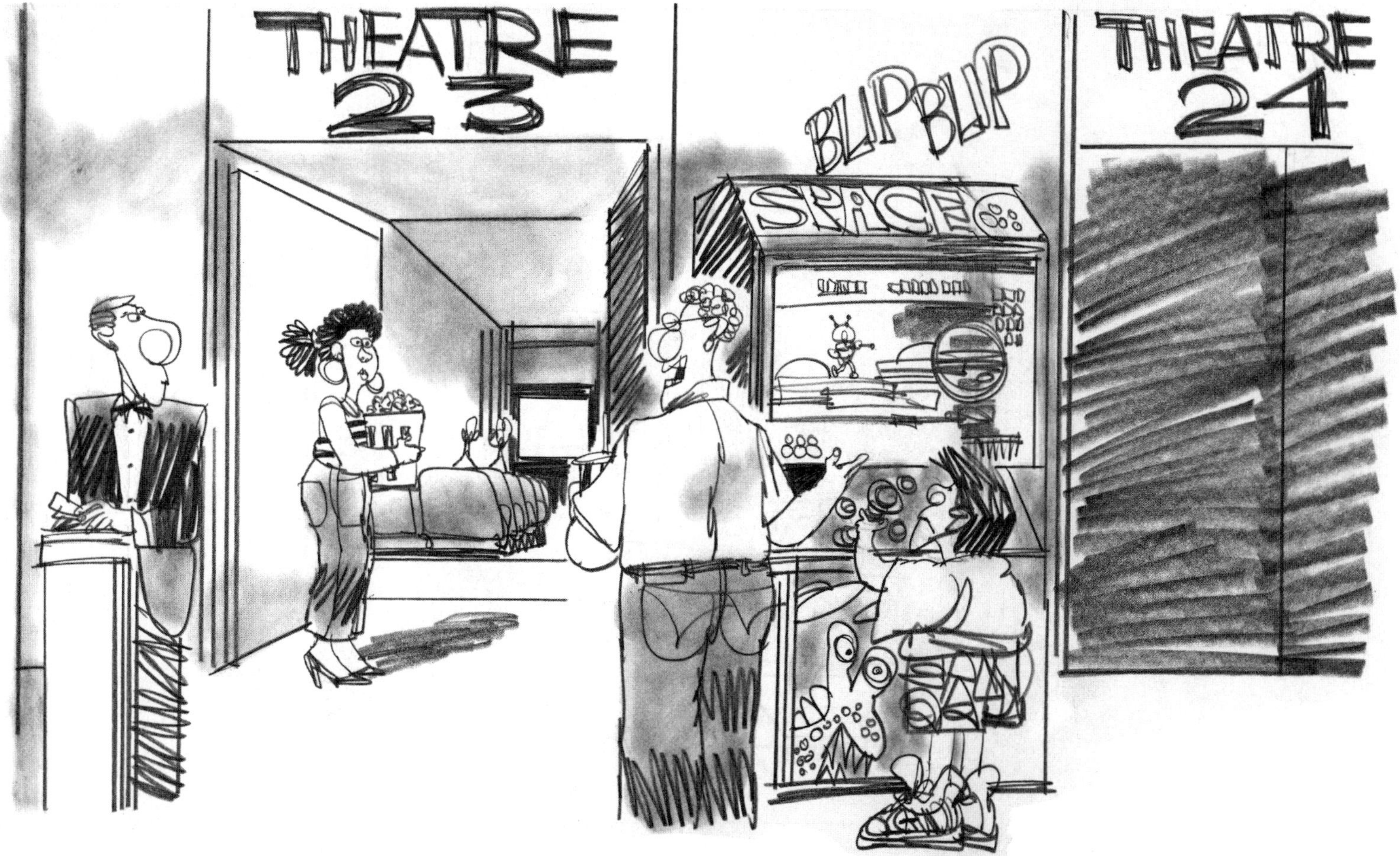
THEATRE
23
BLIP BLIP
SPACE
THEATRE
24

"Let's watch this instead. The screen's bigger."

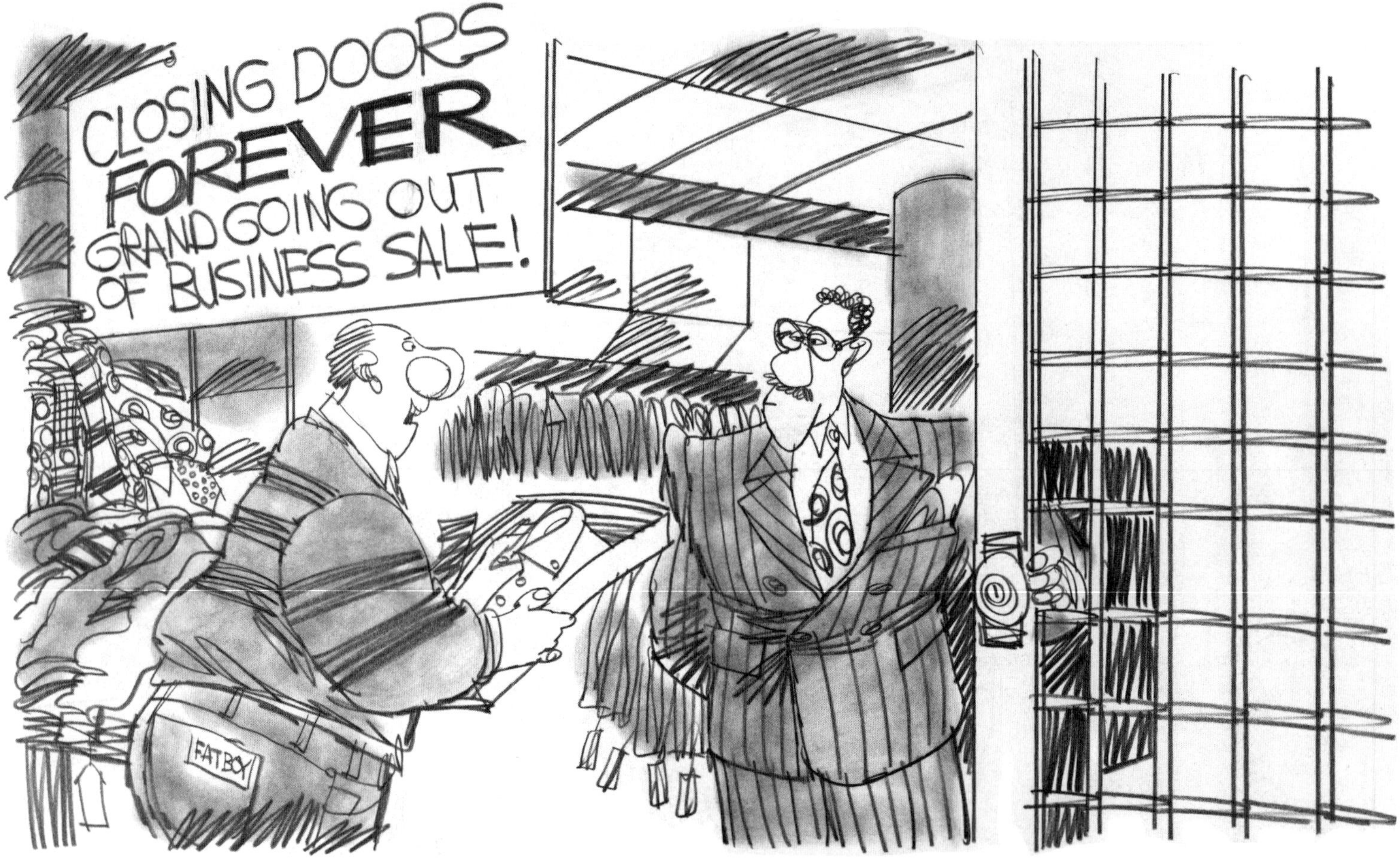
CLOSING DOORS
FOREVER
GRAND GOING OUT
OF BUSINESS SALE!
FATBOY

"I bought this shirt at your grand opening yesterday.
Am I too late to exchange it?"

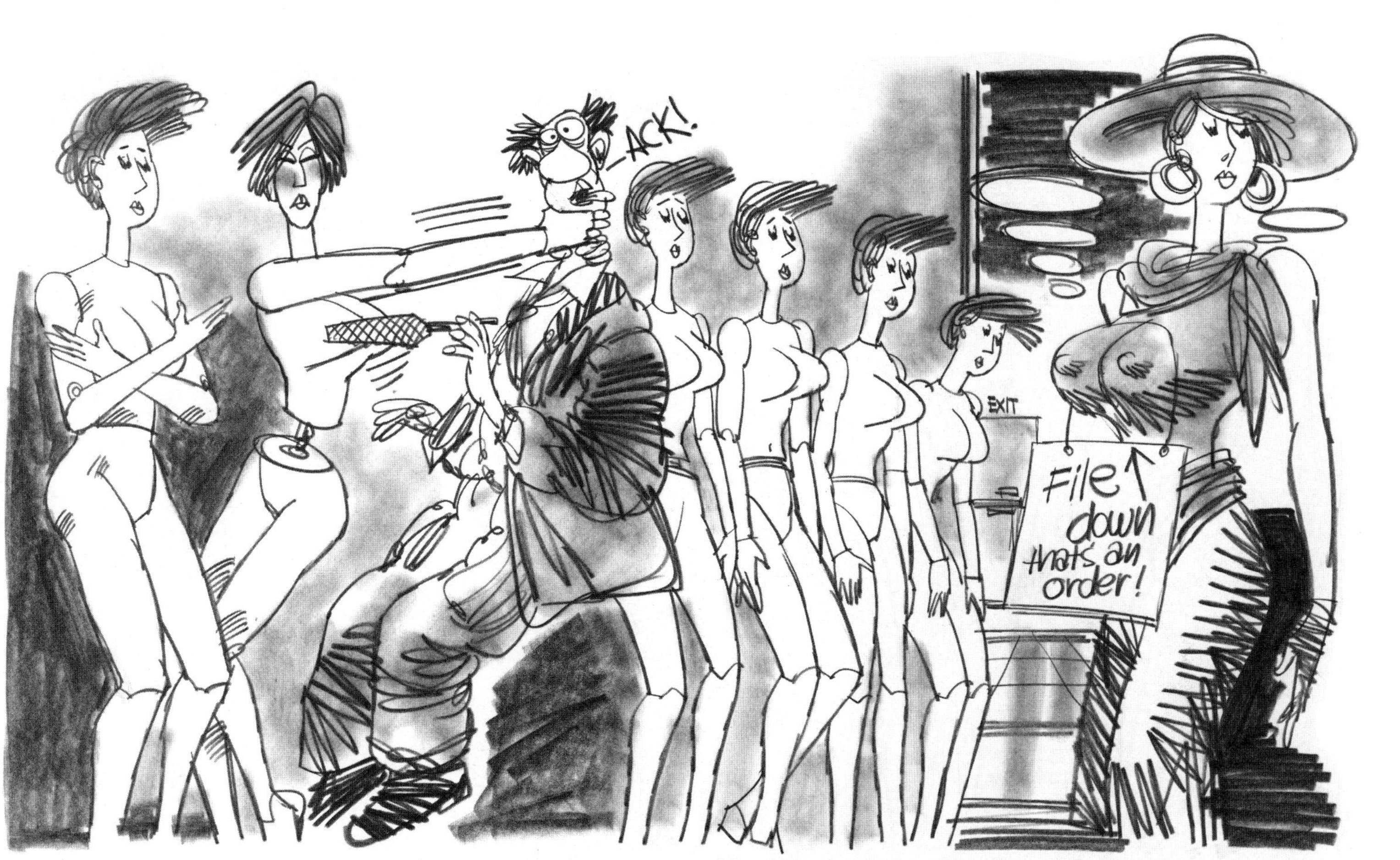
ACK!
EXIT
File ↑ down
that's an order!

NIGHT OF THE LIVING Z.C.M.I. MANNEQUINS

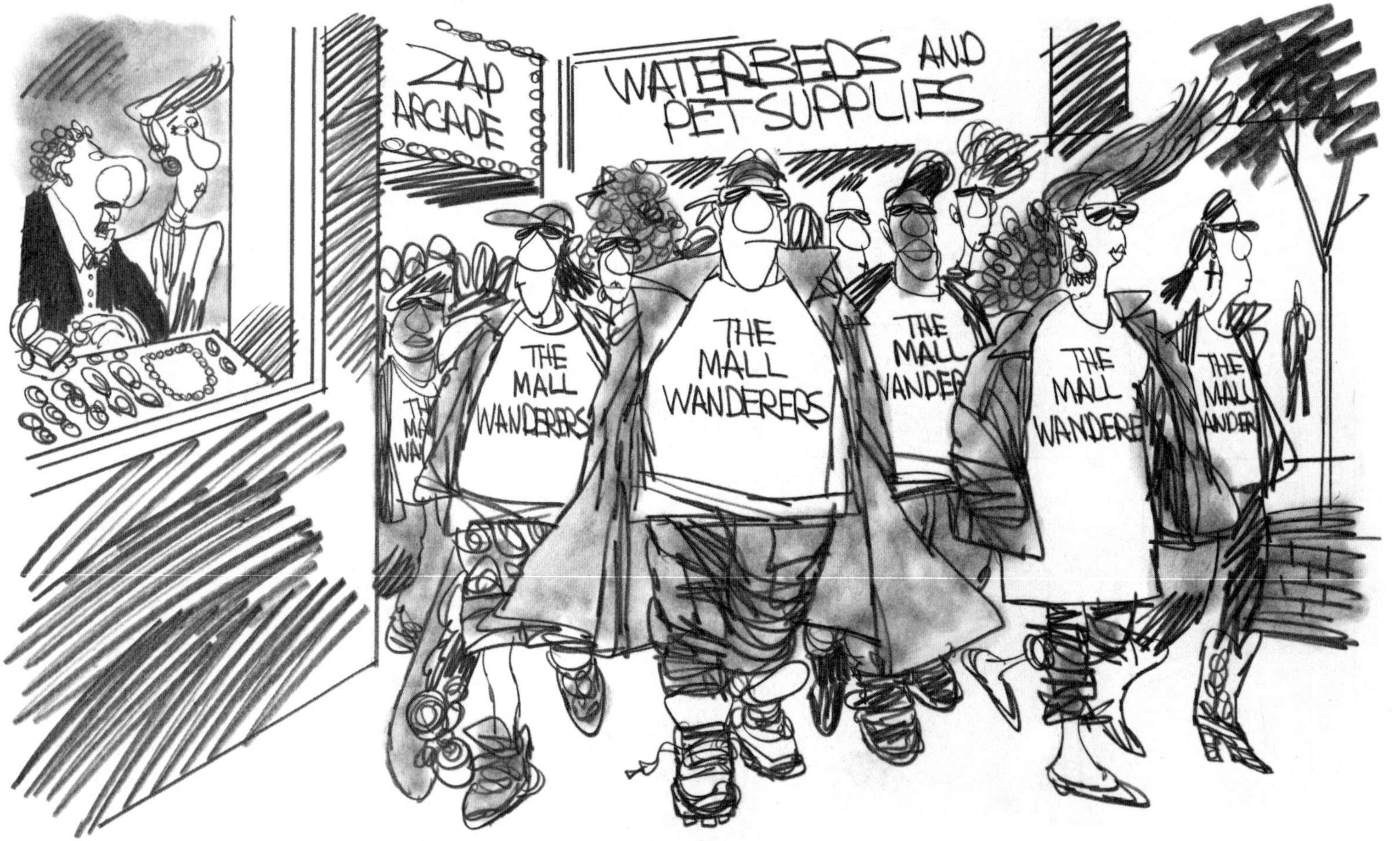
ZAP
ARCADE
WATERBEDS AND
PET SUPPLIES
THE MALL WANDERERS
THE MALL WANDERERS
THE MALL WANDERERS

"Oh, no! Here comes the biggest street gang in Utah."

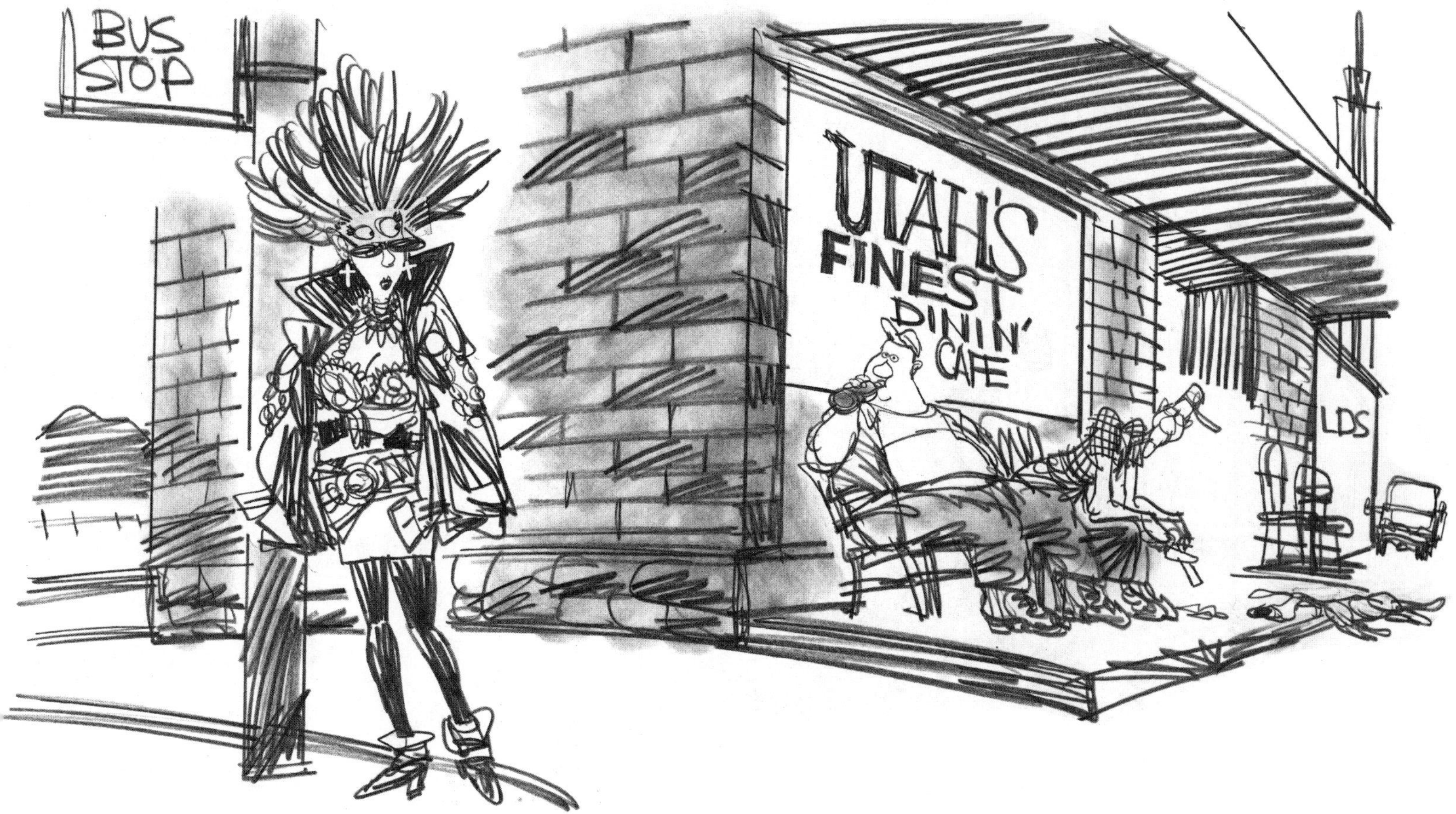
BUS STOP
UTAH'S FINEST DININ' CAFE
LDS

DESPERATELY SEEKING URBAN

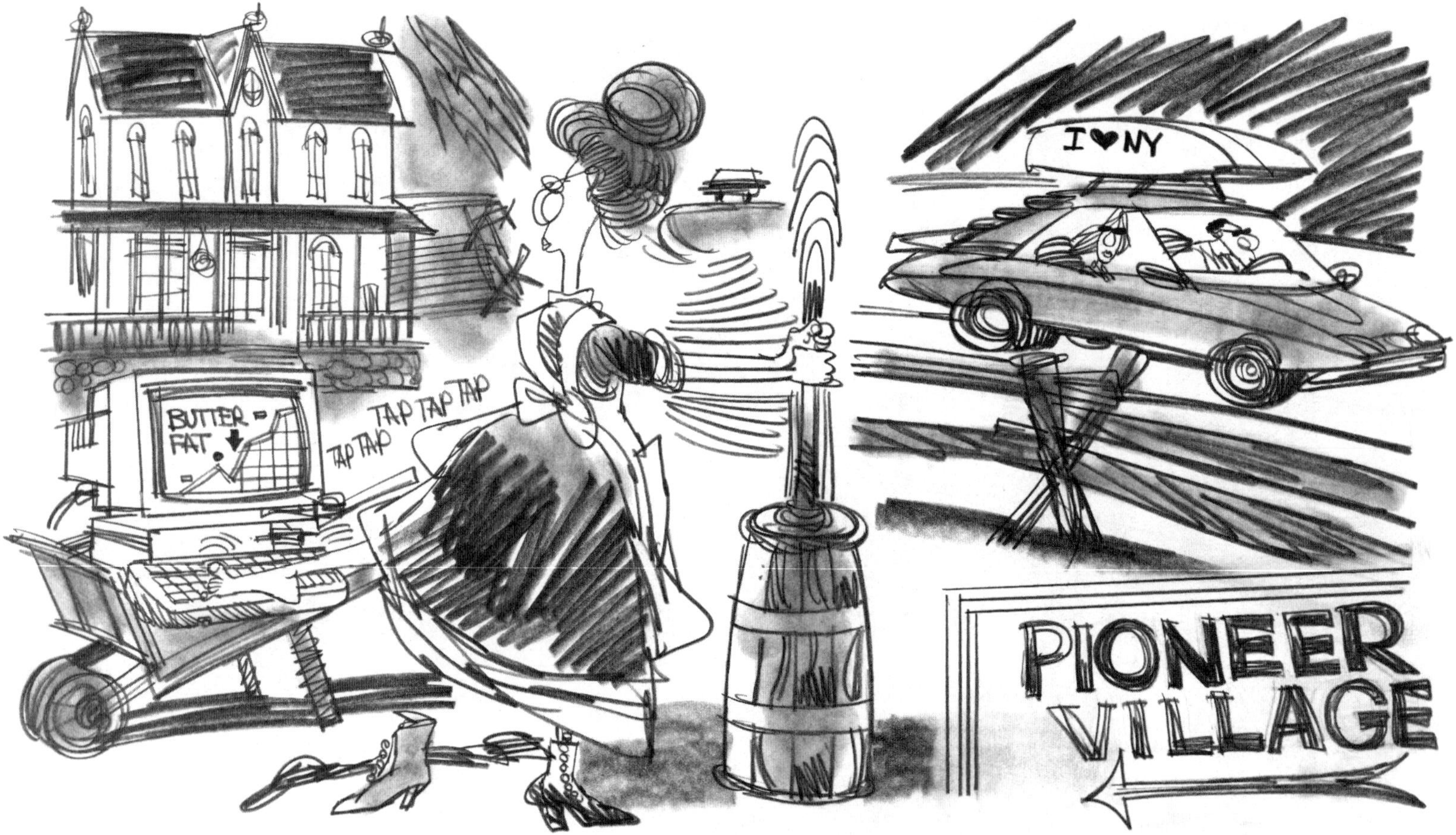
I ♥ NY
BUTTER-FAT
TAP TAP TAP TAP TAP
PIONEER VILLAGE

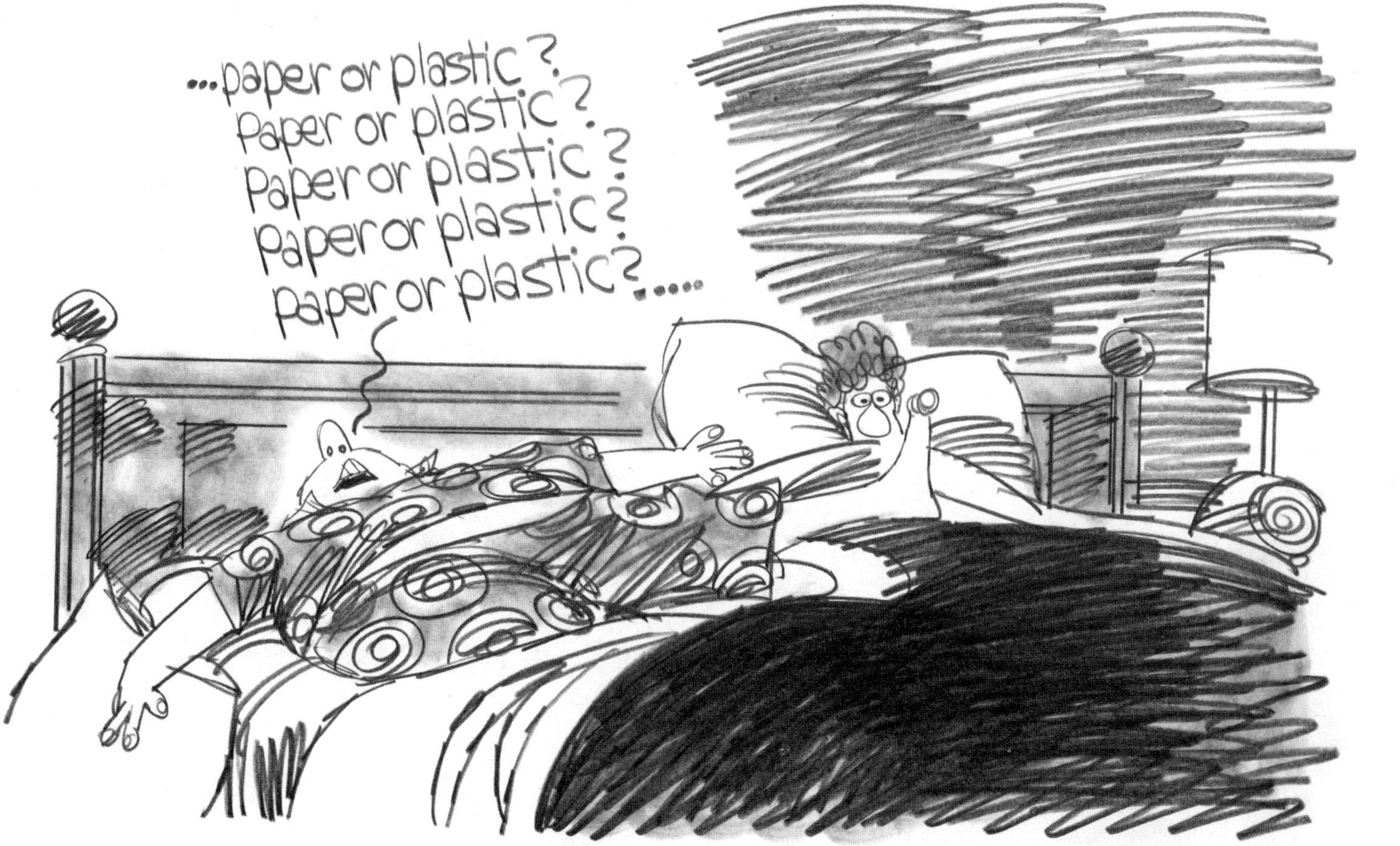
...paper or plastic?
paper or plastic?
paper or plastic?
paper or plastic?
paper or plastic?....

JOE ALBERTSON'S NIGHTMARE

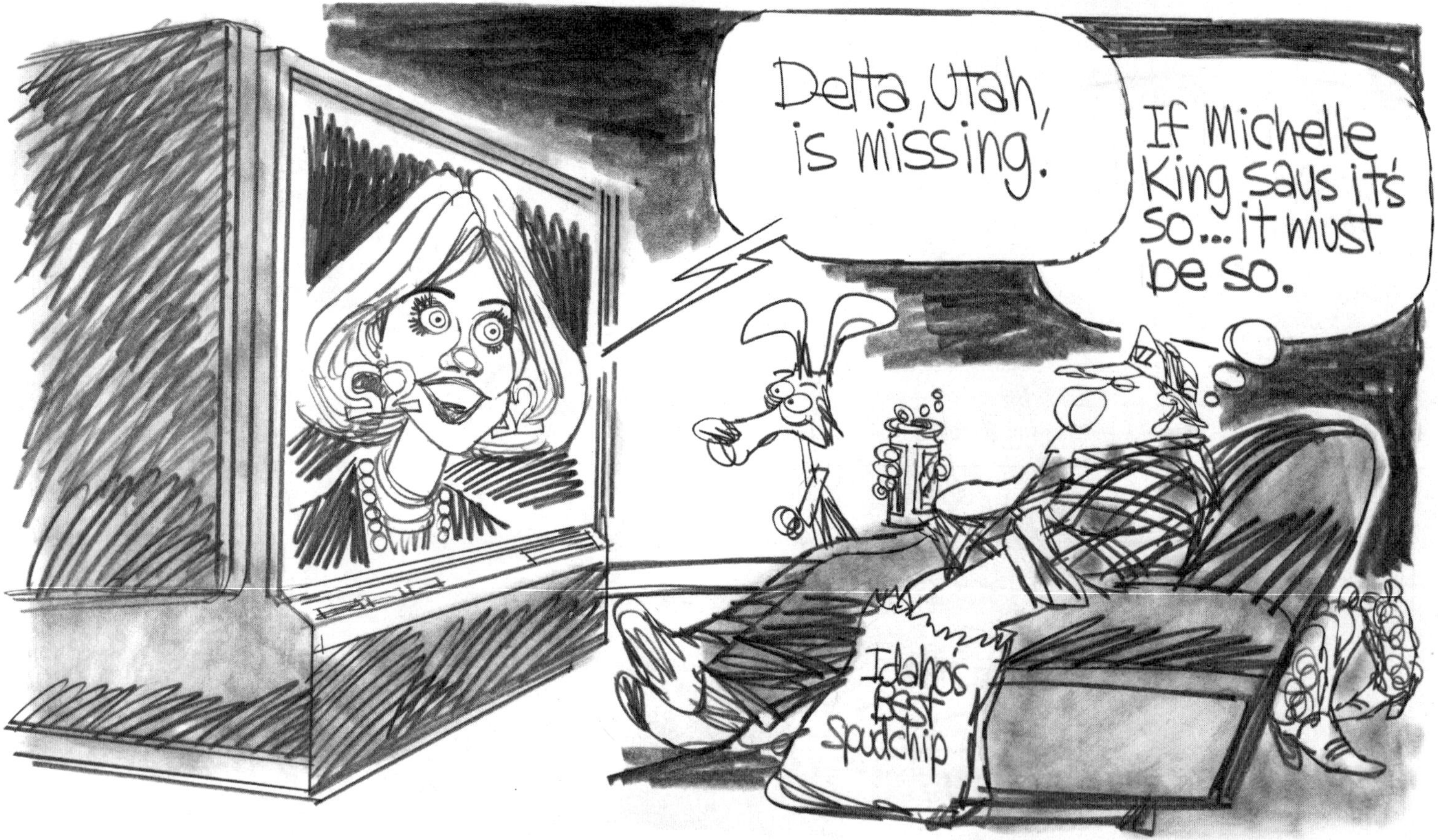
Delta, Utah, is missing.
If Michelle King says it's so... it must be so.
Idaho's Best Spudchip

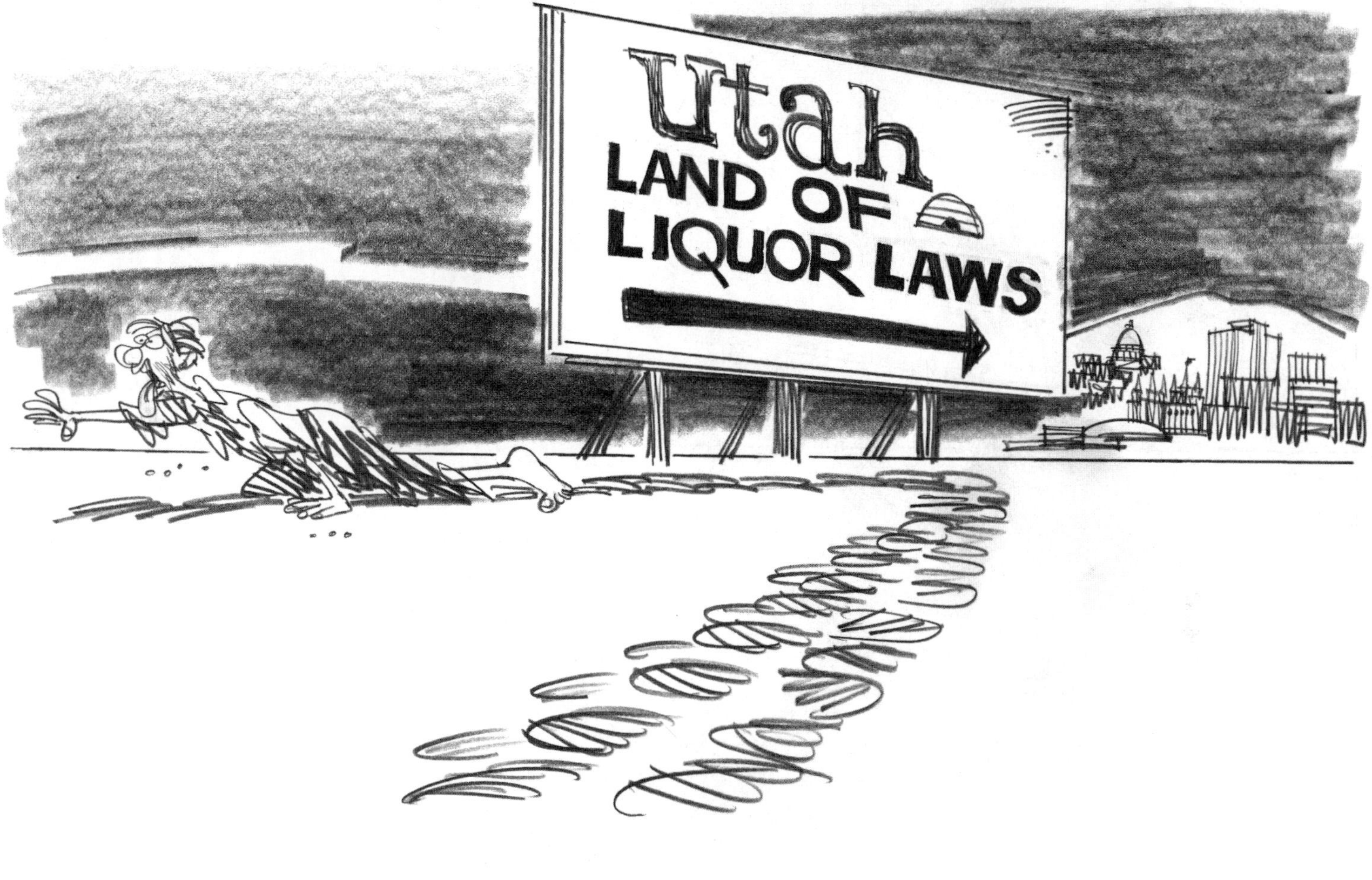
Utah
LAND OF
LIQUOR LAWS

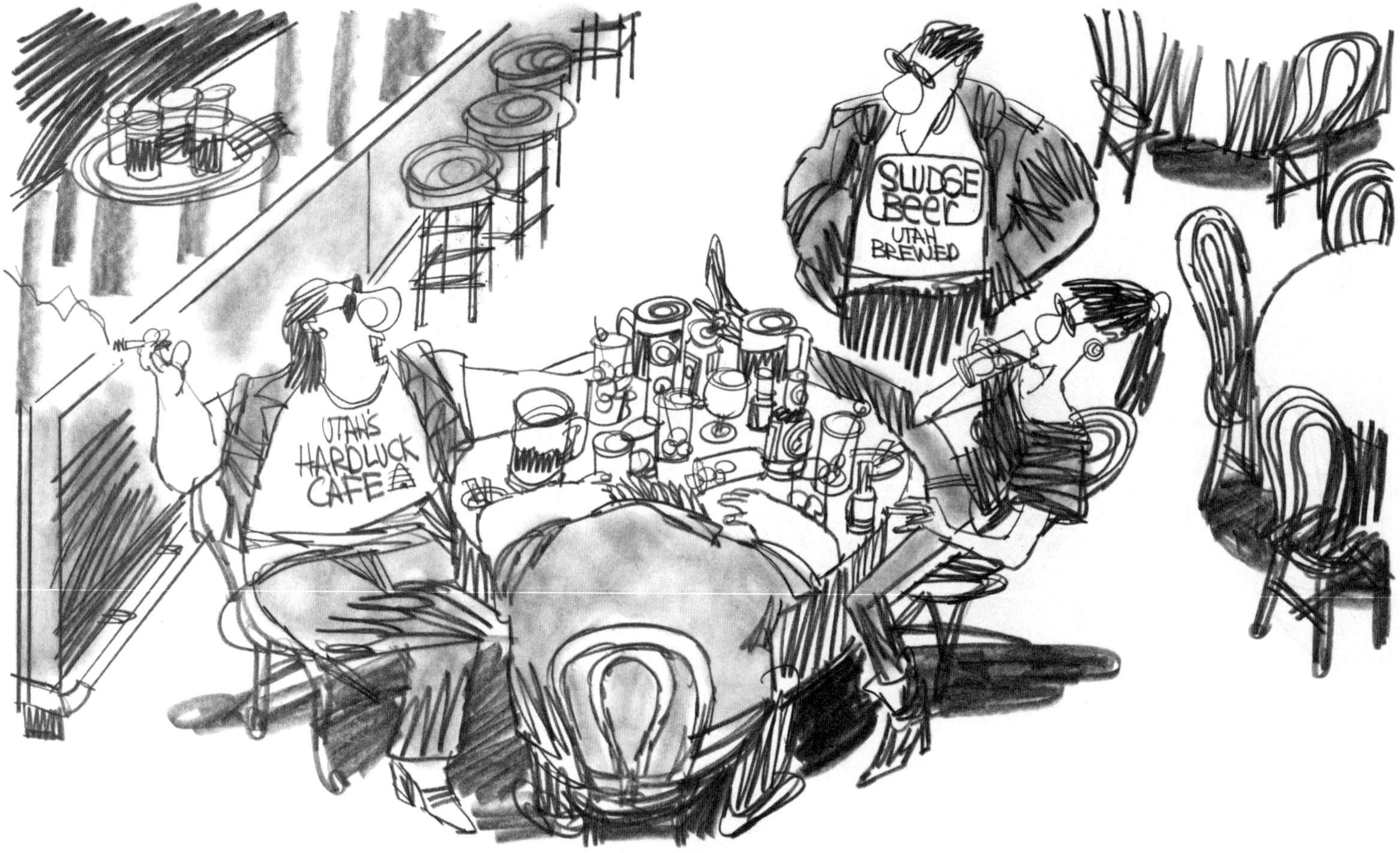
SLUDGE Beer
UTAH BREWED
UTAH'S HARDLUCK CAFE

"We've just been sitting here discussing how hard it is to get a drink in this state."

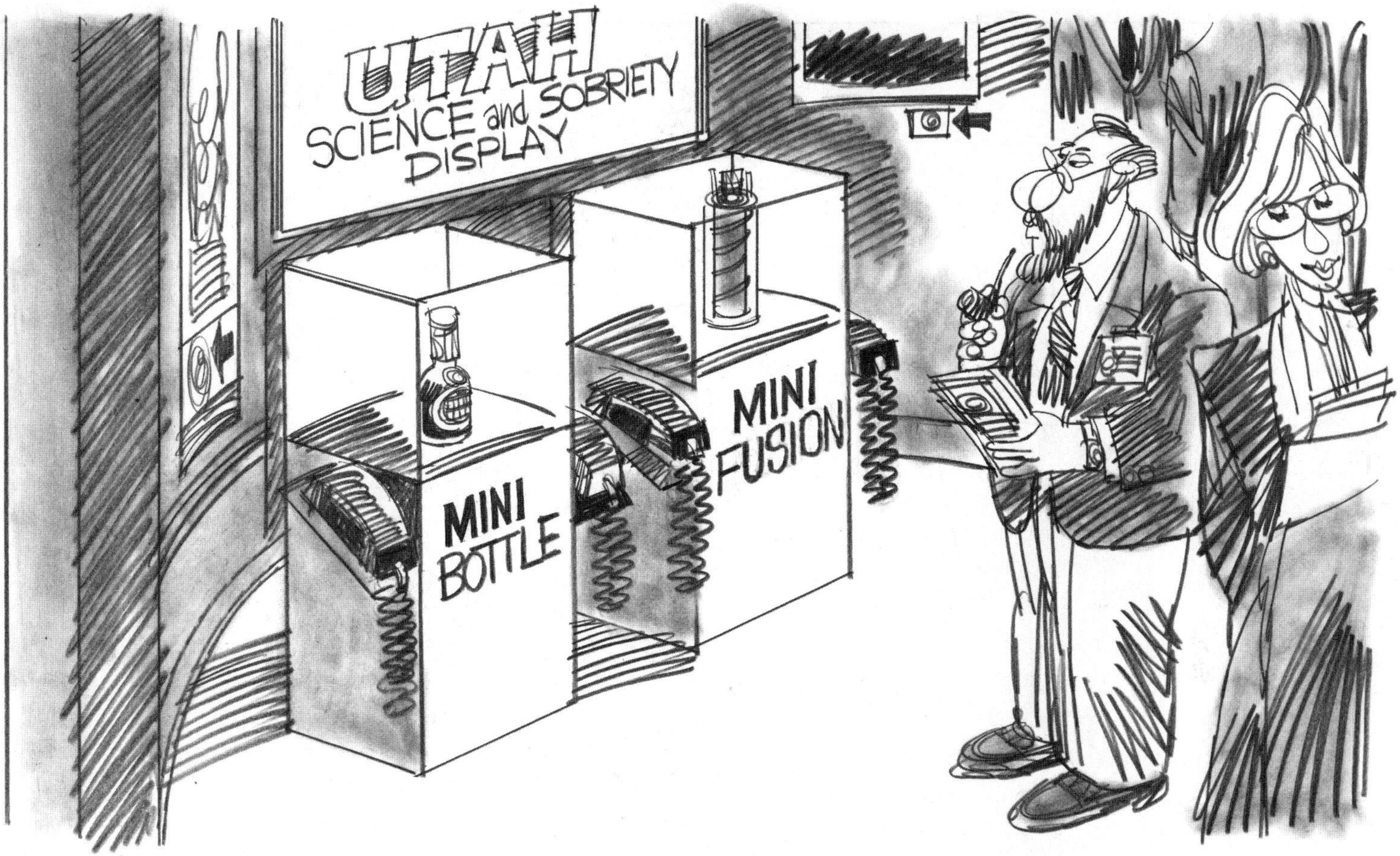
UTAH
SCIENCE and SOBRIETY
DISPLAY
MINI
BOTTLE
MINI
FUSION

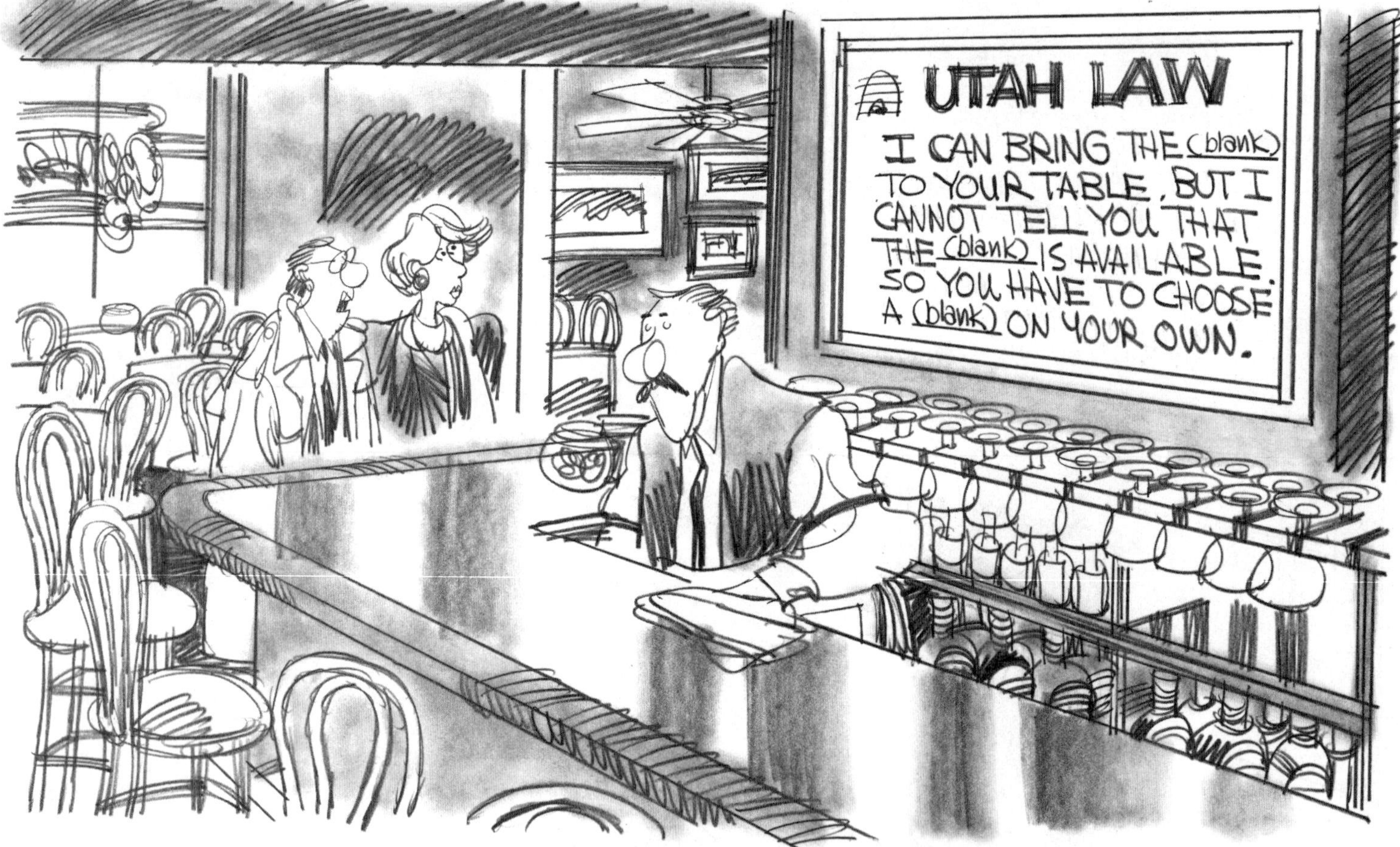
UTAH LAW
I CAN BRING THE (blank) TO YOUR TABLE, BUT I CANNOT TELL YOU THAT THE (blank) IS AVAILABLE. SO YOU HAVE TO CHOOSE A (blank) ON YOUR OWN.

"It's either about mini-bottles or birth control devices."

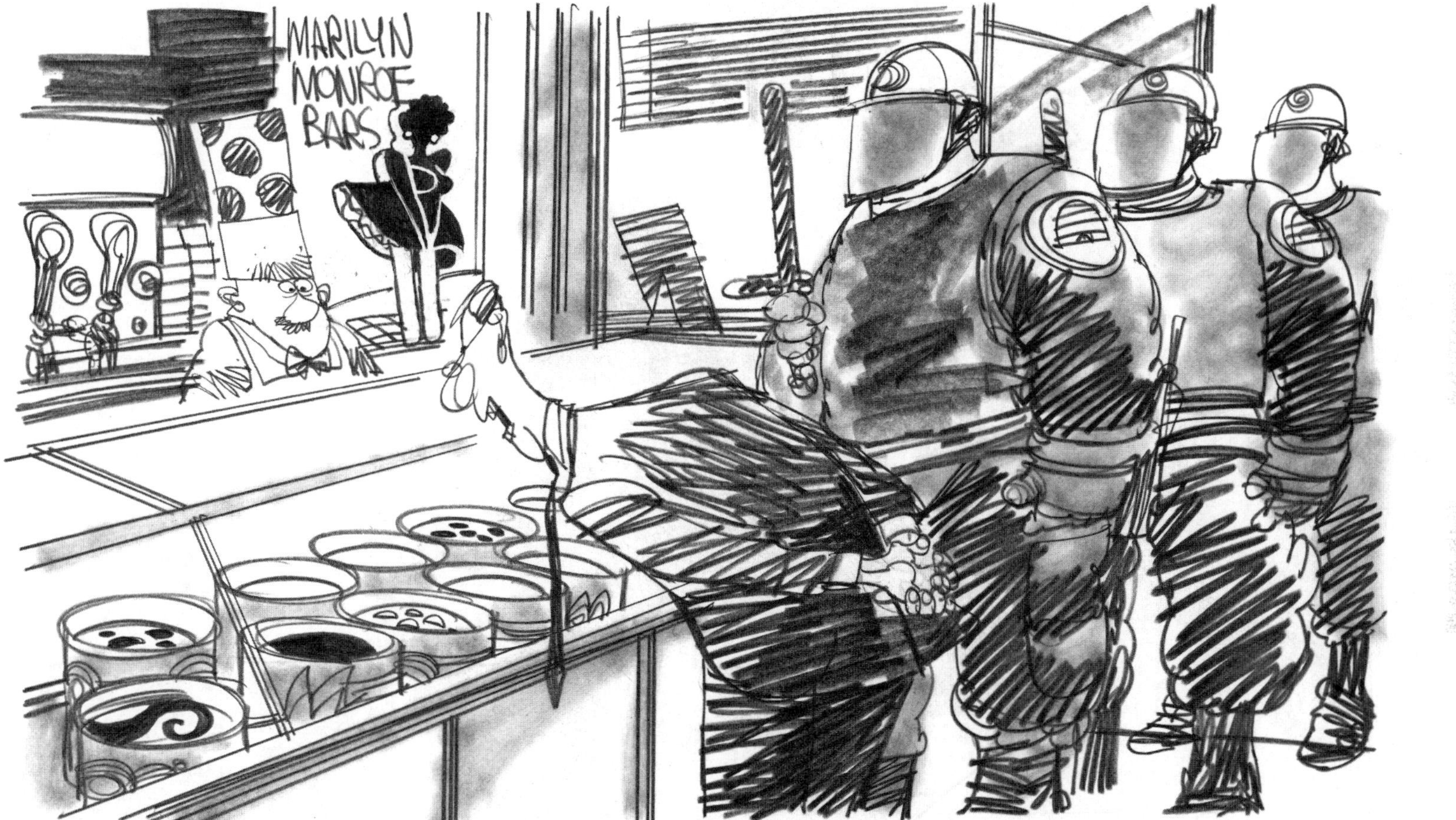
MARILYN
MONROE
BARS
"We're from the Utah State Liquor Control Commission . . .
I hear you use rum in your ice cream."

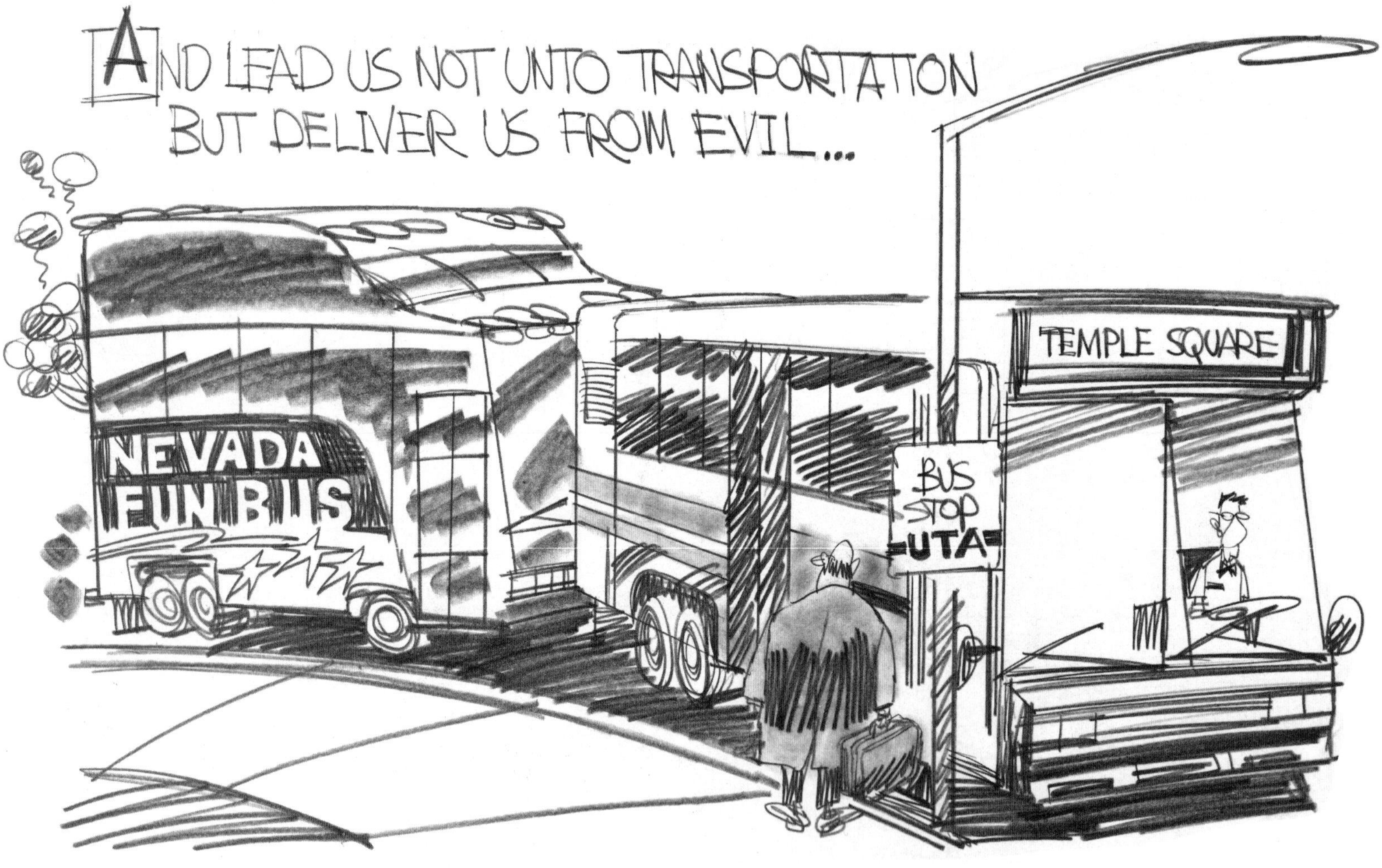
AND LEAD US NOT UNTO TRANSPORTATION
BUT DELIVER US FROM EVIL...
NEVADA
FUN BUS
TEMPLE SQUARE
BUS
STOP
UTA

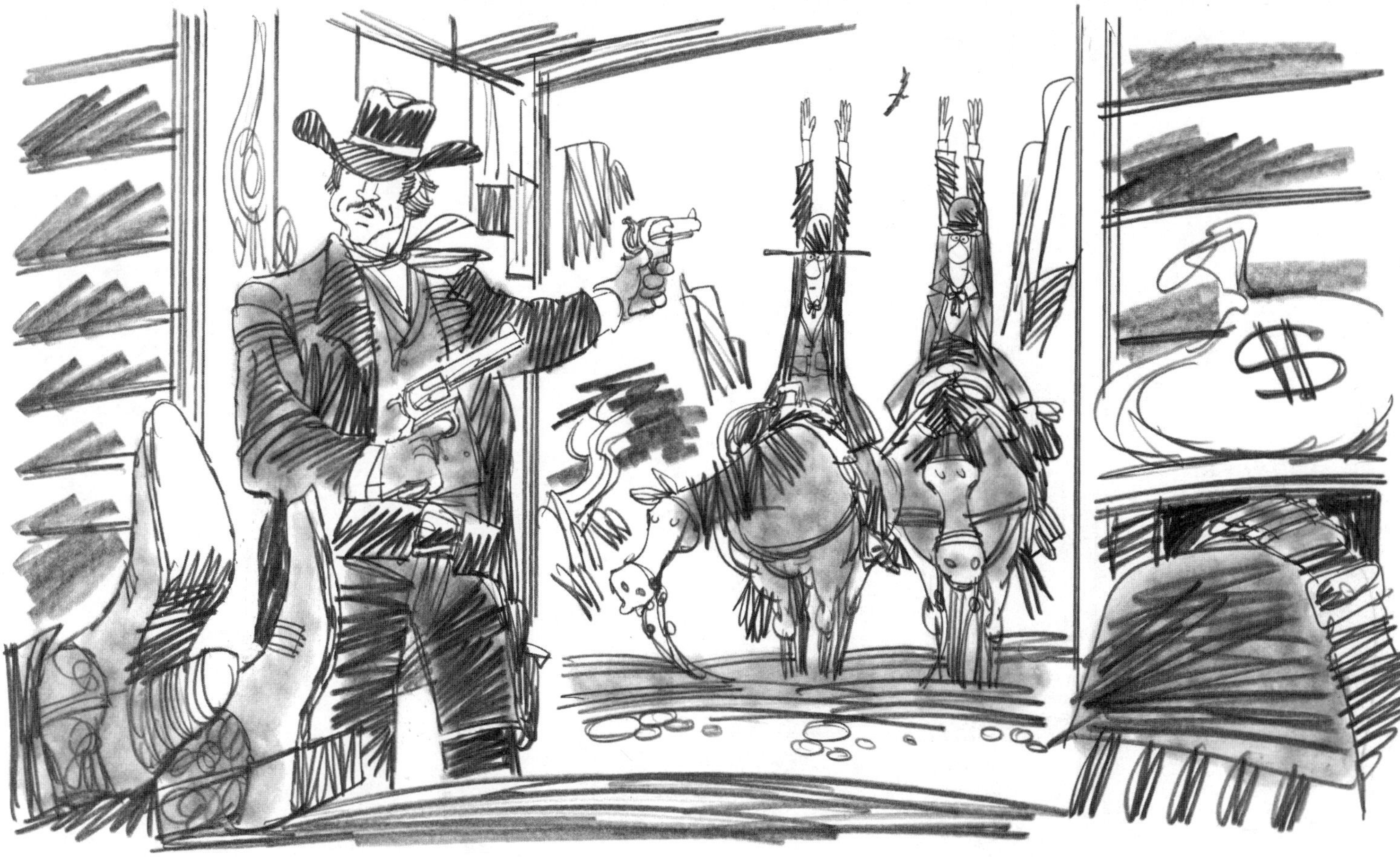

"Butch, your home teachers don't ever give up, do they?"

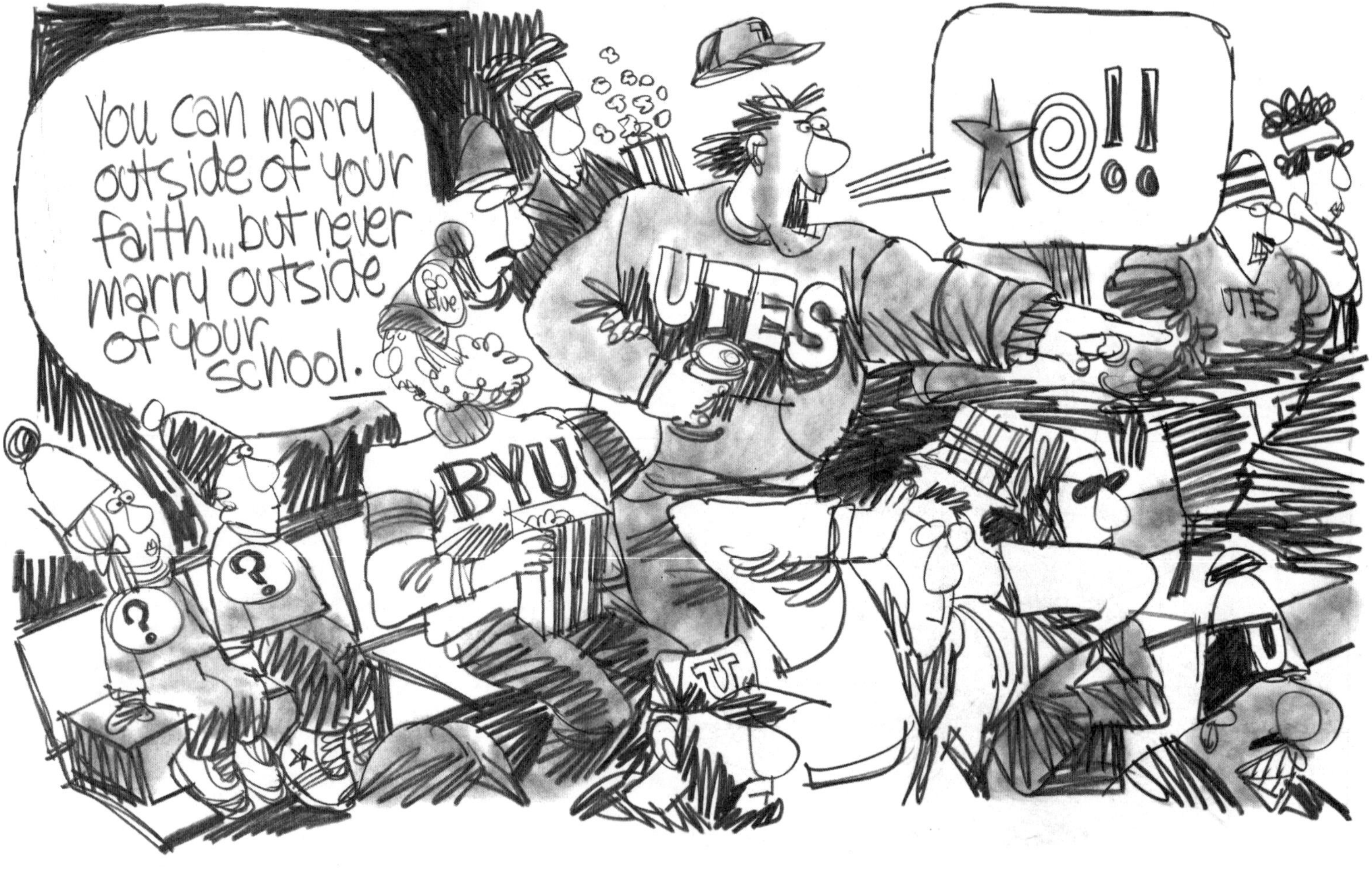
You can marry outside of your faith...but never marry outside of your school.
UTES
BYU

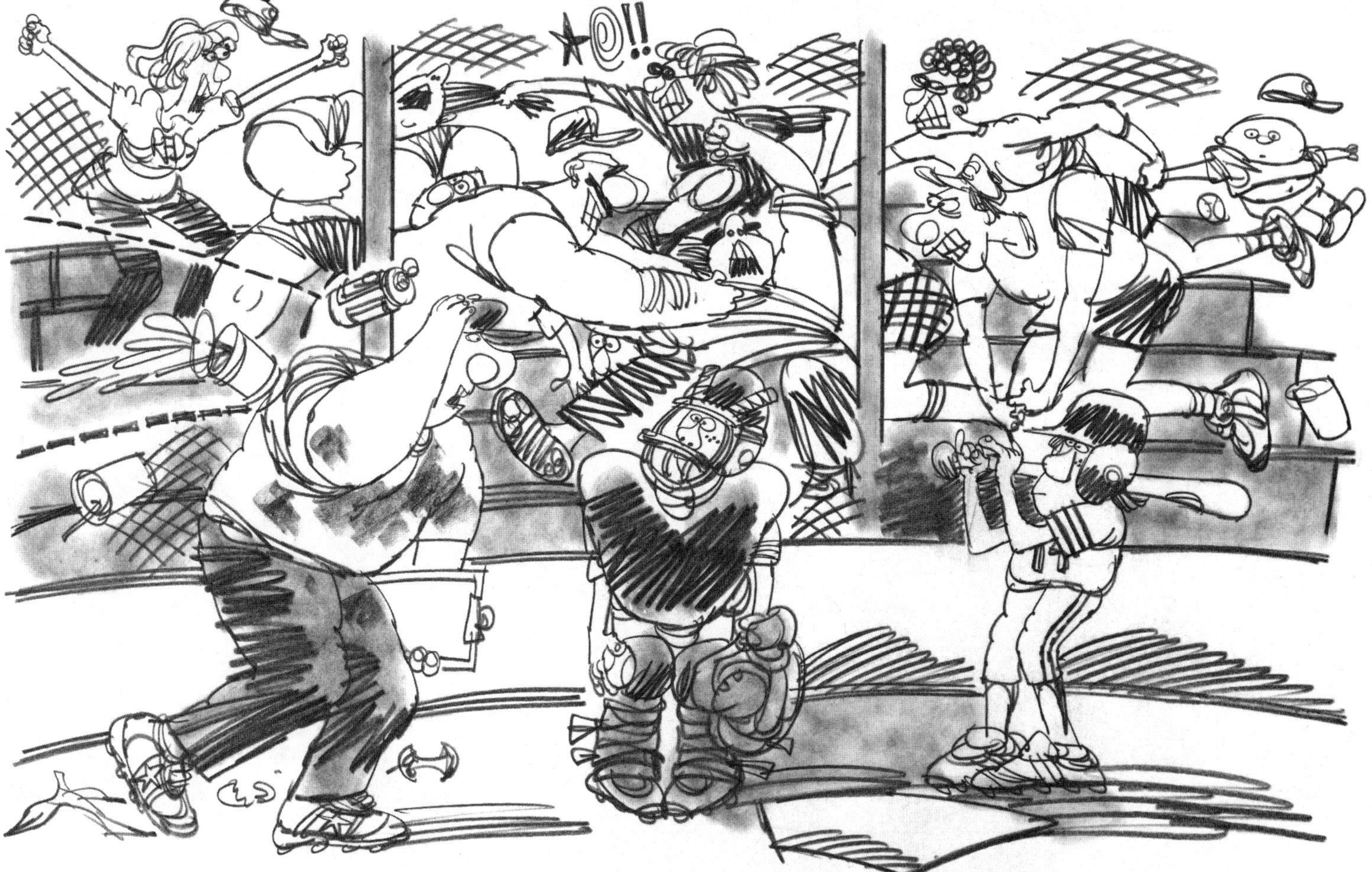
★@!!

"The game's been called off on account of parents."

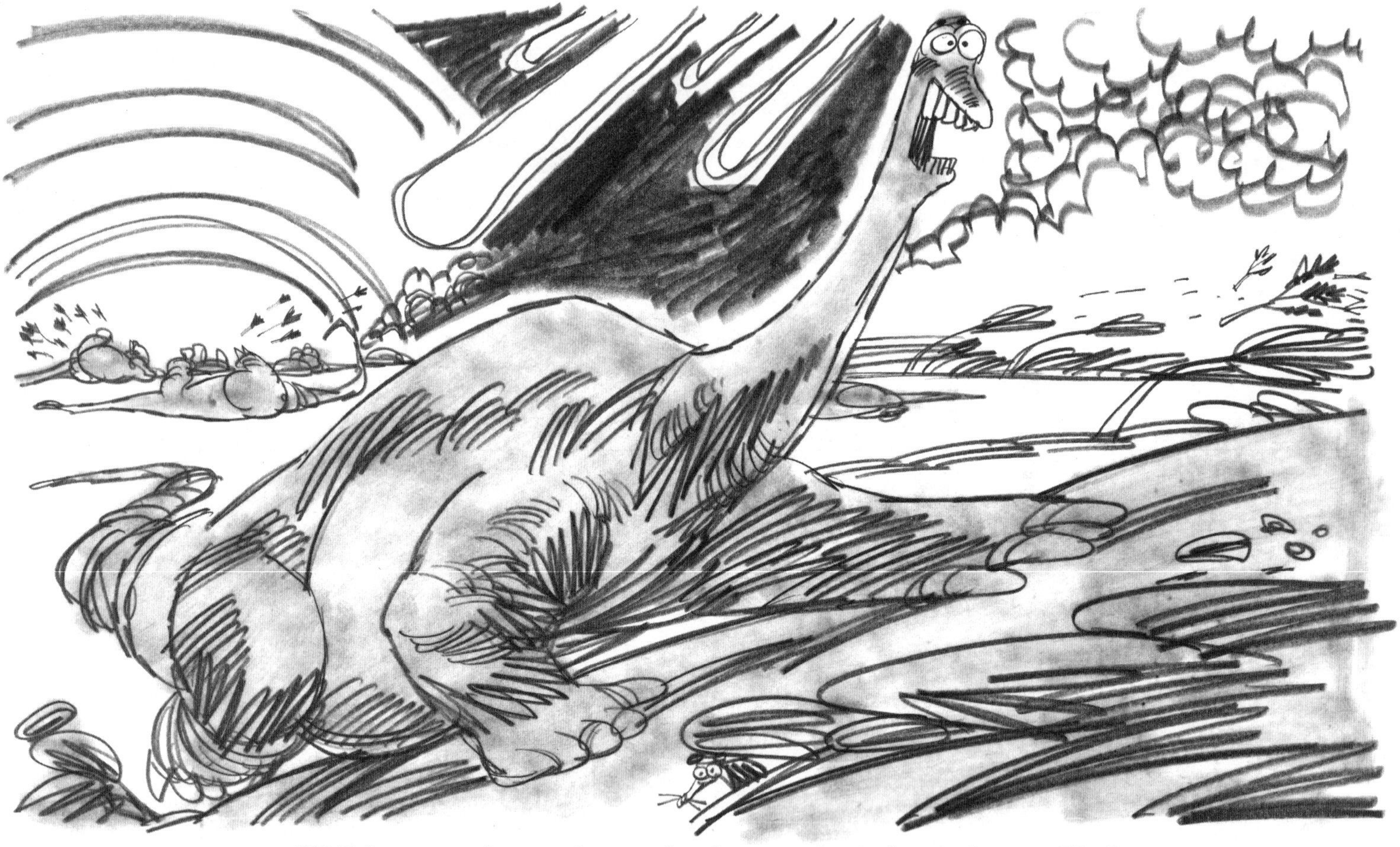

“If I have to be extinct, oh please, don’t let it be in Utah.”

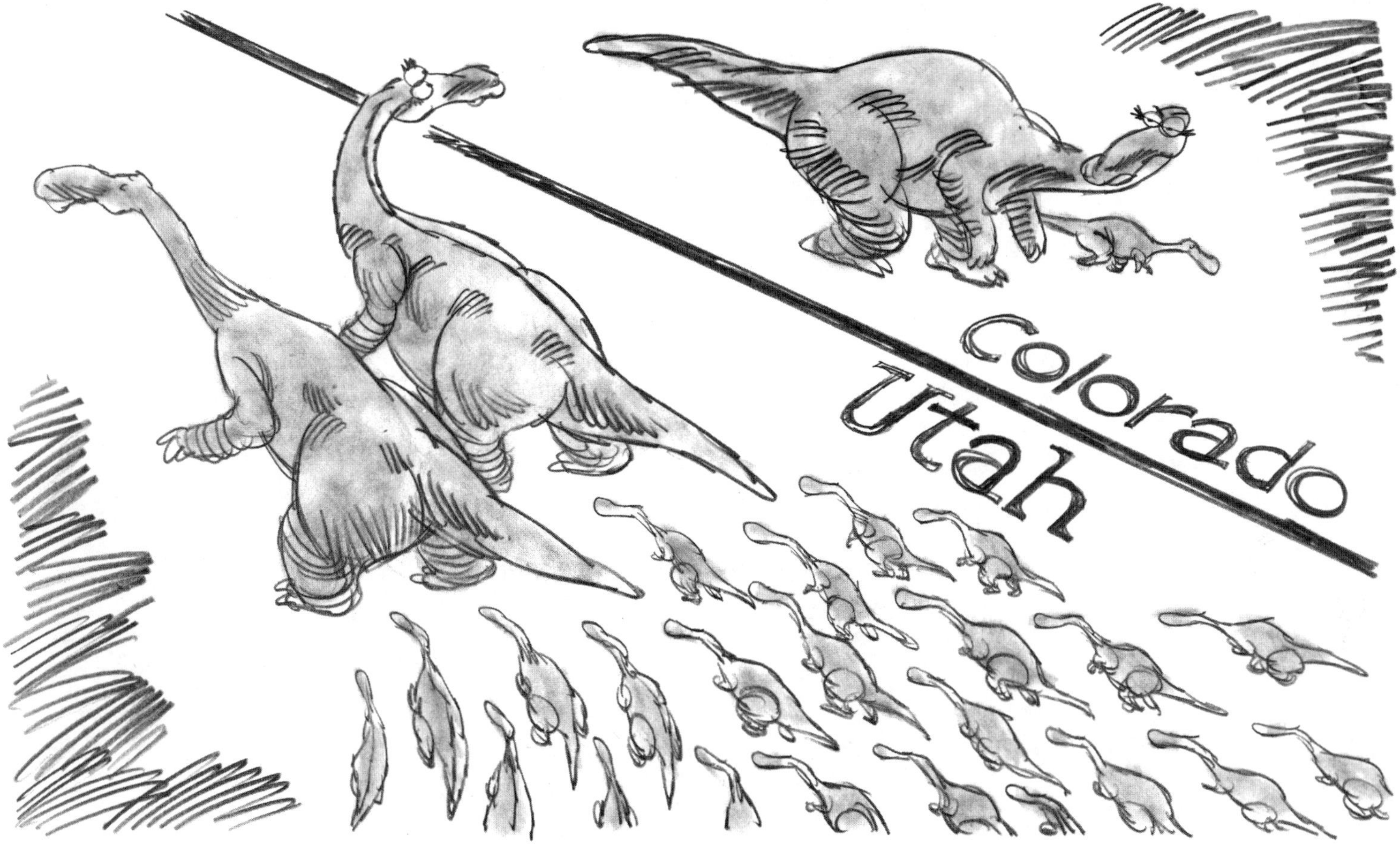
Colorado
Utah

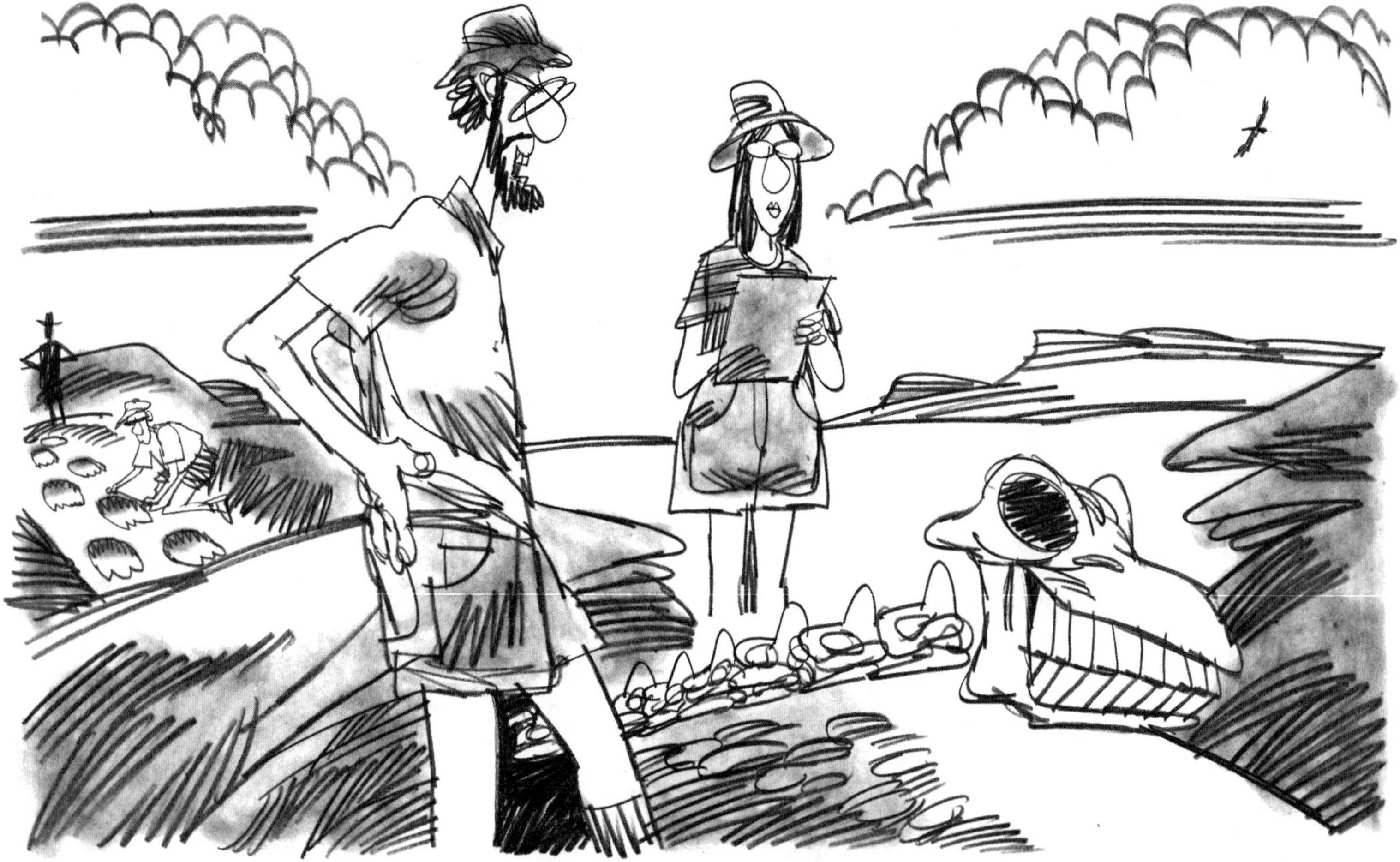

"This one's tracks show that he made it out of Utah just before he died . . . smiling."